Sacred Quest

Sacred Quest

The Evolution and Future of the Human Soul

L. Robert Keck

CHRYSALIS BOOKS

West Chester, Pennsylvania

Library of Congress Cataloging-in-Publication Data
Keck, L. Robert, 1935-
    Sacred quest: the evolution and future of the human soul /
L. Robert Keck.
    p. cm.
    Includes bibliographical references and index.
    ISBN 0-87785-306-1 (hardcover);
    0-87785-389-4 (paperback)
    1. Soul. 2. Spiritual life. 3. Evolution—Religious aspects.
    I. Title.
    BL290.K43 2000
    218—dc21   00-031571

Permissions: Material quoted in chapter 1 from *Origins
Reconsidered* by Richard Leakey, copyright © 1992 by B. V.
Sherma, is used by permission of Doubleday, a division of
Random House.

Edited by *Mary Lou Bertucci*
Cover design by *Caroline Kulp Kline*
Interior design by *Robin Milicevic, Ox and Company, Inc.*
Set in Janson Text and Univers
Printed in the United States of America.

Chrysalis Books is an imprint of the Swedenborg Foundation, Inc.
For more information, contact:

Swedenborg Foundation Publishers
320 North Church Street
West Chester, PA 19380
or
http://www.swedenborg.com.

Diana

Wife, lover, companion, and soul-mate. She personifies the archetype of feminine-nature, and is a skilled artisan in the high calling of compassionate service to others.

After twenty-five years of marriage, I am more certain than ever before in knowing that it is an incredible pleasure to live and love with her, and to learn from her.

and

Bishop James S. Thomas

(United Methodist, retired)

Friend, mentor, and facilitator of my first "wake-up call" regarding God's powerful and transforming presence. He is a wonderful example of the Christian faith's intellectual power and its call for love and justice.

Contents

Gratitudes

I have Parker Palmer to thank for the idea of identifying the usual "acknowledgments" as "gratitudes." It is so much more accurate regarding how I feel about the people who contributed to making this book what it is.

The gratitude that I feel for the Swedenborg Foundation's staff is overflowing. Chrysalis Books' acquisition editor Susan Flagg Poole's intuition got us started, and Deborah Forman, the Foundation's executive director and publisher, followed up with such a generosity of spirit, an integrity, and a warmth that let me know immediately that I was privileged to be dealing with an extraordinary group of people. Indeed, extraordinary they are, including Susan Picard in Marketing, Caroline Kulp Kline, designer of the jacket cover, as well as Alice Skinner and the entire board of directors. Mary Lou Bertucci, the extraordinarily skillful senior editor, deserves very special gratitudes—yours as well as mine. After all, were it not for her, you would have to suffer through a much inferior book. There is absolutely no question but that Mary Lou's suggestions made this a far better book than what I initially turned over to them. The entire staff has been and continues to be a delight to work with, a pleasure to know, and the recipients of my deepest gratitude.

I am also extremely grateful to three particularly wonderful friends who helped me in this project in very important and significant ways—Kent Meager, Paul Jerde, and Kiyoshi Murata. The marvelously visionary Kent showed a belief in, an affirmation of, and a support for this book when it was still "below the radar screen." He initiated the idea of creating a "Deep-value Research Fund" by which to support some of my research and writing time, and then made the initial and very generous contribution to that fund. Paul, who possesses a mercurial mind of quicksilver and a heart of gold, provided moral support and affirmation all along the way, as well as devoting untold hours, on a moment's notice, to assisting his techno-dunce writer-friend with any and all computer-related problems.

And Kiyoshi, as fascinating an entrepreneurial spirit as one could find, hidden beneath a wonderfully low-keyed and understated exterior, surprised me with the gift of a web site—another loving and gentle nudge to get me out into cyberspace. I am extremely fortunate to have such quality friends.

I am also grateful for the generosity of spirit in the Reverend Toni Cook and the St. Paul's United Methodist Church in Denver, Colorado, who responded to Kent's initiative and created and facilitated the "Deep-value Research Fund."

And, finally, I am grateful to you the reader, who will bring to the reading of this book your own special sacred quest. My hope, of course, is that the words and the spirit in these pages will stimulate your mind, stretch your spirit, and nourish your soul. But the real action is in the synergy that is created by what you also bring to the reading, the thinking about, and the living of the thoughts in this book. It is to you who complete the circle of spiritual energy and who empower the sacred synergy that I also express my gratitude.

Introduction

It is time for a breath of fresh air in the realm of the sacred. Stale air not only is unhealthy for inhalation and the continuation of life, but it is simply inadequate for the spiritual inspiration that is so desperately needed at this time in history.

It is time for a mind-boggling and spirit-stretching growth spurt for religions and spiritualities. Arrogance, stagnation, and death are the only alternatives when minds are not humbled by periodic boggling and spirits are not kept fit and flexible with constant stretching.

The human journey, when viewed over an extended period of time, gives us a marvelous model of periodic spurts, boggling, and stretching—a collective human story wherein chapters are usually written from a larger perspective than the chapter before, with more knowledge and greater maturity taking us far beyond the previous point of view. For instance, at one time we thought human life was created just six thousand years ago, but now we think in terms of an evolutionary journey covering at least five million years—or billions of years if we consider that we are actually star-children, made from material created in the heavens long ago. At one time we were so self-centered and small-minded as to think that our world was the only locale for God's creative activity, but we have now been humbled and stretched by learning that we participate in an enormous wonder-filled and awe-inspiring universe.

Oliver Wendell Holmes observed that, when a mind is stretched to a new idea, it can never return to its original dimensions. In contrast, however, original dimensions have often been sacrosanct in the realm of the sacred, where religious history, traditional ritual, and ancient spiritual truths have often been the bedrock of inflexibility.

This book is for those who quest after a spiritual fitness wherein flexible souls can be stretched and spirits can negotiate leaps of faith. It is for those who believe that it simply does not make sense to see everything in the world changing, yet to presume that our religious or spiritual lives should remain static. And it is for those spiritual mavericks who embrace a courageous creativity, those who want never to return to the previous dimensions of truncated theologies, stifled spirits, restrictive religions, ecclesiastical exclusiveness, parochial prayers, or shrunken souls.

You and I are living within an extraordinary time in history: revolutions are occurring in virtually every field, paradigm shifts and "faithquakes" taking place all across the human landscape, while many historians and cultural analysts are observing that ours is one of the most transformational times in all of human history. I developed a passion for trying to understand why all this is happening now at this historical moment and wondered if they are all connected. Is there a deep underlying cause for all the incredible, seemingly unrelated, chaotic changes that we are experiencing in the world today?

At the start of this inquiry, I had no idea where the quest and the questions would lead me. In fact, I intentionally wanted to begin with few if any preconceived conclusions, to let the process of discovery be as fresh and creative as possible, although recognizing that we all have certain preconceived assumptions that influence how we see the world. This book is about my twenty-one-year quest for underlying causes—a spiritual archaeology, if you will, of excavating layer after layer of cultural habits to find what it is that influences human existence at this time in history. It was late in the research—in fact, very recently—that I came to feel that it was appropriate to speak of this inquiry as forging a new science of Soul.

As you will soon see, the comparison with an archaeological "dig" is appropriate because the inquiry took me not only down deep in the human psyche, but far back in time as well. From an inquiry that began with trying to understand our own chaotic time, I ended up exploring what appears to be the entire history of the human Soul. It also led, inevitably, into speculations regarding the future of the Soul—our spiritual lives in the twenty-first century and beyond. In other words, trying to make sense out of today's world invariably led to the quest for where we have been and to questions about where we are going.

For the purpose of introducing this book, it might be helpful to discuss why a new science of Soul is needed in the first place; to introduce the new science of Deep-value Research, its methodology, and some of the key terms that will be used; to identify its primary contributions; and to summarize the big picture it presents of the history and future of the human Soul.

A New Science of Soul

We need a new science of Soul precisely because our other sciences have been too materialistic to help us understand the territory of Soul.[1] Without denigrating the awesome discoveries that the materialistic sciences have made to our understandings, the fact is that all the awe that can be discovered about human nature and our evolutionary journey of development will not be discovered if we look only at physical evidence.

For example, materialistic sciences have discovered a great deal about the history of matter but virtually nothing about the history of spirit. They have taught us about the evolution of the human body but not about the evolution of the human Soul. They have examined "Lucy's" skeleton and told us that she was an upstanding relative of ours who lived some three million years ago, but they have not been able to tell us what Lucy valued in her heart. They can tell us that a particular campfire is carbon-dated at 100,000 years ago, but they cannot tell us what the people talked about as they warmed themselves around that campfire on a cool autumn evening. They have discovered our genetic DNA and impress us with all the potential benefits that can be derived from mapping the human genome, but they have not been able to tell us if there is a spiritual equivalent to DNA, a deep encoding that determines what we value and why we think and behave in the particular ways that we do. Materialistic science cannot tell us why we conceive of God and create religions in the particular ways that we do or why those conceptualizations go through changes from time to time.

We need a new kind of science if we are to discover the Soul's DNA, if we are to discover the spiritual equivalent to the moment when humanity began walking upright—when humanity discovered spiritual fire—or to discover when humanity developed spiritual tools. We need a new kind of science if we are to explore the sacred meaning and purpose within the human journey, if we are to understand what appears to be the current transformation of humanity's Soul, and if we are to speculate reasonably about where religion and spirituality are headed in the future.

Deep-value Research

Deep-value Research is the new science of Soul. The values that this research investigates are the deepest, most fundamental, and causal values that shape mainstream human cultures. In other words, "deep values" are the values that determine why certain ways of thinking, acting, and institutional creating become dominant throughout the human family.

The scope of this research is multinational, interdisciplinary, cross-cultural, interracial, and transreligious, because the goal is to attempt to discover if there are common causal influences throughout human cultures and across all the artificial boundaries we have drawn to categorize our thinking and our research. However, because each culture, each religion, each intellectual discipline has its own language and parochial jargon, a common language was needed—thus, value terminology that crosses all categories. And the methodology considers such a broad scope that one scholar's biases, or one culture's particular take on life, or one religion's unique history or theology will not alone influence our conclusions.

It is important to note that Deep-value Research is not investigating only religion or spirituality. The level of Soul is far more inclusive than that, and deep values are the cause of religion and spirituality, not the other way around. In Deep-value Research, we are attempting to discern the values that shape, determine, and influence all aspects of mainstream human life and the fundamental underlying reasons as to why we create our cultural institutions in the way that we do, including but not limited to religion. Because of their profound influence, it is appropriate to refer to deep values as the DNA of the human Soul. Genetic DNA determines how we look physically, whereas the Soul's DNA determines what we value, how we think, how we act, and why and how we create and run our institutions.

It is also important to be aware of how Deep-value Research deals with the marvelous diversity throughout the human family. The focus of this research is on identifying and understanding the values that *dominate* the human landscape without denying, ignoring, or denigrating the exceptions lived out by various individuals, native and indigenous peoples, subcultures, and countercultures. The hope is that, if we can understand why certain values become dominant, we might understand why dominant cultures deal with nondominant cultures in the particular way that they do and why majorities treat minorities in the particular way that they do—some of the most intransigent and tragic ethical issues of our time.

Let's begin with defining terms that I will use throughout the book. You no doubt have noticed that I am capitalizing the word

Soul. I do so when referring to the collective human psyche, the deepest part of the human being wherein divine purpose for the species is embedded. When I lowercase the word *soul,* I am referring to the individual, assuming that is where the personal spiritual journey is embedded. Obviously, to speak of divine purpose in Soul and in souls is to make a statement of faith: these are not matters that can be "proven" by the empirical research itself but are, I believe, implied. I try to keep the distinction clear throughout this book between the research and my theological assumptions, the evidence and what I believe the evidence suggests.

Spirituality is our response to the Soul's DNA and our sense of a deep, divine meaning and purpose in life. Here we begin to see a great deal of differentiation throughout the human landscape—the same deep values, the same evolutionary purpose, but individual religious, cultural, and spiritual diversity regarding how one chooses to respond to that divine presence.

Religion is the more superficial—not to suggest insignificant—and the institutional ways in which groups of people manifest and facilitate their sense of the spiritual, create meaningful community, and honor their particular history, tradition, rituals, and symbol systems.

The *sacred* embraces and covers all the above. Thus, the *sacred quest* is an attempt to quest after some understanding of the human spiritual journey in general and the individual's attempt to live a spiritually responsive life in particular, and to question where humanity and our lives, our religions and our spiritualities are going in the future as a twenty-first-century Soul grows within us.

With these basic concepts in mind, we can introduce the primary contributions of Deep-value Research before briefly summarizing the big picture it presents. We will consider, in turn, how Deep-value Research enlarges the context of the sacred, introduces an evolutionary paradigm into our thinking about the sacred, discovers periodic transformations of Soul, and utilizes a maturational metaphor.

Enlarging the Context of the Sacred Quest

Traditionally, many religions have held tightly to a microscopic and myopic interpretation of spiritual reality. There have been at least three versions of this.

One version was a restricted historical view. Depending on who was talking, the history of *their* religion was literally the history of both the universe in general and humanity in particular. Since most of today's religions are only a few thousand years old, "pre-history" was out of sight and out of mind—certainly, out of the range of anything that was considered spiritually important.

The second version was theological exclusivity: *their* god was the one and only god, and their rituals were the one and only means to salvation. All others either had to be converted or were damned and doomed. This mind set also tried to make religion and spirituality synonymous: if you were spiritually inclined, you simply had to express that within the accepted institutions of religion. Period. Exclamation point! Of course, fewer and fewer people want to worship "Saint Procrustes," but some religious groups are slow learners.

The third version, particularly manifested during the recent secularization of humanity, assumes that life is divided up into mutually exclusive compartments. Most of our lives are devoted to commerce, national or international politics, sports, technology, etc. Religion, as a compartment, is reserved for certain times, places, and experiences that call out for rituals of the heart, such as birth, marriage, and death.

In recent years, there has been considerable change in the tendency of people to view their own religion as "the one and only true" religion, in spite of the current supernova—a bloating but dying star—of fundamentalism. Ecumenical and interfaith dialogue, a shrinking world, and the greater awareness of humanity's rich diversity of religious and spiritual traditions have all worked to soften the arrogant, exclusive, and isolationist propensities of the past. In later chapters, we will address how this is associated with the current transformation of Soul. In addition, spirituality for many people has become more and more liberated from institutional religion, as the latter is often stuck in the past, more interested in embalming the past than in facilitating an emboldened move into the future.

Deep-value Research enlarges the context of the sacred in several ways. It not only takes seriously the matter of diversity, but celebrates the richness of color and texture in the fabric of the human spiritual experience. It also addresses the reasons that narrow exclusivity and institutional pride are logical outcomes of the former deep values, but are inconsistent with those emerging in our current epoch.

Deep-value Research makes a particular contribution to expanding the historical context. It probes the question, "If we step outside the narrow parameters of any given religion, how far back in history can we find evidence of a human spirituality?" The new science of Soul, the quest that explores that question, has determined that the human Soul awakened about thirty-five thousand years ago. Granted, there is some evidence of spiritual values prior to that time—a few scattered pieces of art and musical instruments, and some evidence that Neanderthals buried their dead—but not enough quantity from which to draw any reasonable conclusions. Additional evidence may be discovered tomorrow, or next year, so we need to be open to whatever emerges with the possibility of changing our theories. However, even a mere thirty-five thousand years of evidence extends the historical context considerably, vis-a-vis what most religions consider relevant.

An Evolutionary Paradigm in the Realm of the Sacred

The thirty-five-thousand-year history of the human Soul, when exposed to the methodology of Deep-value Research, presents a direct challenge to the traditional steady-state paradigm for religions and spiritualities. Just as a snapshot in time gives us no clue as to the vast cosmological changes taking place throughout the universe or the drifting of continents causing the ascension of mountains on the surface of this planet, a truncated historical view of only five-thousand years can give religions the illusion that some things are permanent and unchanging when, in fact, they are part of a very long evolutionary process, moving and changing over great periods of time. Soul-time, just as geological and cosmological time, requires a longer history in order to see the changes.

Religions and spiritualities have often exacerbated the problem of a short view with an emotional need for theological stasis, stability, dependability, and predictability. The primary focus has often been on "ancient wisdom" that is presumed to be unchanging; on the lives and experiences of founders, prophets, saints, or saviors that are honored; and on dogmatic belief systems that are hermetically sealed and protected from any change for posterity.

The need to worship, conserve, and preserve the past leads invariably to envisioning the future through the rearview mirror. As one pundit quipped, some people act as if God wrote the Bible and then died. A steady-state paradigm is intellectually easy and emotionally comforting, whereas an evolutionary paradigm is discomforting and threatening, constantly forcing us to challenge the status quo, to rethink our previous assumptions, to renew, reform, and to be reborn.

Cosmology provides a marvelous analogy regarding the move from a steady-state to an evolutionary paradigm. It is a particularly appropriate analogy because cosmology and theology are, in one sense, twins: the former being the way science thinks about the ultimate context in which we live, the latter being the way religion thinks about the Ultimate.

Not too many years ago, most scientists thought that the universe was in a steady-state—that it was fundamentally stable, dependable, unchanging, and predictable. Albert Einstein, the very name we use to symbolize intellectual genius, was one such scientist. So much did Einstein need the universe to be in a steady-state that he actually fudged his mathematics in order to make it so, modifying his General Theory of Relativity by inserting a "cosmological constant." Only after being challenged by other physicists did he admit that his need for a stable and predictable universe led him into what he personally referred to as "the biggest scientific blunder" of his career.

In similar fashion, many of us need to insert a theological constant into our spiritual and religious thinking because we want God to be stable, static, unchanging, eternal, reliable, and predictable. I will be suggesting that the spiritual and religious realms need to face the same tough growth spurt that science did a few decades ago—being willing to leave behind the illusion of a steady-state reality and to grow into realizing that the divine–human relationship is one that takes place within the flow of time, a journey of growth wherein change, process, formation, reformation, maturation, novelty, innovation, evolution, and transformation are fundamental ingredients.

We have discovered nothing in the universe that holds still. Nothing is static. As far as we can tell, everything constantly changes. We may want things to hold still, but we have no evidence that anything does or that stability is in any way accurately defines reality.

Deep-value Research introduces an evolutionary paradigm into the sacred realms of the human journey. In this book, we will consider how, if we have the courage to realize that everything is changing, we can become spiritually and religiously user-friendly with change, and we will find our souls experiencing new possibilities for growth and maturation. Indeed, deep-value Research suggests that humanity's Soul is going through a growth spurt during our time in history. We can resist it, or we can resonate with it. With the latter, we have the opportunity to live in harmony with the transformational energies that consume the human Soul at this time in its evolutionary journey and to increase the spiritual meaning and purpose within our lives. In fact, the central purpose of this book is to facilitate that correspondence.

Periodic Transformations of the Human Soul

Deep-value Research has discovered what appears to be a large pattern within the history of the human Soul—long periods of relative stability, then a rather sudden transformation (sudden in terms of Soul-time), followed by another period of relative stability. Here, again, there is an interesting similarity with a pattern discovered within the physical evolutionary sciences.

Evolutionary geologist and biologist Stephen Jay Gould and his colleague Niles Eldredge published a paper in 1972 in which they argued that, in contrast to conventional Darwinian gradualism, evolution of the species took place via "punctuated equilibria."[2] They suggested that biological evolution is episodic rather than gradual, jerky rather than smooth, looking more like stair steps than a ramp. After a period of relative equilibrium—a time in which there was very little change in speciation—our evolution was punctuated with a period of dramatic and rapid change. Another period of equilibrium followed, and then another punctuation, with the pattern repeating itself over and over again.

In similar fashion, Deep-value Research suggests that the human Soul goes through periods of relative stasis or equilibrium, only to be punctuated or transformed, to be followed with another period of relative stability. After awakening some thirty-five thousand years ago, the human Soul experienced a twenty-five thousand-year period of equilibrium, with what appears to be a single evolutionary purpose and a stable deep-value system for that entire time. About ten thousand years ago, however, the human Soul was punctuated with its first major transformational change. An entirely new evolutionary purpose displaced the old, and a completely new deep-value system emerged to change human cultures. Humanity experienced another period of Soul equilibrium, this time for ten thousand years, bringing us up to our present time. Our current chaos is occurring because we are living within another punctuation, the second transformation of Soul.

The impact of a Soul's transformation can hardly be overstated. It may, in fact, be impossible even to imagine the full extent to which we will be changed by an entirely new evolutionary purpose and its accompanying change in deep values—after all, our imaginations have been conditioned for ten thousand years in a particular way of thinking and acting. The entire history of civilization, all of so-called "recorded history," has been within one evolutionary purpose and one deep-value system—no wonder we think that encompasses all of religious or spiritual reality. The second half of this book will attempt to explore—albeit, with a hefty dose of humility—the future of the human Soul, the new evolutionary purpose, and the emergent deep-value system.

The Maturational Metaphor

After several years of conducting the research in deep values, I found that a metaphor of maturation did the best job of encompassing and communicating the evidence. Humanity collectively, it appears, has been on a maturational journey akin to that of an individual: growing through a childhood epoch, then an adolescent epoch, and now entering an adult epoch.

As mentioned before, Deep-value Research began with an attempt to make sense out of today's chaotic world. After identifying and analyzing the values that are currently dying and those that are currently being born, I found that the evidence suggests a growth spurt from an adolescent set of values wherein psychological maturation was the primary evolutionary agenda—specifically, ego and mental maturation—into a more mature set of values wherein spiritual maturation became the central evolutionary task.

When eventually trying to discover when the currently dying deep-value system began and what preceded it, I found that Deep-value Research detected only one previous value system. The values of Epoch I suggested a childhood evolutionary purpose of facilitating physical maturation while in the arms of Mother Earth.

A brief summation of the research to date and the subject matter for the rest of this book looks as follows:

Epoch I: 35,000 Years Ago to 10,000 Years Ago

Although humanity's physical evolution covers millions or billions of years, sufficient evidence of humanity's Soul activity from which we can draw legitimate conclusions, as was suggested earlier, emerges in the historical record beginning about thirty-five thousand years ago. This childhood period of humanity's Soul had an evolutionary purpose similar to a child's physical maturation during his or her early years.

The first deep value that appears to have facilitated physiological development was that of a sense of unity with our Mother the

Earth in general and a profound respect for the powers inherent within the animal world in particular.

The second deep value was that of nonviolence. As incredible as that may sound to Epoch II ears, we now have a rather considerable body of evidence suggesting that it was a much more nonviolent epoch than what we have known and experienced in recent millennia. For instance, in over three-hundred cave "art galleries," presenting an extensive display of the spiritual values of this twenty-five-thousand-year period, we find no depictions of war, no celebration of warrior-priests, and no evidence of human or animal sacrifice. One does not have to romanticize humanity's childhood epoch to realize that the ethic of relationship was quite different vis-a-vis violence.

The third deep value of Epoch I, a natural extension from the first, was a celebration of and focus upon the feminine side of Soul, with societies being matricentric and matrilineal. We did not know of paternity at that time; the woman was the most obvious giver and nurturer of life. It is not surprising, therefore, that, when we began to think about giving praise and worship to the divine energy that empowered all of life, we conceived of divinity as an earth goddess.

Epoch II: 10,000 Years Ago to the Present

The punctuation or transformation of Soul some ten-thousand years ago changed humanity's evolutionary emphasis from physical to psychological maturation. We had grown a human body while being in the nourishing arms of Mother Earth, and it was now time to develop our ego and mind. Consequently, a completely new deep value system replaced the old—a transformed DNA of Soul, if you will—so that the new evolutionary purpose could be carried to the surface of culture and change humanity's ways of thinking and acting.

With ego maturation coming to center stage, the first deep value to emerge from humanity's transformed Soul was that of a changed relationship with nature. Just as an individual develops his or her ego by distinguishing "self" from "other," humanity distinguished itself from the rest of nature. The human/nature relationship was changed from one of cooperation to one of separation, manipulation, management, control, use, and abuse. Agriculture, horticulture, and animal husbandry all began at about the same time, launching humanity's ego development and an epoch that eventually led to a human/nature relationship similar to that of an adolescent and the refrigerator—a handy resource for whatever we are hungry for, with the expectation that "Mom" (Mother Nature) will keep it well stocked. Only when this ten-thousand-year-old value began to die in the latter half of the twentieth century did humanity, generally speaking, become aware of how such an immature relationship was unsustainable.

Reducing the whole of the human/nature paradigm into separate and distinct parts of humanity and nature was the initial cause of reductionism, a way of seeing and organizing the world that is expressed in modern cultures by the way we have presumed separated parts to be the functional categories of education, science, health care, religion, etc.

Perhaps the primary consequence of humanity's separating itself from nature, however, was the estrangement from the feminine side of Soul. It made the subsequent deep values of patriarchy and hierarchy inevitable, led humanity into an immature and distorted expression of power—either projecting all essential power externally or exercising power by controlling other people, money, land, and privileged knowledge.

The deep values of power and control were maintained by institutions that demanded subservience and conformity to certain rigid belief systems and ways of living. Violence enforced and manifested such power and control.

Although the recent six-hundred-year period, known as the Modern Age, did not represent a transformation of Soul, a new evolutionary purpose, or a change in deep values, it has been an extraordinarily influential exaggeration and completion of Epoch II. In chapter two, we will use the biblical story of the prodigal son as the framework for our exploration of the Modern Age, not because we will stick closely to the biblical meaning of the story— we won't—but because the prodigal son parable provides a rich and appropriate image by which to understand the past six-hundred years: an immature male concluding his ego development by demanding his inheritance and declaring his independence.

We will also devote an entire chapter to the current transformation of Soul, the chaos that accompanies the shift from Epoch II into Epoch III, since this has such existential meaning for those of us living today. It is significant that the Greek word for soul, *psyche*, is the same word for butterfly. We are, as it were, a chrysalis people. We are the adolescent Soul of the Epoch II caterpillar in the process of dying, while at the same time we are the adult Soul of the butterfly being formed.

It can be very confusing trying to differentiate the dying from the birthing, the deconstruction from the reconstruction, and the devolution from the evolution. How does one discern the caterpillar parts of oneself from the butterfly parts?

Deep-value Research can be helpful in understanding the unique confusion within which we live by providing a larger perspective and identifying the values that are dying and those that are being born. For example, we will see why a deep Soul-change can unleash pent-up hatreds and fear-driven fundamentalism around the world, while at the same time unleash democratic and liberating movements. Deep-value Research can show why a tough-minded hope in the future is both possible and appropriate.

Epoch III: The Emergent Future

The many historians and cultural analysts who say that we are living in a dramatic transformational time for humanity are right; they just have not gone far enough. History may very well prove that, to date, we have all been thinking far too small and substantially underestimating the extent to which this second transformation of Soul will change life as we know it. Adulthood is replacing adolescence, and spiritual maturation is replacing ego and mental maturation as the central evolutionary purpose. We will see that "the good old values" of Epoch II were not nearly as good for human fulfillment as are the new Epoch III values.

Perhaps the most influential deep value currently emerging from humanity's Soul is that of re-membering that which we dismembered ten-thousand years ago—humanity and nature. This value will, in the process, redefine human nature.

For example, one of the many ramifications of this new deep value will be the end of patriarchy: its time in history is over. Patriarchy can only exist when humanity's Soul is fractured along gender lines, elevating the masculine and sublimating the feminine side of Soul. The first deep value of Epoch III will be the healing of that fault-line. The healing has, of course, already begun, as has the sure-to-fail resistance.

The ubiquity of wholeness is the second emergent deep value. Science in the last century, overturning some of the pet theories of classical science, has discovered and proposed that everything in the universe is interconnected and interrelated. We will explore the spiritual and religious implications of that revolutionary idea and new deep value.

The third new deep value of Epoch III is the democratization of power. We will discover how essential power is not handed down from on high or conferred on us from external authorities: it is an emergent quality from within the individual and from within relationships between and coalitions of individuals. We have seen this kind of power manifested in the many human and civil rights movements, and we have seen it demonstrated in the world's dramatic national and international shifts from colonialism, imperialism, and totalitarianism to democratic rule. In a little over two-hundred years, for example, the world has gone from having only one democracy to having one hundred and seventeen. The overall trend is unmistakable.

The fourth and final Epoch III deep value to emerge from humanity's Soul, and probably the most controversial, is the spirituality of time. The religious and spiritual realms may have a particularly difficult time with this one, precisely because of the adolescent emotional need for theological constants.

"There is a grandeur in this view of life"

With these words, Charles Darwin began the final sentence of his book *The Origin of Species*. If there is a grandeur in biological evolution, however, how much more grand it is to consider a synthesis of physical, mental, and spiritual evolution. If there is a grandeur in physical development, how much more so in spiritual maturation. For the Soul gives birth to and embraces our very sense of grandeur. The Soul provides humanity with an oceanic, even a cosmic, view of life.

Both Carl Jung and Joseph Campbell thought and wrote eloquently about the human journey and the meaning and purpose inherent within it. Both, in their own ways, saw that each stage of life has its opportunities and challenges, but that there is a meaningful and purposeful progression. Although using a different metaphor than the one Deep-value Research utilizes, Jung was talking about how each stage of life involves its own unique purpose when he wrote:

The afternoon of human life must also have a significance of its own and cannot be merely a pitiful appendage to life's morning . . . [and] . . . whoever carries over into the afternoon the law of the morning, or the natural aim, must pay for it with damage to his soul."[3]

The same is true for humanity as a whole, and there is a special grandeur in considering the entire history of the human Soul, the different stages of its maturation, its changing purposes, and the values that shape and determine human cultures, while also considering how we individually can relate to that overall journey of Soul. So, let us now join that grand adventure, questioning and questing after the sacred and, in so doing, explore and experience the magnificent grandeur that is the spirit of life.

Sacred Quest

Part One

The Early Development of the Human Soul

Chapter One

Epoch I: *Childhood*

35,000 YEARS AGO to 10,000 YEARS AGO

We are all familiar with legends about an earlier, more harmonious and peaceful age. The Bible tells of a garden where woman and man lived in harmony with each other and nature—before a male god decreed that woman henceforth be subservient to man. The Chinese *Tao Te Ching* describes a time when the yin, or feminine principle, was not yet ruled by the male principle, or yang, a time when the wisdom of the mother was still honored and followed above all. The ancient Greek poet Hesiod wrote of a "golden race" who tilled the soil in "peaceful ease" before a "lesser race" brought in their god of war.

But though scholars agree that in many respects these works are based on prehistoric events, references to a time when women and men lived in partnership have traditionally been viewed as no more than fantasy.

Riane Eisler, *The Chalice and the Blade*[1]

And a Child Shall Lead Us

How wonderfully appropriate that the first discovery of humanity's childhood Soul was made by a child. As this chapter will eventually make clear, it is even meaningful that the discoverer was a female child.

In the late nineteenth century, Don Marcellion de Sautuola owned the old farm of Altamira situated on a high meadowland in northern Spain about three miles from the Cantabrian coast. Only by accident had he discovered a cave under his farm. He made a brief exploration of what he thought was the entire cave and found nothing of interest. Some ten years later, however, he realized that the cave was much larger than he originally thought, actually meandering some three-hundred yards back into the depths of the mountain. One day in 1879, Sautuola and his five-year-old daughter Maria were exploring a low chamber of the cave. Archaeologist Richard Leakey describes what happened:

> Whereas her father had had to crawl through the chamber, Maria could stand up in it. She looked at the ceiling and, in the flickering light of an oil lamp, saw images of two dozen bison grouped in a circle, with two horses, a wolf, three boars, and three female deer around the periphery, images in red, yellow, and black, as fresh as if they had just been painted.[2]

Eventually, it was confirmed that what little Maria had discovered were the artistic renditions of our early ancestors, painted in their cave sanctuary some fourteen-thousand years ago. Her initial discovery of Paleolithic cave art, what in other caves has now been revealed to have taken place throughout the entire twenty-five thousand years of Epoch I, opened one of the most fascinating chapters in the human story: the story of our childhood Soul. Before we get into the analysis of Paleolithic cave art and how it reveals the nature and content of humanity's Epoch I Soul, it might be helpful to place the artists who did that magnificent work, the people in whom the human Soul first awakened, into an historical and evolutionary context.

The Evolutionary Emergence of Human Beings

The first evolutionary "task" for humanity was to develop a human body. That process took millions, or even billions of years, depending on when one wants to locate the beginning—after all, the stuff that makes up our bodies was created in stars, although we tend to speak of human biological evolution only in earthly terms. Although we have no reason to believe that physical evolution has ended, it is on a different time scale, as this book will make clear, than is psychological or spiritual evolution. In addition, each evolutionary epoch has a different developmental emphasis. The primary emphasis of the first evolutionary epoch was physical, whereas the most recent epoch, the past ten-thousand years, has had a psychological emphasis. In contrast, the emergent epoch shows signs of having a spiritual emphasis. Our consideration of the historical and evolutionary context, therefore, begins with the first evolutionary emphasis, physical development.

It is not the purpose of this book to trace humanity's entire physical evolutionary journey, as wonderful and wonder-filled as it has been. An appropriate place for us to dip into that long and complex story, however, would be at the point in time when anatomically "modern humans," or *Homo sapiens sapiens* emerged from pre-humans approximately 150,000 years ago. That was the time when, as anthropologist Ian Tattersall writes, "a totally unprecedented entity . . . appeared on Earth:"

> For the first time since the adoption of upright walking—or perhaps stone toolmaking—a new kind of hominid was around of which it could not be said that it merely did what its predecessors had done, only a little better, or even just a little differently. *Homo sapiens* is not simply an improved version of its ancestors—it's a new concept, qualitatively distinct from them in highly significant if limited respects.[3]

There is an interesting debate among scholars regarding precisely where on this planet human beings finally became physically "modern."[4] Some scholars subscribe to what is called the "multiregional theory," which suggests that, after *Homo erectus* migrated out of Africa about one-million years ago and populated parts of Europe, Asia, and Australia, modern humans evolved independently from *Homo erectus* in many different locations.

The competing theory, what is called the out-of-Africa or "Noah's Ark" hypothesis, argues that modern humans evolved first in Africa sometime around 150,000 years ago. Then, about 100,000 years ago, modern humans began migrating out into the rest of the world and gradually replaced all the premodern humans, including the Neanderthals in Europe. Despite the debate regarding origins, it is generally agreed that by about thirty-five thousand years ago, or shortly thereafter, there remained only one form of human beings on this planet—*Homo sapiens sapiens*.

Molecular genetic research appears to have tipped the balance in this debate in favor of the out-of-Africa theory and is the primary reason that prestigious scientists like Richard Leakey and Stephen Jay Gould, among others, have thrown their hats into "Noah's Ark."

Most genetic information is packaged in the nuclei of cells; therefore, that is where most of the scientific research is focused. A small number of genes, however, are found in the cell's mitochondria. Leakey describes the reasons that mitochondrial DNA has played such an important role in helping us to understand the human evolutionary story.

> Two interesting properties of mitochondrial DNA make it particularly useful for tracking evolutionary history of recent populations. First, the DNA accumulates mutations rapidly, and therefore acts as a fast-ticking molecular clock. Second, because mitochondria are inherited maternally—from mother to offspring—they offer geneticists a relatively uncomplicated way of reconstructing evolutionary events in populations. By looking at patterns of genetic variation of mitochondrial DNA among modern human populations, anthropologists, theoretically, should be able to determine when and where the first members of anatomically modern humans evolved. This, in effect, would be the family tree of *Homo sapiens sapiens*.[5]

In the early 1980s, several scientific laboratories focused upon this challenge; their research placed the beginning of our species about 150,000 years ago in Africa. The *San Francisco Chronicle*, on March 24, 1986, brought this to the public's attention with the headline "The Mother of Us All—A Scientist's Theory." In general, the popular press, with its penchant for hyperbole, led the public to believe that scientists had discovered a singular "Eve." To imply the mother of the human species was one single female, however, is a bit misleading. Our genetic mother was, rather, a population of "first" human females, albeit probably a very small population.

The survival of our first mothers and fathers, however, was evidently not a sure thing. Christopher Stringer and Robin McKie write that "at one stage, according to genetic data, our species became as endangered as the mountain gorilla is today, its population reduced to only about 10,000 adults":

> Restricted to one region of Africa, but tempered in the flames of near extinction, this population went on to make a remarkable

comeback. It then spread across Africa until, by about 100,000 years ago, it had colonized much of the continent's savannas and woodlands. We see the imprint of this spread in biological studies that have revealed that races within Africa are genetically the most disparate on the planet, indicating that modern humans have existed there in larger numbers, for a longer time than anywhere else.[6]

According to this evolutionary theory, all of humanity can trace its lineage back to Africa. We are all, therefore, literally African–_____ (just fill in the blank with your current geographical home). The post-hyphenated period began about 100,000 years ago when some of our relatives caught the traveling bug and became remarkably skilled globe-trotters. Some of our ancestors migrated from Africa eastward through Asia, arriving in New Guinea and Australia by about fifty-thousand years ago—in the latter case, a trip that remarkably included negotiating about sixty miles of open water. Other modern humans were in Europe by about forty-thousand years ago, Sri Lanka by about thirty-thousand years ago, and China about twenty-five thousand years ago.

The first human beings in America, apparently, were neither Native Americans nor European Americans. They were African-Asian-Americans. Nevertheless, precisely when humans first migrated into the Americas is still a matter of conjecture. Some scholars believe that humans first ventured across the now-lost land of Beringia—the land between Siberia and Alaska created during the last Ice Age but what is now the watery Bering Straits—then gradually moved down the entire nine-thousand miles to the tip of South America. Others think that the route was by sea. In either case, there is rather clear evidence of human activity in the Americas by about twelve-thousand years ago, the so-called Clovis People, named after evidence discovered in what today we call New Mexico, as well as evidence as far away as Monte Verde, Chile. Still, some scholars believe humans were in the western hemisphere as long as thirty-thousand years ago. It will be fascinating to see how that picture of the first Americans comes into focus, or perhaps even changes dramatically, as new evidence is discovered.

Our primary interest here, however, is in the spiritual evolution of our species, the awakening of the human Soul. For that, we look to thirty-five thousand years ago.

The Awakening of the Human Soul

Having stated that humanity's evolutionary journey arrived at our current physical state about 150,000 years ago, it may initially seem rather strange to suggest that it took more than 100,000 additional years before the human Soul awakened spiritually to facilitate the physiological epoch.[7]

It may be that the awakening of the human Soul coincided, meaningfully and purposefully, with the time when *Homo sapiens sapiens* were the only surviving human species. It is also possible, of course, that we will eventually discover evidence of Soul from a much earlier time. For instance, there is some evidence that the pre-human Neanderthals—who existed in Europe from about 200,000 years ago to about 30,000 years ago, just after modern humans arrived—buried their dead and that they regularly took care of their sick and aged. As Jared Diamond states:

> Most skeletons of older Neanderthals show signs of severe impairment, such as withered arms, healed but incapacitating broken bones, tooth loss, and severe osteoarthritis. Only care by young Neanderthals could have enabled such older Neanderthals to stay alive to the point of such incapacitation.[8]

That, one would think, is evidence of a spirituality, of Soul-level deep-values. Nevertheless, it is not enough. Indisputable evidence of an awakened human Soul, sufficient evidence from which we can draw reasonable conclusions, does not appear in the historical record until about thirty-five thousand years ago. Consequently, according to current evidence, the gap between humanity's becoming physically mature and the human Soul's awakening is a little over 100,000 years—still but a blink of the eye in evolutionary terms. If we consider this gap in the light of our primary metaphor, that of an individual human being's maturational process, it certainly is not unheard of for a person to reach physical maturity slightly before becoming aware of the spiritual meaning of that significant threshold.

We will focus most of our discussion on European evidence, not only because it provides the greatest quantity that has been discovered to date, but also because it provides a striking contrast between the Neanderthals who had inhabited the region for about 150,000 years and the modern humans who replaced them. For although the

Neanderthals may have buried their dead and taken care of the sick and aged, a dramatic leap forward occurred in virtually every aspect of human culture when *Homo sapiens sapiens* arrived, particularly in what we are here calling evidence of Soul. Modern humans demonstrated symbolic activity in sculpture, elaborate burial practices, musical instruments, and artistic expressions on cave walls, as well as so-called portable art, involving bone and antler carvings, all of which gives powerful testimony to the presence of Soul.

For example, there is no doubt that modern humans buried their dead with an elaborateness that has not been discovered from an earlier time. (These early "modern humans" are referred to with a variety of names. Cro-Magnon is the name scholars have given the Europeans of this period, named after the site in southwestern France in which the first skeleton was discovered; but Upper Paleolithic, Ice Age, or Late Stone Age people are also terms referring to modern humans living at this time in history.) Christopher Stringer, a British researcher who championed the out-of-Africa evolutionary theory before it was confirmed by genetic research, reflected upon the elaborate burial practices of the Cro-Magnon and believes that it suggests "some form of organized religion and belief in an afterlife."[9]

It is important to keep in mind that Epoch I was a very different Soul-time for humanity. The Epoch I human Soul, as we will make clear, was not at all like the Epoch II human Soul that has given rise to what we now consider religious. We should not, therefore, expect to see in the Epoch I evidence of Soul the same religious symbols that are used in today's major world religions.

Later in this chapter, we will specifically examine the spiritual images and symbols of Epoch I, and the meaning and content of humanity's childhood Soul. But, first, we need to set the stage with a couple of important observations.

As already mentioned, most of the evidence we have to work with comes from what today is called Europe. It is important, therefore, to guard against any simplistic Eurocentric bias in our interpretation of the evidence. We need to be careful not to draw species-wide conclusions from evidence found only in Europe, if evidence from the rest of the world is shown to be different. We will take that kind of care throughout.

On the other hand, we should also be careful not to project today's cultural diversity onto the world of thirty-five thousand years ago. Colin Renfrew, professor of archaeology at the University of Cambridge, writes:

> We humans are a wonderfully diverse species. All over the globe, there are habitats of widely different character, with human communities adapted to their fruitful exploitation. . . . But as little as 12,000 years ago, the extent of that diversity was still limited.[10]

The out-of-Africa or "Noah's Ark" theory of human migration may explain a relatively late diversification of human cultures. Our challenge, therefore, is to tread carefully on the cautious path between the oversimplification of diversity and the overdiversification of a collective unconscious and a common Soul.

The most substantial body of evidence that seems to reveal the newly awakened human Soul is the art left by these early humans—portable art in the form of bone, antler, and ivory images, various stone sculptures, and—on what we will concentrate most—an amazing quantity of art painted on the Paleolithic cave walls and ceilings. Little five-year-old Maria Sautuola's discovery in the cave of Altamira first made us aware of the treasure trove of ancient art, but, following her discovery, more than three-hundred caves have been found in which there exists Cro-Magnon artistry. That number, in fact, is growing every year with, on average, one new "gallery" of cave art being discovered.

Using carbon-dating science, it is now known that cave art was painted over a period of at least twenty-five thousand years, from about thirty-five thousand years ago to about ten-thousand years ago. Interestingly, the first cave art that was discovered by little Maria in 1879 includes paintings that have been dated to slightly before and slightly after fourteen-thousand years ago, whereas the Chauvet cave in southcentral France, discovered in 1994, has a phenomenal collection of more than three-hundred animal images painted over thirty-thousand years ago. Cave art does appear, however, to have accelerated throughout Epoch I, with approximately eighty percent of the art that has been discovered to date being painted between eighteen-thousand years ago and ten-thousand years ago.[11]

One of the remarkable things about even the earliest Paleolithic cave art is that "unprecedented though it was," writes Ian Tattersall, "much of this early art was not in the least crude or primitive":

From the very beginning, the finest Paleolithic art showed a perceptiveness of observation and a command of form that rivals anything achieved since. . . . Both monochrome and polychrome paintings were made on cave walls, using naturally occurring pigments; bas-reliefs were carved on the walls of rock shelters; clay figures were molded and sometimes fired in kilns; stone and bone plaques were engraved; animal and human figures were carved in antler, ivory, bone, and stone. . . . [The animals painted were] so acutely observed that we can sometimes tell both by behavior and appearance in what season of the year an animal was depicted.[12]

Another remarkable fact about cave art is that we still do not know the extent of it. As already mentioned, new caves and new "galleries" of art are being discovered virtually every year. One of the most fascinating places where caves might yet be discovered is under water.

At the end of the last Ice Age, some ten-thousand to twelve-thousand years ago, huge amounts of ice melted, releasing water that had been locked up in the glaciers for sixty-thousand years or so and raising the sea level by some four-hundred feet. How many caves, we wonder, with their marvelous sanctuaries of art might have been above sea-level at the time the art was painted, but are now beneath the surface of the water and out of sight? At least one such cave has been discovered.

In 1991, professional undersea diver Henri Cosquer discovered, quite by accident, a cave 120 feet under the surface of the Mediterranean Sea, between Marseilles and Cassis, in the south of France. Thus, the Cosquer Cave, as it is now known, was almost three-hundred feet above sea-level when our Cro-Magnon ancestors crafted their art on the walls of that cave, beginning about 18,500 years ago, some fifteen centuries before the art in the famous cave at Lascaux. An interesting fact that appears to be true of all the caves discovered to date is that the art was painted, in any given cave, over a period of several thousands of years.

As of this writing, the Cosquer Cave has not been fully surveyed; no doubt many more images are yet to be discovered. Yet, to date, researchers have found images of marine life—seals, fish, and jellyfish—that are not found in other caves. Three images of the now-extinct great auk are also unique in all Paleolithic cave art. In addition, there are horses, bison, ibexes, and chamois. The oldest images discovered in the Cosquer Cave are twenty-six stenciled human handprints, an image also found in many other prehistoric caves. They were done, in the best guess of scholars, by a kind of oral spray-painting: the artists apparently put pigment in their mouths, mixed it with saliva, and then spit it over the hand that they held against the wall. It created a silhouette of their hand, the meaning of which may have been in some way becoming one with the wall of the cave.[13]

The actual content of cave art is rarely a matter of debate. On the other hand, the interpretation of what the images meant to the artists who did the work is the stuff of which controversy is made. After all, how can a twenty-first-century person, with any degree of certainty, imagine what an artist tens of thousands of years ago, in a totally different evolutionary period, in an immensely different culture—motivated out of what Deep-value Research suggests was a radically different Soul—actually meant by what he or she was painting?

Of course, regardless of uncertainty and in spite of controversy, we still have to give it a try. How can we encounter such magnificence and such extraordinary artistry from tens of thousands of years ago and not wonder why people were creating it? "Ever since prehistoric art was discovered in the late nineteenth century," writes Richard Leakey, "it has held archeologists in its thrall: the quest for what the images mean has been constant."[14] And it has obvious import for our exploration here, as we attempt to understand the entire history of the human Soul and to ascertain if the content of the Soul changed from time to time throughout our evolutionary journey.

The Spiritual Significance of Cave Art

If we could establish, with reasonable credibility, that Paleolithic cave art was primarily a spiritual expression—in other words, an expression of the deepest and most meaningful aspects of human life at that time in history—then it would provide a good resource for understanding the nature and content of humanity's Epoch I Soul.

For one thing, the number of prestigious, secular academic scholars of cave art who express a feeling of sacredness in their encounter with it is impressive, in and of itself, almost as if the spiritual motivation of the artist was so powerful that it transcends millennia to elicit a spiritual response from the supposedly objective and scholarly modern observer.

As a five-year-old child, Richard Leakey accompanied his famous scientist parents, along with the Abbe Breuil, then France's leading expert on cave art, to Lascaux, perhaps the most renown "sanctuary" of Paleolithic art:

> It was an intense experience for everyone, this visit to Lascaux. I knew I was in the presence of something quite remarkable, but wasn't aware of what it was. I don't remember what was said. I don't even remember which paintings they looked at. I just remember the sense of reverence, veneration that quieted their voices.[15]

Decades later, as an adult and a world-renown archaeologist in his own right, Leakey revisited Lascaux. He was stunned by the "visual bombardment of chaotic activity":

> On the left-hand wall, a cavalcade of prehistoric beasts stampedes toward the deeper recesses of the chamber. Four gigantic white bulls in black outline dominate the long cavern where it widens to form a rotunda; this is the Hall of Bulls. A menagerie of smaller creatures jostles among the legs of the great beasts. Trotting horses, tense stags, and frisky young ponies stand out from the walls and ceiling in black, red, and yellow, sometimes bold drawings, sometimes just tantalizing suggestions. Several images overlap others; some are huge, some diminutive. A fine purple-red horse with a rich, flowing black mane hangs near two great bulls facing each other in head-on challenge. Standing in the Hall of Bulls, surrounded by this wild scene, which exudes so much vitality and power, one is overwhelmed.[16]

"The images have such an urgent presence and energy," Leakey reported, "a tangible power . . . that speaks of their importance in the lives of our ancestors." Lascaux, he said, is a place "imbued with meaning . . . the potency is palpable." He felt a "deep conviction of connectedness, and a humility at the power of the human mind."[17]

Other scholars share this perception that the content of the cave-wall paintings bespeak a spiritual motivation. Henry de Lumley, director of France's National Museum of Natural History, writes, "The fact that the iconography is relatively consistent, that it seems to obey certain rules about placement and even the way animals are drawn . . . is evidence of something sacred."[18]

Goran Burenhult, an archaeology professor at the University of Stockholm and a leading expert on cave art, writes:

> To encounter the [cave art] of Upper Paleolithic people is an experience marked by awe, anxiety, excitement, and wonder. Often it involves an expedition of a kilometer or more (about half a mile) into the depths of a mountain—walking, crawling on one's knees and elbows, and sometimes swimming across underground lakes and rivers. The remote location is characteristic of cave art . . . [and] must have been of vital importance to the people of that age when selecting a sanctuary.[19]

Footprints left over from an ancient dance are an interesting discovery that suggests religious ritual. Unfortunately, in the early years of cave-art investigation, many researchers walked around in the caves studying the walls and ceilings, unaware that they were stomping out valuable evidence on the ground. But in a few sites, footprints, dating back tens of thousands of years, were discovered and preserved.

In one cave, for instance, the footprints of six people—all children—form a clear circular dancing pattern, adding to the suggestion of ritual. Flutes and the remains of what appear to be other musical instruments were also found at the spot. In one of the most spectacular discoveries, researchers found more than five-hundred footprints from a circular dance ritual, involving children thirteen to fifteen years of age, as well as adults. What gives this ritual dance its level of importance is that it took place in a chamber more than three-thousand feet back into the depths of the mountain, a chamber accessible only by negotiating three large underground lakes.[20]

Not only was sacred ritual evidently an important part of human life during Epoch I, but spirituality might have even been a priority, as is suggested by one remarkable area of evidence. Stringer and McKie report that the Cro-Magnon had developed "the technology to make pottery but chose only to make sculptures. In other words, symbolism and art were as important as functional applications."[21]

Ian Tattersall, curator of the Department of Anthropology at the American Museum of Natural History in New York City, reports that, at the Czech site of Dolni Vestonice, female and animal figurines were baked and apparently deliberately fractured in kilns during what were probably homesite rituals of some sort. This kind of production is known from nowhere else; and, indeed, the notion of baking clay subsequently lay fallow for as many as 150 centuries, until pottery was introduced in the New Stone Age, this time in the service of utilitarian purposes.[22]

Our twenty-first-century minds may find this almost unbelievable—that our ancient relatives would use a technology for religious purposes for over fifteen-hundred years before using it for utilitarian reasons, such as making pottery. Nevertheless, it appears that early humans valued spiritual and sacred purposes over more mundane purposes.

Cave art, however, provides the largest body of evidence helping us to understand humanity's childhood Soul. And what may be the most convincing interpretation of cave art that suggests its spiritual significance is that much of the art may have had shamanistic origins.

In the 1970s, Mircea Eliade, the scholar whom many consider to be the authority on primitive mentality and culture, suggested that much of the Paleolithic cave art might have been the work of shamans while in trance.[23] In the 1980s, anthropologist Joan Halifax made a similar suggestion.[24] But what may turn out to be the most convincing analysis of cave art as being the work of shamans, and therefore one of profound spiritual significance, comes from a collaboration conducted in the mid–1990s between Frenchman Jean Clottes, an expert on Cro-Magnon cave art, and South African David Lewis-Williams, an expert on the art of the African San.[25]

We know that virtually every primitive society had (and has) shamans and that they were (and are) the resident experts of the spiritual world. Shamans go into a trance, either passive or frenzied, to heal the sick, obtain a special relationship with the animal world, converse with spirits, etc. Virtually all interpretation of prehistoric cave art has been done in the twentieth century, a profoundly rational age and one in which mainstream cultures have denigrated anyone who was particularly close to nature and anyone who regularly experienced altered states of consciousness—literally, a modern, left-brained, half-brained bias. Most scholars, understandably, never even considered shamanistic trance while studying cave art.

Consequently, although there are many geometric forms found in the Paleolithic cave art in Europe, as well as in the African rock art—dots, grids, zigzags, spirals, and curves—most scholars simply ignored them or passed them off as meaningless and unimportant. Not so with David Lewis-Williams, who had been studying San art for four decades. He was uneasy with the too-easy exclusion and trivialization of the geometric forms and suspected some kind of meaning in the images, even if most scholars thought there was none. Fortunately for us, Lewis-Williams followed his intuition and began an investigation that combined both ethnographic and modern neurophysiological research on altered states of consciousness. Our understanding of humanity's childhood Soul has been greatly enriched because of his creative insight and courage to follow his intuition, albeit against the grain of most scholarship.

In modern neurophysiological research, Lewis-Williams discovered a three-stage process for those who enter a trance. The first, or lightest, stage of trance involves the subject's seeing "entopic images"—which means "within vision"—that are primarily grids, zigzags, dots, spirals, and curves. These images appear to be consistent for people who enter trance, regardless of their cultural or historical context. In the second stage, subjects try to make sense of the images; here, their interpretations are influenced by their emotional, cultural, and historical context. In the third stage, once again apparently consistent throughout all cultures of all times, the subject feels drawn into a vortex or tunnel and changes into a bird or some other animal. "Because they derive from the human nervous system," says Lewis-Williams," all people who enter certain altered states of consciousness . . . [will have a very similar experience] . . . no matter what their cultural background."[26]

Lewis-Williams applied this breakthrough insight to his understanding of African San art and published many scholarly papers describing how the geometric shapes were probably the work of shamans in an altered state of consciousness. He suggested that a similar explanation might be applied to the geometric shapes found in Paleolithic cave art. He also felt that the puzzling images that were part human and part animal, such as the famous "Sorcerer" at Les Trois-Freres, could be depictions, from memory, by the shamans who transformed into animals during the third stage of their trance experience.

Jean Clottes, a recognized expert on the European Paleolithic cave art, approached David Lewis-Williams during an International Colloquium on Rock Art, in June 1994, and suggested joining forces. The resulting collaboration of these two highly respected scholars of prehistoric cave and rock art has given strong credibility to the idea that when studying the artistic renditions painted during the epoch of humanity's childhood Soul, we are given insight into the nature and content of humanity's childhood Soul. "Contrary to what is commonly thought," write Clottes and Lewis-Williams, "we have better access to the religious experiences of Upper Paleolithic people than to many other aspects of their lives."[27]

Before identifying the deep-value system—the Soul's DNA during our childhood epoch—and that which determined human culture for that particular twenty-five-thousand year period, it is important to emphasize three things. First of all, the caves in which we find this art are not caves in which our early human ancestors lived. All the evidence suggests that they were special "sanctuaries," places where our ancestors went for important spiritual, ritualistic, and symbolic purposes. The extremely remote locations, deep into mountains, and the difficult accessibility, often necessitating crawling and sometimes even negotiating large underground rivers and lakes, add to the suggestion that these were very special places.

Second, the scholars who spend their lives studying this evidence are now virtually unanimous in disposing the notion that this art could have been merely random doodling. It is quite clear that this art held great symbolic and spiritual importance to those who did the painting.

Third, as Clottes and Lewis-Williams attest, "despite all the diversity of the art, there is a long-term unity that testifies to some sort of common framework."[28] There is an amazing unity, over a twenty-five-thousand-year period and over great geographical distances, in the techniques used as well as in the animals painted. There is also a profound commonality in what was excluded. In spite of animals being the most frequent images, we find no depiction of insects or rodents. The animals are clearly the focus, with no emphasis upon the landscape within which the animals would be found. In addition, during this extensive period of history, five times as long as what we consider "recorded history" or "the history of civilization," there are no depictions of daily human existence—no images of tents, huts, or tools, and no pictures of human gatherings, families, clans, etc. What is excluded is as revealing as what is included, and we will return to this theme when we consider some of the deep values of this period, such as that of nonviolence.

Deep-value Research attempts to identify, clarify, and interpret precisely this "common framework" and "long-term unity." Taken as a whole, Paleolithic cave art gives us twenty-five-thousand years of evidence regarding the nature and content of the human Soul during its childhood evolutionary epoch and regarding the deep-value system that determined and shaped the details of human existence during that period of history. Thus, judging from the evidence currently available, our Epoch I deep values were (1) a unity with nature in general and a profound respect for animal powers in particular, (2) a relatively nonviolent relationship with the animal world and other humans, at least as contrasted to that of recent history, and (3) a celebration of and focus upon the feminine side of Soul, including a worship of the Mother Earth Goddess.

Epoch I Deep-Value:
Unity with Nature and Respect for Animal Powers

That humanity was within and at-one with nature, throughout Epoch I, would appear to be self-evident. After all, regardless of where one arbitrarily wants to begin tracing the human evolutionary journey—many billions of years ago in stars, four-billion years ago on planet Earth, a few million years ago when there were distinctive thresholds in the human journey, or 150,000 years ago when we finally looked as we do today—the entire history of human development has been within and part of nature.

What we are calling Epoch I was a time in history before civilization was invented and before we lived in cities, both of which tended to separate us from the natural world. Most importantly, it was a time in history before humanity grew into the evolutionary agenda of ego development, when a perception of separation from nature became a maturational necessity.

In Epoch I, humanity lived within the natural world, gained its subsistence through hunting and gathering, and, as far as we can tell, found life's meaning and purpose from within nature. Humanity had a close and cooperative relationship with nature; for as hunter-gatherers, we knew intimately all the nuances of animal behavior and the seasonal cycles—which seasons provided what kinds of food and shelter, the timeliness of certain food availability, etc.

The unity of humanity and the rest of nature was a given in Epoch I. We would probably not even emphasize it, were it not for the critical contrast of Epoch II separation from nature. Life in Epoch I was *in* nature; life in Epoch II was, intentionally and necessarily, estranged *from* nature. We'll deal with the latter in the next chapter, but for now we simply state the obvious: in Epoch I humanity was in and of nature.

The import is Soul-level. Humanity's connection with or estrangement from nature will play a critical role in our understanding of the evolutionary history of the human Soul. What this book will make clear, as we explore this subject in greater detail throughout, is as follows. First of all, nature and the organic feminine principle are synonymous, and so Epoch I emphasized the feminine side of Soul. Second, the ego need for differentiation in Epoch II resulted in estrangement from the feminine side of Soul and an emphasis on the patriarchal. As we shall soon see, it is no accident that humanity in Epoch I worshiped an Earth Mother, whereas much of humanity in Epoch II worshiped a Heavenly Father. And, third, the whole-Souled condition of the spiritual maturity to which Epoch III is "calling" humanity necessarily involves a reunion with the natural world.

When we look at the entire body of evidence that we find in the Paleolithic cave art and when we listen carefully and thoroughly to the scholars who have dedicated their lives to understanding the meaning of that art, we find in our early human ancestors a pervasive preoccupation and a profound respect for the powers in and of the animal world. "Above all," write Clottes and Lewis-Williams, "Paleolithic art, from the beginning to the end, is an art of animal forms."[29]

To discover the spiritual significance in the animal paintings, however, we first need to address and dispel what had been a long and persistent misconception—namely, that the animal art was primarily done for the purpose of enhancing the hunt. There was a long period in which scholars believed that the reason there are so many animals in Paleolithic art was so-called "hunting magic," art for the purpose of magically assuring success in the act of hunting.

By the beginning of the twentieth century, the archaeological establishment had begun to interpret the cave art in this way. The primary scholars responsible for this interpretation were Salomon

Reinach, who wrote extensively on the subject beginning in 1903, and the Abbe Breuil, a Frenchman who was considered the leading expert in cave art and who promoted Reinach's theories up through the 1950s. Breuil dominated prehistoric research during the first half of the twentieth century; his support of the "hunting magic" theory virtually assured its status as orthodoxy. As so often happens when a giant in a particular field dies, as did Breuil in 1961, it opens the way for alternative interpretations.

Of course, hunting was part of our ancestor's lives during Epoch I, and we generally refer to all pre-agricultural and pre-herding peoples as "hunter-gatherers." But the issue for our discussion here is not the matter of hunting per se. Our purpose is very specifically a search for the values revealed in the cave art. In other words, what were the motivations behind the animal paintings on the Paleolithic cave walls and ceilings? The overwhelming percentage of the images painted on the Paleolithic cave walls and ceilings were of animal forms; but what did the artists have in mind as they were painting them? Was the artistry done for strictly utilitarian purposes, making the hunt more successful, or was it done for deeper, more spiritual purposes? Are the animal paintings revealing something about the DNA of humanity's childhood Soul?

A great deal of research throughout the latter half of the twentieth century has discredited the notion that the motivation behind the art was that of hunting magic. Rather, it seems that the cave art had more to do with respecting and celebrating the powers of the animal world in general and shamanic ritual in particular, so as to become one with the animal and to absorb its power.

At least three fields of study have recently converged to reveal the spiritual motivations behind the cave art of Epoch I. First of all, there is the careful analysis of precisely which animals appear on the Paleolithic caves walls and ceilings. A full sixty percent of all the animal images are horse, bison, or oxen. Images of deer, mammoth, boar, ibex, rhinoceros, and goats are also found, but they comprise a much smaller percentage. Also rare are fish and birds, as are carnivores like lions, hyenas, foxes, and wolves. Such analysis reveals that the animals painted do not represent, proportionally, the animals found in the surrounding natural habitat. "There is no doubt," write Leakey and Lewin, "that the images as they appeared on the walls did not accurately represent the animals in nature."[30]

Related to the analysis of the animals painted but also an observation that belies the hunting magic theory is that the number of animals bearing anything resembling implanted weapons, such as arrows or spears, were found to be negligible. In many cases, what was earlier thought to be arrows or spears, "on closer microscopic examination, proved to be plants, leaves, branches and trees."[31]

The second converging field of study undermining the hunting magic theory is the analysis of the diet of Paleolithic peoples. As already mentioned, horses were plentiful in the art, but nonexistent in the Paleolithic diet. On the other hand, reindeer, according to the archaeological evidence, were far and away the animals most hunted for food during this time. Yet, reindeer, comprising a significant part of the Paleolithic diet, are rarely among the animals painted on the cave walls. When we do find the rare painting of reindeer, it does not suggest hunting. As Ian Tattersall has stated,

> The most famous reindeer depiction . . . [on the cave walls] is hardly the kind of image one associates with hunting and killing. In the cave of Font de Gaume, just outside Les Eyzies, France, there is a badly faded but immensely moving painting of a pair of reindeer. On the right is a female, bending down with forelegs flexed, facing a male with magnificent antlers. The male reindeer, on the other hand, is leaning forward and gently licking the female's forehead. The scene is . . . full of tenderness. I, for one, am totally incapable of seeing this image in any violent context.[32]

The third field of study that strengthens the idea that the animal art was motivated by spiritual purposes rather than the practicalities of the hunt is an area we have already touched upon—evidence suggesting shamanic ritual as the cause of much of the painting. "The important point here," say Clottes and Lewis-Williams, "is that the paintings and engravings do not depict real animals that were hunted for food. . . . They are more like visions that were sought in a subterranean spirit realm for their [power]."[33]

Remember that the third stage in shamanic trance is that of becoming the animal so as to absorb its power. Then, as now, shamanic vision-quests were entered into for the purpose of discovering, and becoming one with, one's own spirit-animal. That animal became the shaman's "guide" into personal empowerment.

As Clottes and Lewis-Williams describe the shamanic origins of the art, they suggest that the descent into deep caves is analogous to a descent into the spiritual "underworld" where the shaman-artist, in the first stage of trance, painted the geometric images, and then, in the third stage of trance, became one with the spirit-animal:

> The desired spirit-animals appeared to them out of the rock. Then, as some altered states of consciousness permit, the questers may have swiftly sketched their projected visions in an attempt to fix them, to gain their power. Or, perhaps recovering from a deep trance in which drawing was impossible, they may have examined the rock surface to find vestiges of their visions and then, by painting or engraving a few lines, have been able to re-create them. Sometimes only a few strokes were required, together with the interplay of light and shadow, to bring back a vision.[34]

Interestingly, the research conducted by Clottes and Lewis-Williams closely conforms to what the great mythologist Joseph Campbell observed in what he called "The Hero's Journey," found in cultures throughout the world from time immemorial. Campbell observed a three-stage process of (1) separating from the world, (2) encountering new powers, and (3) returning to the world to teach and share the newfound empowerment. Consider the similarity as Clottes and Lewis-Williams describe the shamanic vision-quest behind the Paleolithic cave art:

> Then, transformed by their visions, filled with new power and insight, the questers returned through the entrails of the underworld, past the communally produced images that had prepared their minds, and out of the cave to rejoin their society in a new role, the role of shaman, seer, and intrepid penetrator of the underworld.[35]

It is challenging to look back ten-thousand to twenty-five-thousand years and attempt to interpret that time in human existence clearly, rather than to let our own historical and cultural filters create a distortion. For those of us who have been thoroughly conditioned by modern civilization, it may take a considerable mental and spiritual stretch to appreciate fully humanity's childhood Soul, particularly as it related to the animal world. We have had a long process of conditioning our eyes to overlook the differences between an animal in a zoo and the "same" animal in the wild. We slip into the fears that accompany unfamiliarity, assuming that those "vicious beasts" in the wild are "out to get us."

Throughout our attempt to understand humanity's childhood Soul, we must guard against the natural and usually unconscious tendency to project our Epoch II images of the animal world back onto a people who existed within a very different deep-value system.

We will fail to empathize adequately with our ancient ancestors if we do not try to grasp the awe and reverence with which they held the animal world and the shamanic rituals that were intended for becoming one with and absorbing the powers of those animals. After all, at this time in our evolutionary journey, humanity lived among the animals and knew that they had many superior powers—animals could see better in the dark, had a marvelous sensitivity to impending danger, many had awesome strength, were faster afoot, and could hear far better than the human species. Paleolithic cave art was evidently a shamanic and ritualized way of tapping into those powers. Native and indigenous peoples today, with nature-based spiritualities, still know this and, with the help of their shamans and through the ritual processes of vision quests, continue to access such powers and insights.

Epoch I Deep Value: Nonviolence

The issue of violence—Epoch I vis-a-vis Epoch II—is one of those subjects that truly tests the issue we were just discussing, namely, the challenge of not projecting our own experience of life back onto the humanity of ten-thousand to thirty-five-thousand years ago. This particular deep-value is, in fact, in such stark contrast to the values of the past six-thousand years of human history that to suggest that humanity was ever nonviolent strains credibility. Who would be so naive to think that the species we have known to engage in war, genocide, torture, rape, domestic violence, slavery, witch-burnings, etc.—yes, that humanity—could have ever been nonviolent? All of recorded history would appear to equate human nature with a violent nature. Or, as some might like to put it, testosterone and violence are synonymous: so as long as we have men, we are going to have violence. Indeed, judging from our current and recent experience , human-*kind* does appear to be an oxymoron.

The first thing to remember, however, is that all of "recorded history" is within Epoch II. Until recently, our entire memory of human history was limited to the past five-thousand or six-thousand years. We now have a longer view of history, a larger view of human evolution and, with Deep-value Research, a greater context of Soul from which to understand the human journey and the maturational changes through time.

In the next chapter, we will examine evidence that suggests that the kind of violence we currently equate with human nature does not appear in the historical record until about sixty-five-hundred years ago. But, for now, we will stay with our attempt to understand the deep-value system of our childhood Soul, the humanity of ten-thousand to thirty-five-thousand years ago.

This very exploration has a great deal of importance for our current struggles to understand and heal the Soul of violence; for if we find a twenty-five-thousand-year period in human history when we were nonviolent—almost five times the length of the time when humanity has exhibited violent tendencies—it at least raises the possibility that there is a nobility within the human species that might once again be recovered. A long enough, and deep enough, view of the past might just be a source of hope for the future of humanity.

There is considerable wisdom in the scientific dictum "the absence of evidence is not the evidence of absence." After all, we need to be careful about drawing conclusions that exceed the evidence. Nevertheless, one does not have to romanticize humanity's childhood epoch to suggest that the evidence we do have appears to reveal a value system very different from that of our recent adolescent epoch, particularly as it concerns violence.

Defining what we mean by "violence" is necessary, since everything from the collisions of planets and comets, to the destructive power of a tornado or hurricane, to predation among animals, to protective and defensive behavior when being attacked seems to slip under the term "violence." In this discussion, we are not talking about random acts of nature or about survival instincts. We are, rather, addressing the uniquely human version of aggressive and initiated human-on-human violence represented by war, witch-burnings, heretic executions, lynchings, rape, torture, and genocide, as

24

well as a history of human and animal sacrifice, the latter being the notion that we have to kill something in order to make it sacred or to appease a wrathful God.

As with the issue of interpreting cave art as "hunting magic," the notion that humanity has an innate and biological propensity for violence appears to be an Epoch II notion and a projection back onto Epoch I. As we saw in the interpretation of animal art, a particular theory can gain the status of dogma, when it is almost automatically accepted by scholars and the general public alike. Dogmatic orthodoxy can persist, in fact, long after there is ample evidence to discredit it. Such is the case regarding the dogma of humanity's genetic proclivity for violence.

Like so many other issues that are synthesized into our brief examination of the entire history of the human Soul, this subject is a big one—entire books are devoted to it—and we can only offer a brief summary.

A very influential strain of this dogma began in 1924 when Raymond Dart, an anatomy professor at Witwatersrand University in Johannesburg, South Africa, was handed a box of fossils that had been dug up in a lime quarry. Dart determined that they were the remains of a transitional species between apes and humans and gave it the name of *Australopithecus africanus* (Southern Ape of Africa). His interpretation regarding the innate nature of *Africanus*, however, had a tenacious and, as it turned out, misleading influence. Dart interpreted the presence of damaged skulls and bones as clear evidence that humanity's ancestral roots were extraordinarily violent, and his enthusiasm for dramatically and colorfully describing his belief in humanity's violent proclivities knew no bounds.

By 1953, Dart had developed his theory of human origins and published an article entitled "The predatory transition from ape to man."[36] He began the article with the words of Richard Baxter: "Of all beasts the man-beast is the worst. To others and himself the cruelest foe." Dart then stated his belief that our ancestors were confirmed killers, "carnivorous creatures that seized living quarries by violence, battered them to death, tore apart their broken bodies, dismembered them limb from limb, slaking their ravenous thirst with the hot blood of victims, and greedily devouring living writhing flesh." Humanity had, according to Dart, a "blood-spattered, and slaughter-gutted . . . history. The loathsome cruelty of mankind to man forms one of his inescapable characteristic features—it is explicable only in terms of his carnivorous and cannibalistic origin." He concludes that "man's taste for flesh is so great that human beings, whether in prehistoric or recent times and whether driven by need or not, have practiced either real or ritualistic cannibalism."

Dart's enthusiasm for his extreme beliefs and his vivid imagery made for dramatic copy. The only problem is that Dart's entire theory, as Christopher Stringer of the Natural History Museum in London puts it, "was based upon flimsy, and as we now know, misinterpreted evidence."[37] *Africanus*, says Stringer, "probably did not use tools at all, never mind weapons, and far from being a hunter, was in fact the hunted."[38] Modern research has confirmed that *Africanus* was primarily a vegetarian, and what little meat was eaten was probably scavenged from what other animals had left behind.

Richard Leakey is another of the many modern scholars who discredit Dart's thesis, saying that it simply does not hold up under scientific investigation:

> Skulls said to have been crushed by lethal blows in fact had been damaged by natural processes during fossilization. What were thought to be weapons turned out to be nothing more than the remains of hyenas's dinners. There is no evidence of frequent violence or warfare in human prehistory until after about ten thousand years ago. . . . Far from being an innately violent species, evolutionary history has endowed our species with an inclination to cooperate.[39]

All the scholarly debunking notwithstanding, it appears that current Epoch II humanity, perhaps anxious to find a genetic justification for our violent proclivities, preferred Dart's more dramatic interpretation of human origins. For it was the general public, in the latter half of the twentieth century, that made the American journalist Robert Ardrey a best-selling author. Ardrey, having become enamored with Dart's ideas wrote a series of books, including his 1961 opus *African Genesis*, that popularized the notion that humanity had violent and bloody origins. In spite of the publisher's warning on the jacket cover that Ardrey is "a dramatist, not a scientist," his words fell on welcoming Epoch II ears:

> Not in innocence, and not in Asia, was mankind born. The home of our fathers was that African highland reaching north from the

Cape to the Lakes of the Nile. Here we came about—slowly, ever so slowly—on a sky-swept savannah glowing with menace.

Our ancestry is firmly rooted in the animal world, and to its subtle, antique ways our hearts are yet pledged. . . . But the most significant of all our gifts, as things turned out, was the legacy bequeathed us by those killer apes, our immediate forebears.[40]

Once again, it is critically important, if we have a real desire to understand the human Soul of Epoch I, to let the evidence speak for itself, and resist the temptation to see it through Epoch II eyes. When we do listen carefully to "voices" coming to us from Epoch I, we hear our ancestors "speaking" a far more nonviolent "language" than what we have heard in the most recent five-thousand to six-thousand years.

Even a contemporary scholar the stature of Jared Diamond is not above projecting an Epoch II value system back onto Epoch I humanity. In trying to understand why and how Cro-Magnons replaced the Neanderthals, Diamond writes that:

My guess is that events in Europe (about 40,000 years ago) were similar to events that have occurred repeatedly in the modern world. . . . For instance, when European colonists invaded North America, most North American Indians proceeded to die of introduced epidemics; most of the survivors were killed outright or driven off their land. . . . By analogy, I guess that Cro-Magnon diseases, murders, and displacements did in the Neanderthals.[41]

Guesses and analogies, however, from humanity's Epoch II experience with violent behavior are neither appropriate nor accurate ways by which to understand what happened in Epoch I. Deep-value Research suggests that the respective epochs in the human evolutionary journey are shaped by entirely different DNA of Soul. Humanity had an entirely different evolutionary purpose and an entirely different deep-value system in Epoch I vis-a-vis Epoch II. Human nature is not static and unchanging over the long course of human history. Epoch I was not the same as Epoch II; and as we shall soon propose, Epoch III will be quite different from Epoch II.

Leakey speaks, once again, to the matter of violence:

The archeology of warfare fades fast in human history, rapidly disappearing beyond the Neolithic, ten thousand years ago, when agriculture and permanent settlements began to develop. . . . Back beyond that, beyond the beginning of the agriculture revolution, and the depictions of battles virtually vanish.[42]

As I have suggested before, a revealing fact is that we have a large collection of artistic representations of the Epoch I Soul, covering some twenty-five-thousand years, in which we find no depictions of human or animal sacrifice, no pictures describing any human-on-human violence, and no glorification of war or warriors. The same, obviously, could not be said of the art of the past five-thousand years. Riane Eisler writes:

> We know that art, particularly religious or mythical art, reflects not only peoples' attitudes but also their particular form of culture and social organization. If [during Epoch I] there was no glorification of wrathful male deities or rulers carrying thunderbolts or arms, or of great conquerors dragging abject slaves about in chains, it is not unreasonable to infer it was because there were no counterparts for those images in real life. And, if the central religious image was a woman giving birth and not, as in our time, a man dying on a cross, it would not be unreasonable to infer that life and the love of life—rather than death and the fear of death—were dominant in society as well as art.[43]

We'll discuss the matter of the Epoch I feminine religious imagery in just a moment. Before we leave the deep value of nonviolence, however, it might be helpful to revisit the African San of the Kalahari Desert, the people we considered earlier through the eyes of scholar David Lewis-Williams as he proposed a shamanic causation to their art. The African San are a particularly relevant people to consider regarding the Epoch I deep value of nonviolence since Dart's "evidence" of violent human origins came from the same basic geographical territory, namely, the Kalahari Desert.

In general, scholars have believed that modern examples of hunter-gatherers, who live in stark contrast to the dominant Epoch II cultures, are the best chance we have of seeing something in our world today that reflects the humanity of Epoch I. The African San have been extensively researched; many scholars believe that they provide a fairly accurate window into the past. Melvin Konner, a biological anthropologist at Harvard University, is one such scholar. In addition to his familiarity with the extensive research on the African San, Konner also lived with them for two years.

They live today, and have lived for millennia, Konner suggests, "in a kind of organic harmony, not only with the world of nature, but with one another. Their knowledge of wild plants and animals is deep and thorough enough to astonish and inform professional botanists and zoologists. . . . They kill only what they can eat and remain in a balance with game populations that has persisted for millennia. They have a great respect for and fascination with the animals they prey upon."[44] He also touches on that which is particularly relevant to our discussion here:

> This deep dwelling in the world of nature is mirrored by the organic harmony of the human social world. . . . War is unknown. Conflicts within the group are resolved by talking, sometimes half or all the night, for nights, weeks on end. Equality is universal. . . . Only intractable violence is more repugnant to the San than selfishness, and the former is so incomprehensible it seems to be classified more as mental disorder than sin.[45]

Konner refers to the traditional stereotype of ancient primitive humanity beings as "solitary, poor, nasty, and brutish." Judging from his research, however, and his own up-close and personal observation of the African San, he writes:

> Yet here . . . we view the most basic of human societies operating as it must have for millennia. . . . Plainly we are watching a sort of human experience with a proven viability vastly more ancient than our own. Far from solitary, it is above all things mutual. Far from poor, it is amply supplied and amply leisured. . . . Far from nasty, it is based on human decency, [and] respect for others.[46]

The Epoch I Deep Value:
Emphasizing the Feminine Side of Soul

Perhaps it was because humanity at this time in history did not understand paternity—after all, the male sexual role in procreation was too far removed from the actual moment of birth to presume a logical connection. Perhaps it was because early humanity was truly enamored with the miracle of birth and the nourishment received by the infant suckling at its mother's breast—after all, it was the female body that was the wondrous provider of both. Perhaps it was, at an unconscious level, what I have suggested earlier as the deep psychospiritual connection between nature and the feminine side of Soul. Perhaps it was a combination of all the above. In any case, and for whatever reasons, Epoch I humanity appears to have had, within its DNA of Soul, a deep-value system that included a celebration of and focus upon the female body's capacity for giving and nourishing life and the understandable religious consequence of worshiping a feminine image of divinity, namely, the Goddess.

Nature as Earth Mother

Because we are considering a time in history that preceded any written records, the notion that Epoch I humanity thought of nature as an Earth Mother is one that we have to draw by inference. Nevertheless, the inference is strong.

The mythologist Joseph Campbell writes:

> There can be no doubt that in the very earliest ages of human history the magical force and wonder of the female was no less a marvel than the universe itself. . . .
>
> The obvious analogy of woman's life-giving and nourishing powers with those of the earth must have . . . led [humanity] to associate fertile womanhood with an idea of the motherhood of nature . . . .
>
> The concept of the earth as both bearing and nourishing mother has been extremely prominent in the mythologies of [early humanity.][47]

Although the important work conducted by archaeology professor Marija Gimbutas focused primarily upon the Goddess image in Neolithic times (ten-thousand years ago until about thirty-five-hundred years ago) she, nevertheless, writes that all the symbolism of the later Goddess worship can be traced back to an earlier time when nature was seen as the archetypical female. "The main theme of Goddess symbolism is the mystery of birth and death and the renewal of life, not only human but all life on earth." Gimbutas also points out a fact that suggests early roots, namely, that "in all European languages, the Earth is feminine."[48]

Matrilineal and Matricentric Societies

It is logical that societies that emphasize the female body's capabilities for giving and nourishing life, especially in a time when male sexual activity was not associated with procreation, would trace their lineage back through their mothers—in a word, matrilineal. It also follows that these were societies centered around the woman—matricentric. Merlin Stone comments on this:

> The mother would have been seen as the singular parent of her family, the lone producer of the next generation. For this reason it would be natural for children to take the name of their mother's tribe or clan. Accounts of descent in the family would be kept through the female line, going from mother to daughter, rather than from father to son, as is the custom practiced in western societies today.[49]

Marija Gimbutas suggests that the emphasis upon birth and nourishing life, from the earliest Paleolithic evidence, "can be explained not only by the indestructibility of deeply ingrained life-giving and maternity symbols, but also as a strong memory of a matrilineal system when paternity was difficult to establish."[50]

Riane Eisler points to other evidence, found in early Paleolithic burials, where carefully arranged cowrie shells, along with red ocher, indicate a belief in the female body's being the source of rebirth or resurrection:

> Both the ritualized placement of the vagina-shaped cowrie shells around and on the dead and the practice of coating these shells and/or the dead with red ocher pigment (symbolizing the vitalizing power of blood) appear to have been a part of funerary rites intended to bring the deceased back through rebirth.[51]

Perhaps the strongest evidence suggesting any epoch's deep-value system is what is chosen for veneration and worship. As stated earlier, deep values are the creators and shapers of religion, as well as all other aspects of culture, rather than the result of religion. As Joseph Campbell put it, "In the Paleolithic period . . . the female body was experienced in its own character as a focus of divine force, and a system of rites was dedicated to its mystery."[52]

Vulvas and Goddess Figurines

Vulvas were among the earliest, and the most plentiful, of all the human images found in the Paleolithic cave art, as well as in sculpted portable art. Anne Baring and Jules Cashford report that

> there are more than 100 images of the vulva in Palaeolithic France alone, suggesting that stories of the goddess who gives birth were so familiar that they could be instantly recognized. Sometimes the vulvas have seeds and sprouts drawn over or beside them, or even rippling movement of water, suggesting that the cosmic womb was recognized as the source of the vegetative world and also the waters of life.[53]

The isolated depictions of the vulva, as we have been suggesting, were part of a larger emphasis upon the life-giving and life-nurturing aspects of the female. This all came to focus, in a more comprehensive sense, on the primary symbol of Goddess worship, carved figurines of what are sometimes referred to as "Venus" figurines. One remarkable fact is that Goddess figurines were sculpted over the span of about thirty-thousand years. A second remarkable feature is that they are found over a wide geographical range, from western Europe to Siberia. But perhaps the most remarkable thing of all is how similar they all are, suggesting a powerful unanimity within the human Soul. With little or no definition of the face, head, or limbs, the emphasis was always on the elements of birth and nourishing life: a female with large breasts and hips, frequently pregnant, usually showing a clear definition of the vulva.[54]

The consistency of the Goddess figurines, and their extent both geographically and historically, is, as Baring and Cashford state it, "a testament to a surprisingly unified culture—or at the very least, a common nexus of belief—lasting for a much longer period of time than their successors, images of the Father God."[55]

I have stressed several times the importance of not projecting the value system of Epoch II back onto Epoch I. It is important enough to repeat once again, this time in relation to masculine and feminine images of the Divine. Several archaeologists, earlier in this century, viewed the discovery of Goddess figurines as erotic images, evidence of Paleolithic pornography. This would be unthinkable were it not for the Epoch II assumption that God is masculine, for only when divinity is conceived of as masculine, could the feminine body be considered pornographic. Consider, for instance, how the conventional tendency is to de-sex anything considered divine and how virtually any discussion of Jesus' possible sex life is automatically viewed as heresy for many Christians. Anything erotic—certainly anything considered pornographic—is usually reserved for the profane, definitely not considered to be divine.

Along the same lines, Baring and Cashford reject the often-used term for the Goddess figurines as "Venus" figurines, for to do so "is to reduce the universality of a first principle—the Mother—to the name of the Roman goddess of love, who was by then only one goddess among many, all of them long superseded by the Father God as ruler if not creator of the world."[56]

One interesting observation is that, although vulvas are prevalent in cave art, alongside the aforementioned and numerous animal paintings, full images of the Goddess are not. Virtually all of the Goddess images are sculpted. I am not sure anyone has yet come up with an adequate explanation for this, and it may remain a mystery.

In any case, the bulk of the evidence we have from the Paleolithic era, or Epoch I in the human evolutionary journey, suggests that humanity's religious impulse was focused upon the female body and its capacities for giving birth and nourishing life. The object of worship was the ever-present Mother, the immanent Earth Mother, the Goddess. This stands in stark contrast to an Epoch II deep-value system that was decidedly focused upon the masculine side of Soul and, when conceiving of a God at all, conceived of a transcendent Heavenly Father.

Humanity's adolescent Epoch II, to which we will now turn, has demonstrated a profound childhood amnesia. Until recently, most of us thought, or at least consented to belief systems that proclaimed, that the only part of human existence that really mattered was the past five-thousand years of "recorded history." All the rest was lumped into one general and unimportant category—prehistory. Prehistory was pre-important, pre-civilized, defacto pre-human, and pre-religious as far as we were concerned.

But we are finally awakening to the fact that to forget our childhood epoch is to live in a poverty of Soul and to view our history with a tragic myopia. For the story of our childhood Soul, as we are beginning to remember it, gives us an additional perspective on the innate capacity, indeed, the nobility of the human species. In vivid contrast to what was to follow, we were in a close symbiotic relationship with our Mother the Earth. We were at home with all of nature and, therefore, with our innate feminine nature. We emphasized that which gives and nourishes life. We had a great appreciation of the powers represented by the animal world. We were nonviolent in comparison to our attitudes today. And we worshiped a feminine image of divine power.

Our childhood story was, all in all, a wonderful and wonder-filled story, a story of being whole-Souled, of peace and cooperation, of nature and nurture, and of art and spirituality. It was a paradise remembered in Epoch II creation myths all over the world.

Nevertheless, the time came in our evolutionary journey when, for necessary maturational purposes, we had to leave our childhood and to grow into and through the developmental purposes of our adolescence. That is what individuals do in order to live full and complete lives, and that is what our species apparently had to do in its evolutionary journey toward health and wholeness.

Questions for Those on a Quest

To quest is to question,
and the quality of the sacred quest
has more to do with the questions we ask today
than with answers entombed within past dogma.

1. When and how do you use the word *ancient*? Is something several hundred years old ancient? Should the Anasazi Indians of the American southwest (the word *Anasazi* literally means "the ancient ones"), who inhabited the region about one-thousand

years ago, be considered ancient? If so, what term do we use for our ancestors of thirty-five thousand years ago? What is your paradigm of the past?

2. How do you define *primitive*? Is there a judgment in your use of that word?

3. How do you define *uncivilized*? Is there judgment in the way you use that word?

4. Regarding the Epoch I respect for the powers of the animal world, in what ways, if any, is such respect applicable today?

5. How do you feel about humanity's worshiping the Earth Goddess for twenty-five thousand years? What perspective does that give to our recent ten-thousand-year long worship of a Heavenly Father?

6. If God's purpose for humanity has changed from time to time throughout history, and if our Soul's deep value system has been epoch-specific, what does this do to "traditional religious values?" What does it mean for our future?

7. How do you explain the twenty-five-thousand-year absence of any art glorifying war or warriors, and the lack of any evidence of human or animal sacrifices? Does that provide any insight relative to our concern today for a nonviolent world?

Chapter Two

Epoch II: *Adolescence*

10,000 Years Ago to the Present

. . . bonding of the human with the natural world was progressively weakened. Humans, in differing degrees, lost their capacity to hear the voices of the natural world. They no longer heard the voices of the mountains or the valleys, the rivers or the sea, the sun, moon, or stars; they no longer had a sense of the experience communicated by the various animals, an experience that was emotional and esthetic, but even more than that. These languages of the dawn and sunset are transformations of the soul at its deepest level.

Brian Swimme and Thomas Berry, *The Universe Story*[1]

The First Punctuation of Soul

Evolution is about as factual as you can get in science. There is simply no doubt in the scientific mainstream that life evolves. The details of evolutionary theory, on the other hand, are constantly in flux as we learn more. In other words, we have known for some time that life evolves, but our understanding of the precise process by which evolution takes place is . . . well, evolving.

Deep-value Research suggests that the human Soul is also engaged in an evolutionary process. As we mentioned in the introduction, the evolutionary history of our Soul appears to follow a pattern similar to Gould and Eldredge's theory of "punctuated equilibria," namely, an episodic evolutionary process rather than a continuous one, looking more like stair steps than a ramp. The human Soul apparently experiences long periods of relative stability, stasis, and equilibrium before being punctuated with a rapid transformation, only to be followed by another period of equilibrium.

We have just finished examining the first evolutionary epoch of humanity's Soul, a twenty-five-thousand-year long equilibrium in developmental purpose, as well as stasis in the Soul's deep values or DNA. About ten-thousand years ago, however, our Soul was punctuated with a "sudden" transformation of purpose, resulting in the emergence of an entirely new deep-value system or spiritual DNA .

Possibly related to the Soul's punctuation is the fact that a major geological punctuation took place about the same time. Following what had been a sixty-thousand-year long Ice Age, a massive global warming took place, what science calls the Holocene Period. It changed the physical landscape dramatically, as massive glaciers melted raising the oceans by some four-hundred feet, submerging a great deal of previously usable land, including nearly half of western Europe. It drowned sanctuaries of cave art; we don't know how many. It altered humanity's habits of habitation and isolated the Americas, England, and Japan, as well as the offshore islands of southeastern Asia.

Many scholars believe that the climatic and geological changes were, in fact, the cause of changes in the human psyche. They may be right, at least in part, for such major changes in the environment would undoubtedly have a deep and profound effect on the human Soul. The suggestion of Deep-value Research, however, is that that interpretation overlooks the most fundamental and influential cause of cultural, psychological, and spiritual change—namely, the transformation in the human Soul's evolutionary purpose and spiritual DNA. It was simply time, ten-thousand years ago, in the maturational journey of the human species for the natural organic process of growing out of childhood and into adolescence.

The extent and the significance of the psychological and spiritual changes that adolescence brought into the human experience can hardly be exaggerated. And, once again, we will try to do justice to an enormously complicated and complex period in history, the past ten-thousand years, with our necessarily brief generalizations.

Prior to this transformation, all of humanity, on every continent, lived as nomadic hunter-gatherers, apparently were nonviolent, and worshiped an immanent feminine image of the Divine, the Earth Goddess. After this transformational "moment," most of humanity turned to agriculture, began clustering in settled communities, grew in number, began to value the masculine over the feminine and humanity over nature, became an extremely violent species, and turned away from worshiping an earthly Mother to worshiping a heavenly Father.

Today, at the beginning of the twenty-first century, we conclude Epoch II with a strong human ego, considerable intellectual ability that has developed awesome technological powers of weaponry, travel, communication, and exploration—mind-boggling, spirit-stretching, and Soul-quaking changes that have taken place over the past ten-thousand years.

As diverse as those ten-thousand years appear on the surface—from the "dawn of civilization" to instant communication around the world, and from hand-held weapons to rocket-delivered nuclear warheads—this chapter will try to make clear that, throughout that entire time, humanity had only *one* stable Soul-level evolutionary purpose—ego and mental development—and one consistent deep-value system with which to facilitate that purpose.

Before exploring Epoch II deep values in some detail, however, there are a couple of considerations that will enrich our understanding of this time in human history. One is the transformational phenomenon itself, what is generally referred to as "The Stone Age," "The Neolithic Revolution," "The Agriculture Revolution," or what archeologist Goran Burenhult calls "The Great Transition." The other is how we might think about our traditional "creation stories."

To better understand the transformational period, we will utilize the metaphor of the chrysalis.

The Goddess and the Chrysalis

The metaphor of the chrysalis is helpful in understanding the first punctuation, or in this case, the first transformation of Soul. After all, these changes do not take place overnight. Something as dramatic as an epoch-sized transformation of evolutionary purpose and DNA of Soul—the agony of death for one deep-value system and the pain of birthing another—needs the passage of time. The caterpillar of humanity's childhood Soul, in other words, needs a chrysalis period of time in order to accomplish the substantial and challenging process of death and rebirth, disintegration and reintegration, destructuring and restructuring, dissolving and resolving. The DNA of Soul needs time to go through its metamorphosis; and the caterpillar identity, which had twenty-five-thousand years of habitually having its feet firmly on Epoch I ground, understandably needs a bit of time to grow a new identity and to get over the fear of flying.

As mentioned earlier, a new Epoch II butterfly Soul is an appropriate image because the Greek word for *soul* (*psyche*) is the same as the word for butterfly. Interestingly enough, Marija Gimbutas suggests that the butterfly was used as a symbol of transformation as early as 6,500 BC in carvings and on pottery.[2] Is it possible that humanity not only intuitively used the butterfly as a symbol of Soul, but also knew that they were living within a transformational period in history?

Given the chrysalis phenomenon, the first transformation of Soul began approximately ten-thousand years ago and took several millennia to complete the change. Paleolithic cave art apparently stopped rather abruptly ten-thousand years ago, but it is not until the second or third millennium BC that we can see Epoch II deep values gaining a general dominance over the human landscape.

If we were to pick one symbol for Epoch I, it would probably be the Mother Earth Goddess; after all, that is the image that Epoch I humanity chose as the embodiment of divine power. In this transition from Epoch I to Epoch II, therefore, we can say that the feminine Goddess went into the chrysalis and a masculine God came out.

It is important to recognize, however, that the evolutionary shift from an emphasis on the feminine side of Soul to an emphasis on the masculine side of Soul was not the "fault" of men. It was not a conspiracy thought up in some private men's club and imposed on human societies by which to shift the Soul-level emphasis from the feminine to the masculine. Once again, these evolutionary epochs, with their respective maturational purposes, are organic and Soul-level. The "Soulquake" that established the Epoch II fault line between the feminine and masculine sides of Soul was a divine initiative, if you will, for the purpose of facilitating the adolescent epoch in the overall maturational journey of humankind.

Humanity had developed a physical body, and it was time to develop an ego and mind. For that, in spite of how much we now view elements of that adolescent epoch as ugly and downright regrettable, we evidently had to experience a period of time in which we lived with a fractured Soul, emphasizing the illusion of separation.

A case in point is that agriculture, perhaps the primary catalyst for humanity's separation from nature and the eventual estrangement from the feminine side of Soul, was apparently, and ironically, an invention of women. "The sowing and reaping of grain," write Baring and Cashford, as well as "the transformation of grain into bread . . . may have been, to begin with . . . the invention of women, whose skills were transmitted from mother to daughter."[3]

It is significant, also, that the very image of the Goddess, in its metamorphosis within the chrysalis, became increasingly diversified, before it was eventually trivialized and demonized. There were goddesses of light and goddesses of darkness, bird, snake, and fish goddesses. And there were goddesses of agriculture, as Merlin Stone attests:

> In Mesopotamia, where some of the earliest evidences of agricultural development have been found, the Goddess Ninlil was revered for having provided Her people with an understanding of planting and harvesting methods.[4]

In spite of the various "faces" of the Goddess, the feminine image of divinity was always "the symbol of the unity of all life in Nature," as Gimbutas put it:

> Her power was in water and stone, in tomb and cave, in animals and birds, snakes and fish, hills, trees, and flowers. Hence the holistic and mythopoetic perception of the sacredness and mystery of all there is on Earth.[5]

Then, according to Baring and Cashford, within the chrysalis as it were, images appeared of a "sacred marriage between goddess and god, which was to endure for 5,000 years until it formally died with Hebrew and Christian monotheism."[6] After that, a masculine image of God ruled all the major theistic religions.

The transformation was complete. A feminine earthly Goddess went into the chrysalis, and a masculine heavenly God came out. The patriarchal warrior God either supplanted or assimilated the feminine side of Soul and a critical part of that was what the Goddess represented—the sacredness of the earth and all its creatures. Taking the place of a respect for nature was a prejudice against the outer world, a growing fear of nature and animals, an ego concern that humanity might fall back into its original animal state, and a self-proclaimed right to dominate and manage the rest of the world.

As we will see in our examination of the Epoch II deep values, mainstream cultures and religions grew to reject most of what was important in the epoch of the Goddess. From an ethic of relationship, mutual respect, and affirmation of the sacredness of all life, Epoch II became preoccupied with the "God-given right" to dominate and control, with the consequential ethic of aggression and combat. An immanent Mother Goddess was buried, sublimated, disempowered, and disenfranchised, while an emergent and adolescent masculine Soul emulated an image of the Divine personified in a violent and transcendent Father God. (We will revisit this theme, utilizing the parable of the prodigal son, later in this chapter.)

Creation Stories

Virtually every culture and every religion have stories that purport to describe the creation of the world. The question for us in the twenty-first century is how we relate to these stories.

One option is to take them literally. To do this, however, we have to ignore virtually everything we have learned scientifically about the universe in the past four- or five-hundred years. We would have to deny that the universe is about fifteen-billion years old, that this planet itself is about four-and-a-half-billion years old, that humanity became physically mature about one-hundred-fifty-thousand years ago, and that the people who were writing down those creation stories four- or five-thousand years ago knew nothing of all this scientific evidence. This option is untenable for those of us who think that science is extremely valuable in our ongoing attempt to understand the universe and life within it.

Another option is to discount out of hand anything religious or spiritual. Some scientists believe that the scientific creation story is the only one that counts, that evolutionary processes are completely devoid of divinity, meaning, and purpose, that everything happened and is happening completely by random chance, and that any spiritual explanation is an emotional need by those who don't have the courage to face ultimate meaninglessness. That option, too, is untenable for those of us who feel that scientific materialism is good for some things but not good for a complete explanation of reality— that physics and metaphysics are both participants in the real world.

To paraphrase Shakespeare, there are more dimensions to reality than are thought of in a materialistic philosophy.

These are subjects, of course, that deserve far more elaboration and nuance than is possible here. They are mentioned only to set the stage for two perspectives on creation stories that are relevant to our discussion about the end of Epoch I and the beginning of Epoch II. One perspective comes from a cross-cultural, multiethnic, and transreligious study of creation stories throughout the world, and the other perspective is a very particular interpretation of the favorite Jewish, Christian, and Islamic creation story, namely the Garden of Eden.

When the superb independent scholar Richard Heinberg spent a decade researching creation stories from throughout the world, he found a common theme: they represent a collective memory of a once but now vanished paradise, a memory that became codified in official religious creation stories. In other words, it might very well be that the world's creation stories, although written down well into Epoch II, actually incorporated a memory of Epoch I thousands of years earlier.

> Nearly all ancient peoples had traditions of a primordial era when humanity lived a simple yet magical existence in attunement with Nature. The ancients said that this original Golden Age came to an end because of some tragic mistake or failure that forced a separation between Heaven and Earth. Further, they said that the rupture between the two worlds precipitated a descent into the separateness, fear, and greed that characterize human nature as we know it today.[7]

Heinberg found a remarkable similarity in the creation stories of all peoples, ranging from the native and indigenous peoples on virtually every continent, to the ancient Greeks, to the scriptures of today's major religions. Anthropologist Roger Williams Wescott agrees, writing that,

> The fact that so much of our religious iconography . . . depicts a world radically different from any known (in historical times) may indicate, in terms of formative causation, that our paradisal realms are in fact group memories. Perhaps we resonate to the concept of Paradise because we once dwelt in Paradise.[8]

Deep-value Research sees this explanation as completely plausible. What we now know about the twenty-five-thousand years of

Epoch I, if remembered in the mythological and symbolic unconscious, passed down through millennia of storytelling, might very well come out looking like our creation stories—stories that purport to tell about the beginning of the world but that may, in fact, tell about the beginning of the Epoch II world and include memories of the Epoch I. The Garden of Eden story in the Bible provides a particularly fascinating suggestion that the Hebrew(s) who wrote that story may have had a remarkable intuition regarding the evolutionary purpose of humanity's adolescent epoch.

I am not suggesting that the author(s) of Genesis, written down sometime in the middle of the first millennium BC, would have consciously understood it in the way I will be suggesting. Nevertheless, consider the amazing correspondence as we look at that story in light of Deep-value Research and the maturational metaphor.

The book of Genesis actually contains two creation stories, Genesis 1:1–2:4 and Genesis 2:5 and following. A patriarchal Epoch II has favored the second version because it is the one in which Adam is created first and Eve is created out of Adam's rib. There has been little interest in the first creation story, in which male and female are created simultaneously. For our purposes, however, we will stick with the second story, for it is the one in which we sense an intuitive wisdom about the Epoch II evolutionary purpose.

Remember that the evolutionary and maturational purpose of humanity's adolescent epoch has been that of ego and mental development. Indeed, parents know that an adolescent develops a healthy ego, an independent sense of self, by experimenting with independent thought and action, no matter how scary that prospect may be to those of us who attempt to live within that wisdom as parents. Many times such development involves a rebellion against external authority. In the Garden of Eden story, God, like a wise parent, can be seen as prompting humanity's ego development through that normal process of rebellion.

Genesis 2:9 tells us that "the Lord God made trees spring from the ground, all trees pleasant to look at and good for food; and in the middle of the garden he set the tree of life and the tree of the knowledge of good and evil." Adam and Eve are told by God that they are free to eat the fruit from any tree in the garden but forbidden to eat from just one. In other words, all the trees but one are fair game; that particular tree is off-limits. Like typical adolescents, and precisely as

God would have expected, Adam and Eve become interested in that one forbidden tree. They exercise their ego, rebel against external authority, make an independent decision (unless you buy their attempt to scapegoat the serpent), and taste the forbidden fruit.

Are we to think that God was surprised by such typical and absolutely necessary adolescent behavior? Or are we to believe that God is so small and vindictive as to set humanity up intentionally for "The Fall," just waiting to impose harsh punishment? Sounds like an idea of God that an adolescent might create.

Through the lens of Deep-value Research, we read a story in which God not only facilitates humanity's ego development through the natural and understandable process of adolescent rebellion, but also facilitates humanity's mental development by means of the forbidden tree.

Remember that there were two trees in the middle of the Garden of Eden—the tree of life and the tree of knowledge. In the story, however, God forbade eating only the fruit from the tree of knowledge. We could stretch the meaning of this story a bit farther and suggest that the author(s) knew that humanity needed to be nourished by the fruit from the tree of knowledge— that is, the evolutionary development of the human mind—before being ready and able to consume the fruit from the tree of life, representative of the spiritual maturity of Epoch III.

I have no idea whether or not the authors of this creation story had this in mind when they wrote it—they probably did not. But we could approach this interpretation in the same way that the Oglala Sioux medicine man Black Elk thought about the legend of the White Buffalo Woman: "This they tell," he said, "and whether it happened so or not I do not know; but if you think about it, you can see that it is true."[9]

The primary purpose of this chapter, in addition to understanding the evolutionary purpose of humanity's adolescent epoch, is to clarify the nature and content of the DNA of the Epoch II Soul: the deep values that facilitated ego and mental development and thus shaped and determined mainstream human cultures for the past ten-thousand years. The deep values of Epoch II have been (1) reductionism (reducing wholes to parts), (2) patriarchy and hierarchy, (3) adolescent notions of power and control manifested through orthodox belief systems, and (4) the excessive use of violence. It is to those deep values that we now turn.

Epoch II Deep Value: Reductionism

The first deep value to emerge from humanity's Soul in order to facilitate ego and mental development, was reductionism, the process of reducing wholes to parts and then becoming preoccupied with the parts. At the beginning of the epoch, we reduced the human/nature whole in order to develop our ego; at the end of the epoch, for the purpose of intellectual development, we binged on analysis (literally, the taking apart), specialization, categorization, and compartmentalization.[10]

Consider the normal process of maturation. A growing individual develops his or her sense of self, an ego, by learning to distinguish "self" from "other," learning the difference between what is "I" and what is "not-I." In a similar fashion, humanity as a species had to go through the process of reducing the human/nature whole to the distinguishable and separate parts of humanity on the one hand and the rest of nature on the other. We now know that it is an illusion to think that we are separated from nature—we do, in fact, participate in a wonderfully complex web of relationships with all of nature —but the illusion was necessary for a period of time so that humanity could develop an "independent" sense of "self."

The illusion of separateness had a powerful influence for ten-thousand years. The previous whole of the human/nature paradigm had respectful, cooperative, and symbiotic internal relationships. That changed to a perception of fundamental distinction and separation, along with a self-proclaimed right of domination, manipulation, management, and control. We increasingly valued the small rather than the large, the micro instead of the macro, the specialist rather than the generalist, the clan rather than the cosmos, and the individual rather than the community.

The Introduction of Agriculture, Horticulture, and Animal Husbandry

The transition ten-thousand years ago from hunter-gatherers to settled herding and farming represented one of the most radical and wrenching changes in human history. Revealing its Soul-level quality, rather than simply an innovation in technology that then spread throughout the world, is the fact that it occurred throughout the world at approximately the same time: the beginning of Epoch II.

Countering what had been a previous misunderstanding—that agriculture had begun in the Near East and spread out from there, archaeologist Goran Burenhult states flatly that "we now know that agriculture developed locally and independently in many parts of the world."[11]

Agriculture and animal herding have often been credited with enabling civilization, humanity's pride and joy, to come into being. With the "dawn of civilization," humanity could settle down in one place and not have to be constantly on the move. Increasing specialization enabled larger and larger communities to manage their lives, enabled population expansion, and facilitated a variety of other consequences that we will explore in the following pages.

Because we have spent ten-thousand years being proud of our agriculture, horticulture, animal husbandry, and civilization, it may be important for us to be aware that some of that is also an illusion—or at least an exaggeration. For instance, physical stature and dental health apparently were not immediately better off due to the introduction of agriculture. Physiologist Jared Diamond reports that the average height of hunter-gatherers in Greece and Turkey ten-thousand years ago was five feet ten inches for men and five feet six inches for women. After three-thousand or four-thousand years of agriculture, men averaged five feet three inches, and women five feet one inch.

Indeed, on the American continent, agriculture brought about a deterioration of physical health. With the domestication of corn, the average Native American experienced rampant tooth loss and abscesses, and went from an average of one to seven cavities. There was a substantial increase in anemia, osteoarthritis, and in the general mortality rate. Diamond points out that,

> hunter-gatherers enjoyed a varied diet with adequate amounts of protein, vitamins, and minerals, while farmers obtained most of their food from starchy crops. In effect, the farmers gained cheap calories at the cost of poor nutrition. Today just three high-carbohydrate plants—wheat, rice, and corn—provide more than 50 percent of the calories consumed by the human species.[12]

Australian anthropologist Max Charlesworth suggests that, based upon current aboriginal cultures, our hunter-gatherer ancestors may have devoted only about twelve to twenty hours per week to the process of obtaining food, deliberately choosing "a simple technology and style of economic life so that they could devote themselves to the elaboration of a rich and intricate social and religious life."[13]

As we prepare to enter Epoch III, it would be helpful for us to see with clear eyes both the benefits and the drawbacks of the deep-value system that has held prominence for the past ten thousand years. Unquestionably, affluent societies enjoy a higher standard of living and a greater state of health, generally speaking. Nevertheless, most of us spend the majority of our waking hours "making a living" so as to retain our technological toys and the trappings of civilization. Most of us frantically rush into and out of our "relaxing" activities. And too few of us have a rich and deep soul life. Could it be true that we have gained the world and lost our soul?

Individualism and Anthropocentrism

It makes sense that the process of reductionism, combined with an adolescent ego, would eventually lead to individualism and anthropocentrism, the latter being, as *Webster's Encyclopedic Unabridged Dictionary* defines it, the belief "that humanity is the central fact of the universe . . . the final aim of the universe . . . [viewing] everything in terms of the human experience and values."

Consider, first of all, the rise of individualism. It would seem natural that, after millennia of falling apart and going to pieces, we would eventually reduce the group to a collection of individuals. After all, that is what a developing ego does.

Burial practices may provide the first evidence of how the emerging deep value of reductionism moved toward an individualistic focus. Professor of Archaeology Anthony Harding, an expert on Bronze Age Europe, writes that during the Neolithic period in Europe, most of the burials were "collective in the sense that the same space was used again and again":

> One of the most remarkable changes that heralded the arrival of new beliefs and practices after 2500 BC, and marked the beginning of the Bronze Age, was the shift to individual burial throughout much of central and western Europe.[14]

Mats Malmer, professor of Prehistoric Archaeology at the University of Stockholm, expands on this theme:

> In the first centuries of the third millennium BC, a surprising change occurred in Europe. . . . [A] new social system seems to have evolved giving greater freedom and rights of personal ownership to the individual. . . . They were the first individualists.[15]

Another natural outcome of reductionism and the adolescent ego is the reduction of our understanding and appreciation of the world in general to a self-centered focus upon our species in particular—anthropocentrism. That self-centeredness is a quality of adolescence is not exactly a news flash. But, in the overall big picture, we can see how inevitable it was that humanity, after separating from nature for the purpose of developing an ego, eventually cuddled up with the artificial and illusory teddy bear of anthropocentrism.

Consider religious conservatives, particularly modern-day fundamentalists, in this context. They have an accurate intuition regarding the changes taking place deep in the human Soul; they frequently know precisely what it is that is changing and don't like the changes one bit, cannot possibly attribute the changes to divine initiative, and try with all their might to resist the changes. The fundamentalist God is the caterpillar God; the butterfly, in their view, is a creation of the Devil. But you've got to give them credit: they intuit fundamental changes more accurately than those who worship materialism, consumerism, or, to use John Cobb's term, "economism."

As a consequence, history is full of religious folks trying to conserve and preserve the caterpillar, trying desperately to pound life into the corpse, via a frantic but doomed theological version of CPR. We saw it happen when the cosmological caterpillar of an earth-centered universe died and when the butterfly of a magnificently huge and mysterious universe birthed our imaginations to mind-boggling and spirit-stretching concepts of space and time. We saw it happen when the biological caterpillar of anthropocentrism died and when the butterfly of evolutionary time baptized creativity, change, novelty, and diversity. As we all know, even today, some public-school boards are still trying to envision the future through the rearview mirror and are rendering an enormous disservice to the children in their care as they attempt to constrict and restrict their minds for the purpose of maintaining religious dogma.

Fundamentalism is antihistorical, so its adherents will not pay attention to the lessons of history. If they were to understand history, however, they would know that the religious idolatry of worshiping temporary human concepts of God's world does not have a chance of survival. Their children, or their children's children, will eventually grow up and grow on. Idolatry, in the long run, does not stand a chance against the divinely inspired innate curiosity of the human spirit and the natural propensity for learning, growth, and development.

Even more tragic than humanity's having some growing pains, however, is what anthropocentrism has done to our relationship with the animal world. In humanity's childhood epoch, we considered animals to be the "first beings," ensouled kin and treasured teachers. We were in awe of and had great respect for their powers, considering them to be messengers of divine power from the Goddess. We had ritual processes by which our own "power" animal would be discovered. Our individual identities were usually linked to the particular characteristics of that animal. We hunted only what we needed to eat, did so in a sacred and ritualized manner, asked the animal to give of itself, and gave thanks for its sacrifice. It was a primal belief in "you are what you eat," combined with a sacred gratitude for the ongoing processes of life, death, and rebirth. Many native and indigenous peoples today still hold this sacred relationship with the animal world.

All that changed in mainstream human cultures during Epoch II. The past ten-thousand years have witnessed a mad rush to distinguish ourselves from the animal world emotionally, psychologically, and spiritually. We have done so in classic adolescent fashion, maintaining that we are not only "different" from the animals, but that we are "better" and "higher."

Insecure about maintaining this artificial division between humanity and nature, we constantly worked to accentuate the difference and to protect against the possibility of "falling back" and losing our hard-won gains. Civilization is the crowning human achievement. Cleanliness is next to godliness. *Webster's Encyclopedic Unabridged Dictionary* defines *animal* as an "inhuman" human, "brutish," referring to the "physical or carnal nature" of a human being "rather than to the spiritual or intellectual nature." We even introduce into our language pejorative expressions regarding our nearest evolutionary relatives. When we feel we have acted in a humiliating manner, we have "made a monkey" out of ourselves. When we are out of control, we "go bananas." When we act in an uncivilized manner, we say that we have "gone ape." And our strongest epithet, applied to someone who is found guilty of the most heinous of crimes, is that such a person is "nothing more than an animal."

To get to where we are today—having turned the ancient sacred hunt into a modern-day sport—we had to de-soul conceptually the animal world, creating an emotional and intellectual distance. We give the label "sportsman" to someone who is so unsportsmanlike as to consider it fair game if one side has a gun and the other does not. From killing only that which was needed for food and doing so in a highly ritualized and ensouled fashion, we started the game of shooting "game." Sacred ritual became sport, spiritually empowered souls became moving targets, and a messenger from God became a decapitated "trophy."

Thus, in our adolescent stage of Soul development, we began to treat animals and the natural world in a strictly utilitarian manner. If it is not good for humanity, it is good for nothing.

Reduction of the Human Soul

If there is a single most influential consequence of separating humanity from nature, it would be what this division did to humanity's Soul. As mentioned before, to separate from nature is to separate from the feminine side of Soul. However necessary for humanity's process of growth and maturation, that act of reduction caused a fracturing, a truncation, and a diminishment of the human Soul. Make no mistake about it, that loss of Soul has had an enormous range of consequences.

Without that loss of Soul, Saint Augustine, in the fourth century, surely would not have come up with the misguided, disempowering, and tragic idea of "original sin." In contrast, an Epoch III recovery of a whole-Souled condition leads Matthew Fox to proclaim humanity's "original blessing," a statement about our original at-one-ment with nature. Nevertheless, we needed at least a temporary Soul-quake along the gender fault-lines, what Morris Berman calls humanity's "basic fault" or what Chellis Glendinning has termed our "original trauma":

> Because we are creatures who were born to live in vital participation with the natural world, the violation of this participation forms the basis of our *original trauma*. . . . Original trauma is the

disorientation we experience, however consciously or unconsciously, because we do not live in the natural world. It is the psychic displacement, the exile, that is inherent in civilized life. It is our homelessness.[16]

The suggestion here is that the poverty and homelessness of our Soul was the fundamental cause of all the other Epoch II deep values: patriarchy and hierarchy, immature notions of power and control, and violence. A feminine impoverished Soul most certainly made the institutionalization of patriarchy and hierarchy inevitable.

Epoch II Deep Value: Patriarchy and Hierarchy

Our alma mater, in today's parlance, refers to the college or university from which we were graduated. If we return to the Latin meaning of that phrase, however, it suggests something relevant to this discussion.

Alma mater literally means "nourishing mother." We might say that, when we separated humanity from nature, we separated from our nourishing mother. With typical adolescent arrogance, we thought we humans were ready to "graduate" from our alma mater and no longer needed the close, symbiotic, and nurturing relationship with our Mother the Earth. Adolescent humanity thought that the time of symbiotic cooperation was over and it was time for competition and battle, domination and control.

The word *patriarchy* comes from the Greek *pater* (father) and *arche* (ruling power). Patriarchy refers to any institutionalized system of male dominance. Masculinity is fundamentally valued over femininity, maleness over femaleness, or as *Webster's Encyclopedic Unabridged Dictionary* defines it, "the father is the supreme authority in the family, clan, or tribe and descent is reckoned in the male line."

Although the seeds of patriarchy were planted in humanity's Soul ten-thousand years ago, patriarchy did not emerge on the surface landscape of human culture for several millennia. For reasons that we may never know, the seeds of patriarchy needed to germinate in the human Soul for a good long time, before rising to the surface of human culture.

Patriarchy is, of course, a hierarchy, so we will treat them as essentially the same deep value. In fact, although we will attempt to discuss all the Epoch II deep values separately, it will become increasingly obvious that there is no way to separate any of them neatly and completely. There is, in fact, a synergy between them. As professor of theology Rosemary Radford Ruether states,

> the patriarchal reordering of the family, its definition of land as patrilineal property, the scribal religious elites who controlled written records, the development of war, and the warrior nobility probably all emerged as part of an interconnected process.[17]

At least in terms of the evidence that we currently have available, all additional Epoch II deep values appeared in the human record about the fifth millennium BC. In other words, there was a germination period within the human Soul in excess of three-thousand years. At the level of Soul, however, a time schedule such as that should not be surprising. As mentioned earlier, cosmic, geological, and spiritual time operate on a very different time scale than that measured by the clock on the wall, the watch on our wrist, or the calendar on our desk.

Marija Gimbutas has suggested that patriarchy and violence appeared simultaneously about 4500 BC, with people from the Volga basin of southern Russia. She dubbed them the "Kurgans" because their dead were buried in round burrows, *kurgan* being the Russian name for "burrow." The Kurgan invasions of the peaceful Goddess-worshiping cultures represent the earliest evidence we have of both patriarchy and violence. The prime characteristics of the Kurgans, in addition to patriarchy, were the herding and slaughtering of large animals, the domestication and importance of the horse, and a reliance upon weapons.[18]

Other institutionalized forms of patriarchy seemed to sprout shortly thereafter all across the human landscape. Evidence found in Sumerian cities of the fourth and third millennia BC suggests that families began tracing their lineage back through their fathers, and that there began the hierarchical prominence of male priests, the institution of slavery, and the male control of and rule over land and other possessions.

Among the propensities of patriarchy are male authority, the exclusive ownership of land, and control, domination, and management of animals. Those beliefs and priorities eventually lead to authority over and ownership, control, and management of wives, concubines, and slaves. For at least seven-thousand years, patriarchal cultures have dealt with women in the same fashion as they dealt with nature: viewed as private property and commodities to be owned, enslaved, managed, used, and abused.

Megaliths and Masculinity

One of the early interesting manifestations of patriarchy, perhaps an unconscious symbol of hierarchy, was the megaliths that began to appear along the coastal areas of western Europe about six-thousand or seven-thousand years ago. The earliest known megaliths are found in France and Ireland. These stone monuments, many of which were large vertical monuments, may have been phallic symbols for the male generative power in nature, or they may have symbolized the hierarchal reach for the heavens. What we do know is that most of them were constructed over burial sites of male leaders.

The megalith tradition reached its height in Europe about 3000 BC with magnificent monuments such as Stonehenge in England, Newgrange in Ireland, and the stone alignments that span more than a half mile at Carnac in Brittany, France. The tradition died out shortly thereafter in Europe, however; and their precise religious, communal, and/or astronomical significance remains a mystery. One can speculate, however, on the possible link with the Egyptian pyramids, the building of which reached its zenith during the fourth dynasty—2575 BC to 2465 BC. The Egyptian pyramids were also tied closely to the patriarchal and hierarchal deep values. As Egyptologist Boyo Ockinga writes,

> [t]heir massive structures are apt symbols of the Egyptian state, with the king at its apex, his officials (drawn mainly from members of his family) at the higher levels, and the mass of the people forming the bulk of the pyramid.[19]

Other megalithic-type structures are found in Central and South America, as well as in Polynesia—the tombs of Tongan chiefs, the temples of Hawaii, and the famous giant stone statues on Easter Island—but those were from a much later time. The Easter Island statues, for instance, as well as the pyramids in Mesoamerica, were probably crafted as late as the first millennium AD.

Throughout the last two millennia BC, the deep values of patriarchy and hierarchy completed the transformation of virtually all the major cultures of the world. Gerda Lerner tells us that "[t]he period of the 'establishment of patriarchy' was not one 'event' but a process developing over a period of nearly 2,500 years, from approximately 3100 to 600 B.C."[20]

This book is not, however, simply an academic survey, analyzing historical and institutional processes, with an objective eye, at arm's length, in a cold, detached, uninvolved, manner. We are concerned here with what these deep-value shifts did, and are doing, to the real lives of real people. This is not a disembodied "head trip," but a full-bodied, full-spirited, and ensouled sacred quest.

History as "His-story"

Consider, for instance, the fact that the art of writing emerged on the human scene at about the same time that patriarchy was becoming firmly established in the human Soul. Virtually all of "recorded history," therefore, is written from a patriarchal bias. All official literature, including religious scriptures, was written by men, for men, and from a patriarchal perspective of the world. Self-centered, adolescent humanity thus defined all of *his*-story as "human history." Everything prior to was generally passed off as simply "prehistory."

It is important to recognize the special and powerful arrogance that is possible with any perspective or system of thought that is "baptized" by religion. "Believers" tend to think that their scriptures are "revealed truth"—uninterpreted, unadulterated, direct messages from God Almighty. The deep values on which they are based, therefore, are not viewed as temporary, appropriate only for a given period of time and for a particular evolutionary purpose. Once a deep value like patriarchy creates religions, as happened in Epoch II, the patriarchal perspective is perceived as divinely ordained, permanently and absolutely. It then becomes orthodox dogma and is thought to be beyond human questioning. It should not be tinkered with, challenged, or changed. In fact, to question the essential deep values enshrined in official religious scripture is viewed as heresy, apostasy, and sacrilege. Many people have been killed for raising such questions. For many people, religion is meant to provide answers, not to entertain questions.

Consider once again the Garden of Eden creation story in the book of Genesis. We referred earlier to the fact that there are actually two creation stories and also mentioned why the first story, in which male and female were created simultaneously, is not the one most people think of when thinking of "the biblical story of creation." It is understandable, given a patriarchal Soul, that the second story is the most familiar one—the story that has Adam's being created first and Eve's being created out of Adam's rib; the story that has Eve responsible for the rebellion against God, the consequences for which are the pain of childbirth, man's labor, and death itself; and the story that tells Adam that he is supposed to rule over Eve. The second creation story became not only the more familiar but, as Gerda Lerner points out, has been "interpreted in the most literal sense for thousands of years to denote the God-given inferiority of woman."[21]

Because of this long his-story of patriarchal sexism, many people, women as well as men, assume without question that God is male. It is the reason men have been assumed to be the only ones eligible for positions of power and influence in the religions of Epoch II. It is the reason all the books in the Bible, as far as we know, were written by men, the reason slavery is accepted in the Bible and never fundamentally challenged, and the reason there is no female in the Holy Trinity. And it is the reason some factions of the Christian Church still maintain that "God's earthly representatives," those who broker the Kingdom of God, have always been, are now, and forever should be men.

Even though there have been men who were kind and benevolent towards women throughout Epoch II, kindness and benevolence within a system of dominance and submission are neither sufficiently kind nor adequately benevolent. A biblical justification for injustice does not make it just. A theological rationalization for and a presumption of a "God-ordained" bigotry do not change the fact that it is still bigotry. A tepid dominator is still a dominator. Sexism, like racism and anti-Semitism, is just plain wrong—it stinks, no matter how much cologne you splash on it.

Theologian Elizabeth A. Johnson exposes both the power and the consequences when patriarchal language is given the status of divine fiat:

> Women have been robbed of the power of naming, of naming themselves, the world, and ultimate holy mystery, having instead to receive the names given by those who rule over them. Since language not only expresses the world but helps to shape and

create it, learning to speak a language where the female is subsumed grammatically under the male gives girl children from the
beginning the experience of a world where the male is the norm
from which her own self deviates.[22]

And Jungian analyst and author Jean Shinoda Bolen points out
that "as long as what is considered sacred is always in the image of
men, a whole aspect of what divinity is for women is not accessible
to us."[23]

Christiane Northrup, a prominent physician specializing in the
care of women, writes about what happens in the delivery room:

> I have been in the delivery room countless times when a female
> baby is born and the woman who has just given birth looks up at
> her husband and says "Honey, I'm sorry"—apologizing because
> the baby is not a son! The self-rejection of the mother herself,
> apologizing for the product of her own nine-month gestation
> period, labor, and delivery, is staggering to experience. Yet when
> my own second daughter was born, I was shocked to hear those
> very words of apology to my husband come right up into my brain
> from the collective unconscious of the human race. I never said
> them out loud, and yet they were there in my head—completely
> unbidden. I realized then how old and ingrained is this rejection
> of the female by men and women alike.[24]

Dr. Northrup touches upon one of the most insidious consequences of any system of oppression—when the oppressed unconsciously accept the perspective of the oppressor. It is not difficult to
find women who thoroughly accept—indeed, endorse—the patriarchal assumptions of their culture and religion. Examples of that,
however, say more about the power of an epoch-long deep-value
system than they do about what is really right, best, and most
empowering for a woman's soul.

Epoch II Deep Value: Power and Control

After we fell apart (reductionism) and then arranged the parts in a
vertical order of importance (patriarchy and hierarchy), the flow
and use of power and control were essentially set—power-wielding
hierarchies that control people's lives from the top down.

A love-hate relationship with authority is characteristic of an adolescent—wanting authority figures, participating in creating certain authority figures, worshiping authority figures (hero worship), engaging in codependent relationship with authority figures, while at the same time rebelling, separating, and declaring independence.

Epoch II humanity has manifested adolescent notions of power and control in two general ways. One way has been to project authority upwards to the top of the hierarchy and then acquiesce to that power and control. The other way has been to claim hierarchal power ourselves so as to wield control over those whom we have identified as below us on the hierarchal ladder. Although we cannot, in reality, neatly separate and compartmentalize the social and political realm from the religious and theological, for the purpose of our analysis here we will do so artificially, while examining the upwards and downwards flow of Epoch II power and control.

Social and Political Manifestations

As agriculture and herding were adopted, a social organizational process began that had never been seen prior to this time: people began clustering together in ever-increasing numbers, with an increasingly patriarchal and hierarchal social structure and with power and control becoming concentrated at the top of those hierarchies. From small egalitarian social organizations based on the extended family, we gradually moved in the direction of larger groups being controlled from the top down. We moved from kin to kings, kin-doms to kingdoms, clans and tribes to chiefs and chiefdoms. Eventually, we established city-states, then nation-states, and dynasties and empires. By the time the Epoch II DNA of Soul had completed its work, but before the Epoch III transformation of Soul began, the entire world was dominated by monarchies, empires, and totalitarian states and dictatorships, wherein the strategy of colonialism—taking control over greater amounts of land and larger numbers of people—became accepted throughout the world as the way a nation became a great nation.

A brief global overview of this epoch-long tsunami that flooded human cultures would look as follows.

Evidence of social stratification and status is found as early as the seventh and sixth millennia BC in the burial customs found in Catal Huyuk and Hacilar, the Anatolian towns in what today we call Turkey. Likewise, evidence of chiefdoms are found in the Fertile Crescent by around 5500 BC. Jared Diamond reports the following:

> As regards population size, chiefdoms were considerably larger than tribes, ranging from several thousand to several tens of thousands of people. . . . Instead of the decentralized anarchy of a village meeting, the chief was a permanent centralized authority, made all significant decisions, and had a monopoly on critical information.[25]

In Mesopotamia, the early dynastic city-states, some of which had come into being as early as 4000 BC, were superseded when the Semitic military ruler Sargon of Agade formed the Akkadian empire in 2350 BC. "This empire," writes Arizona State anthropologist Charles Redman, "was so integrated that many scholars consider it the first nation-state in world history."[26]

Our purpose here is not to analyze in great detail the precise timing and all the various nuances of how all the major cultures worldwide adopted the patriarchal and hierarchal manifestation of power and control. It would seem obvious, in an overall general sense, that the vast majority of humanity gradually moved in this direction, beginning with the Egyptian dynastic tradition about 3000 BC, followed by dynasties and empires developing throughout the rest of the world that exhibited Epoch II hierarchal power—the Ottoman Empire, the Holy Roman Empire, the Byzantine Empire, the Han Empire in China, and the imperial tradition in Japan. And then there were the Inca, Mayan, and Aztec empires in the Americas.

The overall process of building bigger and bigger sociopolitical pyramids—power and control concentrated at the top as rulers took over more and more land and greater and greater numbers of people—continued even up through the first half of the twentieth century, although the Epoch III model of political empowerment (democracy) began its inevitable ascendancy in the eighteenth century. We will examine that transition much more carefully in chapter six.

Before we leave the building of social and political pyramids of power throughout Epoch II, however, we might take a brief look at the exceptional experience of India. About 2400 BC, a diversity of cultures merged into one distinctive culture that became known as the Harappa culture. Unlike many other cultures around the planet at this time in history, however, the Harappa culture lacked evidence of royal burials, symbols of priestly, or other hierarchal authority, and showed no clear evidence of a wealthy class. "So it would seem," write scholars Ian Glover and Himashu Ray, "that the usual model of a kingdom or empire, headed by a 'priest-king' . . . holding authority through dynastic succession, does not apply in this case."[27]

Yet, paradoxically, the people on the Indian subcontinent manifested the Epoch II deep value of adolescent notions of power and control through their caste system. The caste system apparently began about 1500 BC as structured racism: the original term for the caste system was *varna*, which means "color." Over millennia, the determining factor in the caste system became occupation rather than skin color, but it was still a system of power and control, domination and oppression. Indian scholar Shashi Tharoor writes:

> Members of the same caste usually worked in the same profession, married and ate within their caste groups, and tended to look down (or up, depending on their place on the social ladder) on other castes. Caste rules acquired rigidity over millennia: Brahmins would not eat food cooked by non-Brahmins; Untouchables, who performed such "polluting" tasks as disposing of waste or handling carcasses, could not draw water from wells reserved for the upper castes, or live in upper-caste areas; Brahmins would feel obliged to bathe afresh if the shadow of an Untouchable fell across them. . . . Intimate contact, let alone marriage, across caste lines became unthinkable, except in the context of a master-servant relationship.[28]

In India, we also have an example of what was mentioned in the introduction about one aspect of Deep-value Research—that we are interested in the values reflected by how people actually live, not what their religions officially proclaim or what some of the more spiritually evolved leaders or prophets may have said. For instance, Hinduism, the primary religion in India, is a religion about as free from hierarchal power and control and free of adolescent ego needs such as exclusive claims to "The Truth" as any religion on this planet. Hinduism proclaims that all religions are of value, and Hindus may venerate the saints and scriptures of other religions, a remarkable degree of religious tolerance in Epoch II. Nevertheless, the hierarchal and disempowering caste system continued to dominate the culture.

In spite of the Buddha's denouncing the caste system in 500 BC, as did Mahavira, the founder of Jainism, the institutionalization of Epoch II power and control continued. Also preaching against the prejudice and discrimination of the caste system were Nanak, the founder of Sikhism, and more recently, Gandhi. Nevertheless, the caste system prevailed because the people of India, as well as most the rest of humanity, participated in the Soul-level Epoch II deep value of hierarchal power and control.

Religious and Theological Manifestations

The religious and theological version of Epoch II deep values shares in the need to reduce and separate reality into pieces: heaven and earth, spirit and matter, good and evil, divine and human, and, all too often, the one and only True Religion versus all the others. As we have already discussed, there are the patriarchal assumptions that ultimate divinity is a masculine God and that most of his representatives on earth must be men.

When our image of divine power shifted from an immanent Mother Earth to a transcendent heavenly Father, ultimate power was projected up and out. With the deep and unconscious influence that the epoch-long DNA of Soul has, patriarchal and hierarchal authority seems obvious to us today. Whoever controls, of course, is above who- or whatever needs to be controlled. The ultimate power, of course, is God "up in his heaven." Men, of course, are ordained by God to assume the next level of power, over nature, animals, women, and everything else. Humanity, of course, is sinful and powerless to do anything about its fallen state, and must, therefore, submit to the authority of God mediated down through God's earthly representatives, men. Of course, of course.

We can see this pattern manifested all around the world throughout Epoch II. Take Egypt as one example:

> Egyptian history is described according to its dynasties of rulers.
> . . . [W]hat we call the Predynastic period (about 5000 BC to 3000
> BC) was a time when the gods ruled on Earth; later, they handed
> over the kingship to earthly rulers . . . .

The institution of kingship was central to ancient Egyptian civilization, and although it sometimes failed, it was never replaced by another form of government. . . . (All four of the female rulers we know of acted out a male role.) . . . The king shared in the divinity of the gods to a greater or lesser degree . . . [and] from the fourth dynasty onwards, the title "Son of Re" appears proclaiming the king as the son rather than the incarnation of the sun-god.[29]

Throughout the world, we can see various versions of the same theme: an all-powerful and all-controlling heavenly Father God and/or a Son of God, who is considered to be the incarnation of the ultimate divinity, and/or human kings, so-called "sage-kings," emperors, patriarchs, pharaohs, or popes, ordained by God to be his representative on Earth, to wield unquestioned and unchallenged authority. Throughout the ages, throughout the world, proclamations of "the Son of God," validated by a legend of a virgin birth and/or either immortality or resurrection are the typical trappings of Epoch II power and control.

An example of this that many of us in the western world are familiar with is the history of Epoch II Christianity. In it, we can recognize much of the reductionistic, patriarchal, and hierarchal theological structure just discussed. Once we had separated heaven and earth and the divine and human, and once we had projected goodness and power up into heaven, as well as established the sinfulness and depravity of humanity, the perfect gap was created into which an imperialistic institution could step: the Church then proclaims itself to be the one and only conduit from earth to heaven, the only means to get from sin to salvation.

The claim to exclusive salvic power carried control to an extreme, for if one wanted to be "saved," one had to play the Church's game and believe the Church's official dogma. Anything less, any creative or independent thought, anything even remotely rebellious signaled doom. If one had the audacity to challenge the Church's demand for absolute conformity to official orthodoxy or if one had a proclivity for independent thinking, excommunication was the consequence, or, as we will examine shortly, violence was one's due. In other words, not conforming to the Church's line led one to removal from the only institution that provided "salvation" or to death, so the thinking went, in order to save one's soul. Eternal damnation was the threat and, presumably, the consequence. *Heresy*, by the way, literally means "to choose," and anyone making independent choices regarding his or her life and thought was, well, in one hell of a mess.

Given the overall deep-value system, the time inevitably arrived when the Church would feel that the threat of excommunication for independent thinkers would not be enough to gain and maintain sufficient control. Resorting to violence would be the next inevitable step. In the thirteenth century, the Church decided that heretics should not only be excommunicated, but should be put to death. Consequently, when the threat of eternal fire and damnation did not bring people into line and assure proper conformity, temporal fire was literally applied , and the heretic would be burned at the stake.

That gets us into the last Epoch II deep value: violence.

Epoch II Deep Value: Violence

The subject of violence is so huge and complex that we cannot attempt to give it a thorough and careful treatment here. At the same time, that violence has been a prominent deep value throughout Epoch II is self-evident, so we need not document it extensively. Just a couple of observations may give the subject an important nuance or two.

First of all, violence as we know it has been exclusively an Epoch II phenomenon, emerging on the historical scene in the fifth millennium BC. The suspicion, therefore, is that the causes of violence can be found in the Epoch II DNA of Soul—in other words, an inevitable result of the Epoch II deep values—and that there is the reasonable hope, therefore, that we can grow up and out of our violent proclivities in Epoch III when the DNA of Soul is transformed.

A Prism of isms

Reductionism had us preoccupied with differences. Patriarchy and hierarchy had us arranging those differences in a vertical ladder of importance, or what might be described as a socio-political-theological pyramid whereby power and control flowed downwards from "the man at the top." All these values conspired to create a worldview seen through a prism of isms—anthropocentrism, individualism, sexism, racism, anti-Semitism, nationalism, colonialism, materialism, rationalism, etc.

In virtually every case, when a sacred relationship is fractured, when a "thou" is conceptually transformed into an "it," the rationalization for the use of violence is not far behind, particularly when combined with an adolescent ego. When the "it" doesn't obey, when the "it" gets in the way, when the "it" does not conform to the controlling efforts of the ruling person or class, violence is easily rationalized and justified.

There is the natural tendency to fear that from which we are estranged, and it is the fear of category pollution that has justified a great deal of violence—the fear that human nature might be polluted by animal nature, that men might be polluted by women's sensuality, that our "pure" race might be polluted by interracial marriage, that savages might pollute civilization, that homosexuals might pollute heterosexuals, etc.

Consider just a few examples. First of all, human and animal sacrifice are found only in Epoch II. It is only with our current deep-value system that we would think that we had to kill something in order to appease an external God or that something would have to be killed in order to make it sacred, the literal meaning of the word "sacrifice."

Second, consider how the Epoch II deep-value system laid the official ecclesiastical and theological foundation for one of the sickest, most hideous, and tragic periods in Christian history—the witch-craze. From the fourteenth through the seventeenth centuries, the Church and the state conspired to exterminate systematically anyone who did not conform to what the Church deemed proper and orthodox. Women, because they most closely represented nature, sex, and sensuality, were singled out. Somewhere between a half-million and nine-million people, mostly women, were tortured and killed for being witches and heretics.

The excessive need for power and control, the fear of nonconformity, and the prism of isms created a lens through which suspicion of anyone who looked different or lived or believed differently led to centuries of incredible violence. The Italian philosopher Giordano Bruno was burned at the stake simply because he articulated a cosmology that was before its time, suggesting that the Earth moved around the sun. A religious group known as the Cathars, presumably because they were capable of ecstasy, visions, and trances, were singled out, with entire towns being put to death. Babies were butchered so that they would not grow up to be a Cathar. So zealous were these protectors of right belief that they actually tried and convicted people of heresy after their death, and then exhumed the body so as to burn it properly!

Third, consider how the invading Europeans engaged in widespread genocide among Native Americans. After all, through the prism of isms, the invaders saw "savages," not fellow human beings, and saw a "pagan" spirituality that had to be destroyed in favor of "white man's religion." And the same deep-value lens kept many good people from seeing the horrible injustice involved in the institution of slavery.

Nor do we have to go back into the annals of history to find examples. Consider the recent life and death of Nora Marzouk in Islamic Egypt. Nora and her lover eloped. Nora's father, rather than being able to celebrate her love and her marriage, saw only a violation of religious and cultural tradition. He attacked his daughter on her honeymoon and cut off her head—after all, it was a traditional value in their culture that whenever a woman engages in premarital sex, elopes, is seen in public with a man who is not a relative, or goes outside without a veil, there is every justification for her to be beaten or killed by her father, brothers, or husband. In this particular case, the father carried Nora's head through the streets of his town saying, "Now, the family has regained its honor." "Honor and integrity in Egypt have become warped," wrote a leading Egyptian feminist. "For many Egyptian men, integrity is now linked to the actions and behavior of the women in the family."[30]

As another example, consider how the regret at having girl babies can result in an epidemic of infanticide. Today, in a hospital in Madurai, India, " . . . out of 600 female births, 570 babies vanish every year."[31]

As a final example of Epoch II violence, consider the practice of female circumcision. In some other parts of this world, women family members deceive and trap the young girls of the family, holding the child down as her clitoris is cut away, usually without any form of anesthesia—a patriarchal "cultural tradition" of genital mutilation that has scarred the bodies and lives of "some one hundred million women and girls worldwide," according to poet, novelist, and activist Alice Walker.[32]

It has been a patriarchal and violent world for ten-thousand years. It is not, however, a world without hope. As long as this world has people like Alice Walker, there is reason to hope that it can be a world that will grow into a higher level of sensitivity, compassion, love, justice, and spiritual maturity. Walker is one of the prophets of Epoch III, writing in 1997 that "as we approach the millennium, I think it is necessary to consider that the human race, like the living organisms that left the oceans for dry land, is at the beginning of learning an entirely new and different way to be on the planet. The way of *conscious* harmlessness."[33]

Walker was in Bolgatanga, in northern Ghana, making a film dedicated to the abolition of female genital mutilation. She was sitting next to a tree during a break in the filming. Alongside her was Samuel Zan, the general secretary of Amnesty International in Ghana. After a long silence, Zan spoke: "Alice, do you know what I believe? I believe that if the women of the world were comfortable, this would be a comfortable world."[34]

A Modern Parable of the Prodigal Son

Historians and other scholars refer to the past six-hundred years in human history as "the Modern Age." This extremely influential period of time in history deserves its own treatment. It is often seen as representing a radical break from prior times, many historians and cultural analysts describing it as one of the major transformations in human history. Deep-value Research, however, suggests that it is but a natural extension and exaggeration of the Epoch II evolutionary purpose, namely, ego and mental development, as well as the logical conclusion and culmination of the Epoch II deep values.

The parable of the prodigal son provides an appropriate image with which to consider the past six-hundred years. The biblical story found in Luke 15:11–32 is not our interest here, only the image and the metaphor: an adolescent son's completing his ego development by choosing to leave his home and father and go out on his own.

First of all, because Epoch II has been humanity's adolescent evolutionary epoch and patriarchy has been one of the epoch's primary deep values, the image of the adolescent male is appropriate.

Second, in the journey of life, what we decide to leave is often as important as what we are drawn to. In the big evolutionary picture, we left our Alma Mater at the end of Epoch I and moved in with Dad. For most of Epoch II, we thought that our Father served our needs. Nevertheless, before Epoch II could be finished, before humanity's mental and ego agenda of maturation could be completed, we—the Epoch II adolescent, in the persona of the Prodigal Son—needed to distinguish and separate ourselves from the Father and go it alone.

Third, as we explore the nature and content of the Prodigal Son's sojourn, we will also recognize why the term *prodigal* is appropriate for the metaphor of the Modern Age. The word literally means to be wastefully or recklessly extravagant.

In other words, humanity at the end of Epoch II has been like a male adolescent demanding his material inheritance while, at the same time, declaring his spiritual and psychological independence. In today's parlance, it is "Show me the money" and "I am out-a-here."

We are trying in this attempt to understand humanity's grand evolutionary journey, to transcend narrow and parochial perspectives. Consequently, it is important to note that, although the Modern Age was born in Europe and grew up within western culture, it became a world traveler, and its influence cast a long and wide shadow over virtually all mainstream cultures worldwide.

A Near-Death Experience

The Modern Age began in the fourteenth century when the Prodigal Son got very, very sick. He almost died. It was a near-death experience that would have a profound impact upon him and would dramatically change his life.

Historian Barbara Tuchman describes in her book *A Distant Mirror* how trading ships from Asia arrived in Sicily in 1347 with their crews either dead or dying. The sailors carried an especially virulent disease, the bubonic plague, which latter came to be referred to as the Black Death or simply the Plague. The disease was extremely painful, extraordinarily contagious, and so lethal that people went to bed well but died before morning.

The Plague ostensibly started in China and spread through India, Persia, Mesopotamia, Syria, and Egypt before reaching

Europe. The word was out that all of India had been depopulated and that entire territories were covered with dead bodies, with no one left alive to bury the dead. The Plague ravaged North Africa, Spain, Italy, France, England, Switzerland, and Hungary. Pope Clement VI estimated that as many as 23,840,000 people died. In point of fact, there were no precise or completely accurate records at the time, but most estimates suggest that about one-third of Europe was wiped out by the Plague.

The emotional, psychological, and spiritual toll upon the Prodigal Son was severe, even extreme. Without a concept of contagion, there was no strategy for prevention and no hope for a cure. The Prodigal Son thought that it was, literally, the end of the world. As Tuchman puts it, "the sense of a vanishing future created a kind of dementia of despair."[35]

Not surprisingly, people prayed to God for help. They prayed often, and they prayed fervently. They prayed out of extreme desperation; but God, it seemed, was either not listening or had become an absentee Father. No matter how hard they prayed, people kept dying. Even those presumed to be God's chosen, the priests, were dying in massive numbers.

Again, without the knowledge of contagious diseases, no one could understand why those within the cloistered and enclosed monasteries were experiencing such a death in such numbers. If anyone would be protected by God, would it not be the most religious? Yet, if one monk became infected, it usually meant that all within that monastery would die. "Watching every comrade die, men in such places could not but wonder whether the strange peril that filled the air had not been sent to exterminate the human race," Tuchman asserts.[36] Was God, they wondered, angry and punishing them for some terrible misdeed, some unforgivable sin?

The life-changing effect the Plague had on the Prodigal Son was an archetypal tale, told over and over throughout human history—a crisis, often a severe illness or a near-death experience, provides the catalyst for a dramatic and substantial change in one's life. From the uncommon experience of the indigenous shaman to the common experience of you and me, a major health crisis can often change us dramatically. It can change our direction in life. It can even trigger a deep spiritual transformation. In critical experiences throughout life's journey, pathology often provides the path, and tragedy often changes the trajectory of life. The Plague did all of that and more for the Prodigal Son.

Like many an adolescent before him, the Prodigal Son discovered that his God-like Father was not as infallible and all-powerful as he had presumed. The heroic image of the Father was shattered. God, apparently, was incapable of healing the sick or of easing the suffering. God the Father, previously thought to deserve awe, worship, fear, and respect, was discovered to be nothing more than a stumbling, bumbling, and fumbling old man. When the situation was important, he was impotent. When it really counted, when his children needed being saved, he simply was not up to the challenge. For the Prodigal Son, the Plague triggered a confidence-shattering, faith-quaking, personality-changing, earth-shaking, and heaven-destroying realization.

Consequently, with a surge of testosterone, the desire for self-determination, the evolutionary necessity for identity, rebellion, and freedom, and with a growing self-confidence and an emboldened ego, the Prodigal Son decided to save himself. He no longer needed to depend on the old man. He had the guts; now he wanted the glory. No more disgusting, demurring, despicable, dastardly, and damnable dependency! It was time for asserting himself.

The Prodigal Son set out on his journey of self-discovery and, in the process of trying to find his own identity, experimented with several different personae. In the fifteenth century, he traveled through Italy as "the Renaissance Man." In the sixteenth century, he donned the cloak of "the Reformation Man," hiked through Germany and, in a particularly rebellious mood, nailed ninety-five protests on the church door at Wittenberg. His Luther subpersonality had no idea at the time that such an action would end up labeling as "Protestants" the millions of people who were to follow in his tradition. However, not all Protestants protest, not all Methodists are methodical, and not all Roman Catholics are liberal and broad-minded in a catholic manner.

During the seventeenth and eighteenth centuries, the Prodigal Son became even more radical: the reformer escalated to a revolutionary. The Scientific Revolution, arguably the Prodigal Son's greatest single accomplishment and crowning achievement, completely changed how most of humanity goes about establishing "the truth." The locus of authority was shifted from divine revelation to human discovery, from the authority of God passed down through holy scriptures and the institutional church to human rational abilities armed with the methodologies of modern science. In matters of this world, science was deemed the ultimate truth-giver and the standard against which everything had to be measured for legitimacy.

In the nineteenth century, the Prodigal Son launched another revolution—the Industrial Revolution. With the gender propensity for toys, tools, and technology, the Prodigal Son revolutionized virtually everything in the material world—commerce to communications, manufacturing to management, and electronic storage and retrieval to e-mail.

It was, all in all, a successful ego-building venture, and the Prodigal Son raised self-aggrandizement to an art form, as historian Richard Tarnas writes:

> The direction and quality of [the Modern Age] character reflected a gradual but finally radical shift of psychological allegiance from God to man, from dependence to independence, from other-worldliness to this world, from the transcendent to the empirical, from myth and belief to reason and fact . . . .
>
> Modern man's capacity to understand the natural order and to bend that order to his own benefit could not but diminish his former sense of contingency upon God. Using his own natural intelligence . . . this new sense of human dignity and power inevitably moved man toward his secular self. . . . Man was responsible for his own earthly destiny. His own wits and will could change his world. Science gave man a new faith—not only in scientific knowledge, but in himself. . . . And as modern man continued to mature, his striving for intellectual independence grew more absolute.[37]

So proud was the Prodigal Son of his late adolescent intellectual accomplishments and so impressed with how enlightened he thought he had become that he summed up the entire period with the not-too-humble title "The Enlightenment." Such autobiographical arrogance is not particularly surprising, considering that we are the species that dubbed ourselves *Homo sapiens sapiens*—the doubly wise! (Doesn't it bring to mind the common experience of the adolescent who at one stage of maturation thinks he knows everything and thinks his parents are rather hopelessly stupid, only to grow into a modification of those judgments?)

The Need for Control

"Ideas," writes sociologist Peter Berger, "do not succeed in history by virtue of their truth but by virtue of their relationships to specific social processes."[38] So it was with the issue of control. It was an Epoch II deep value, and the Prodigal Son fell in love with it.

As we have just seen, the important social process that shaped the personality of the Prodigal Son was the traumatizing and hope-destroying bubonic plague. As a result of the Plague, his life was out of control and even his Father-God was unable to do anything about it. Such was the soil of his Soul within which his particular personality traits would flourish. Consequently, and understandably, his declaration of independence was infused with a powerful need to gain and maintain control over his world—not because it was a good or even a possible goal, but because it was an idea consistent with the Epoch II DNA of Soul. In other words, it was an idea that fit the physical, psychological, and spiritual foundations of the time, what the Prodigal Son needed and what he was confident he could achieve: the Holy Grail of absolute control.

In *A History of God*, Karen Armstrong describes this time in the Prodigal Son's life:

> There was a new optimism about humanity as control over the natural world, which has once held mankind in thrall, appeared to advance in leaps and bounds. People began to believe that better education and improved laws could bring light to the human spirit. This new confidence in the natural powers of human beings meant that people came to believe that they could achieve enlightenment by means of their own exertions. They no longer needed to rely on inherited tradition, an institution, or an elite— or, even, a revelation from God—to discover the truth.[39]

The Prodigal Son rewrote the gospel truth: "With religion we saw through a glass darkly, but now, with science, we see the Truth face to face," and "The Truth shall put us in control." The worship of science and rationality replaced the worship of the Father, and the Prodigal Son proclaimed his ultimate faith in the scientific trinity of prediction, control, and repeatability.

The Belief in Disbelief

The ultimate in ego development, the pinnacle of self-confidence, the illusion of personal self-sufficiency, and the arrogance of thinking that our thinking ability is all we need—in other words, the summation of the adolescent evolutionary journey—culminated in the Prodigal Son's decision that God was no longer needed. That, as we discussed earlier, is precisely the reason the Prodigal Son is the appropriate metaphor for the Modern Age. Real men don't buy the religious line, and they are cynical as hell, so the thinking goes.

Like the adolescent that he was, the Prodigal Son not only left his Father-God to go out on his own, he became rather extreme about it. He developed an almost religious belief in the necessity of disbelief. He declared that God was dead and that it was childish to be dependent upon religion.

Friedrich Nietzsche (1844–1900) gave voice to what had been building for several centuries when he pronounced "the death of God." And Sigmund Freud, who greatly influenced the twentieth century's understanding of the mind, participated in the celebration of God's demise. Freud's overall influence, in fact, may have been the result of his fitting so well into the Prodigal Son persona. As a doctor of the psyche, Freud ironically proclaimed the absence of Soul. He considered religion to be childish wish-fulfillment: now that our mind had gained a level of independence, we had no need of God or religion. Both were figments of the infantile imagination.

Make no mistake about it, the disbelieving Prodigal Son is alive and well today among our scientists, in our universities, throughout the media, and with much of the general public. Among the more thoughtful, the rejection of the spiritual is explicit. Among the less reflective, a defacto agnosticism and atheism are overlooked, while lip-service is given to a "belief in God." Our "ultimate concern," to use Paul Tillich's phrase, is not God, but "economism," to quote John Cobb Jr., again.

A similar trend can be seen in higher education. Colleges and universities in the United States were, by and large, started as Christian institutions. But that influence, and that loyalty, did not last. The Prodigal Son, in today's parlance, engaged in a "hostile takeover." George Marsden, in his book *The Soul of the American University*, argues that, although higher education began as a "Protestant establishment," it has now arrived at "established non-belief."[40]

Even among those who teach religion there is, if not "non-belief," at least a culture that discourages any personal witness of faith. James Wall, when he was editor of *The Christian Century*, spoke of his observations at a meeting of the American Academy of Religion:

> The greatest fear you sense in the corridors, apart from the fear of not landing a job, is that a professor might be suspected of harboring a genuine religious commitment in the midst of all that intellectual conversation.[41]

And the media? As Wall also points out, the media do not so much have a bias against religious faith, as a bias in favor of the Modern Age rationality—what we are calling the Prodigal Son mind-set. Wall raised some appropriate questions about the Sunday morning talk shows on the major television networks:

> Why do the networks present the programs geared for the more thoughtful segment of the audience during the traditional hours for Sunday worship? Do they assume the intellectual community is staying at home on Sunday morning? The ads for the Sunday morning programs make it clear the corporate sponsors believe that their image-building campaigns are reaching the "thoughtful" community which ponders serious matters on Sunday morning rather than spending time on less important matters, like worship.[42]

One survey of 240 top journalists—working on newspapers and magazines, as well as in television—showed that only 14 percent regularly attended a church or synagogue, in sharp contrast to the 60 percent of the general public who say they worship regularly.[43] Although other surveys have varied in their numbers, all show that the media are more secular than the general public—or, we might say, more a pure incarnation of the Prodigal Son than is the general public.

This is not to demonize the "liberal" media and university professors, nor to suggest that secularization is the ruination of all that is right and good, conclusions that the Religious Right might make. Quite the contrary, the suggestion here is that secularists, atheists, and agnostics may be contributing more to our movement from Epoch II into Epoch III than those traditional believers who try desperately to hold onto and to conserve and preserve an old and dying image of God. The incarnation of the Prodigal Son was a necessary stage in humanity's overall maturational journey, the natural completion and culmination of the ego and mental development of Epoch II humanity.

Atheism is *not* the wave of the future or the essence of Epoch III. As we will soon see, Epoch III's central evolutionary purpose is that of spiritual maturation. Epoch III will be a very "faith-full" epoch, and spirituality will take center stage. Immature and outdated notions of God and of religion, however, must die before more mature ones can be born. Old faith must be buried before new faith can be resurrected. The imaginal cells of humanity's adolescent caterpillar must surrender to the reimagination of spiritual maturity, the emerging adult evolutionary epoch. But before turning to the chrysalis between Epoch II and Epoch III and examining the Soul of Epoch III, there is one more personality characteristic of the Prodigal Son that needs highlighting.

The Worship of Perpetual Material Progress

It may appear ironic at first, if not down-right inconsistent. Nevertheless, there is a logic to it: while the Prodigal Son increasingly disbelieved anything approaching worship of God and involving any spiritual meaning and purpose, he ended up worshiping at the altar of material progress.

Consider what happened to the Prodigal Son in the nineteenth and twentieth centuries; it is not surprising that he raised materialism and progress to the status of divine fiat. The nature and rate of the material progress we have experienced in the past two-hundred years are incredible; it is truly awesome what human inventiveness has accomplished.

For millennia, prior to the Industrial Revolution, progress was so slow as to be imperceptible. For centuries at a time, the conditions of life scarcely improved. But then, almost suddenly in historical frames of reference, it happened. The Prodigal Son's mental development and technological skills burst forth with amazing productivity.

There are reasons," writes Owen Paepke, "that a pervasive assumption that rapid economic growth is the norm, and any departure from it is the result of policy errors or malevolent scheming by the villain du jour":

Famine, never more than two bad harvests away before the nineteenth century, has been buried by mountains of surplus food in every advanced economy, with even India occasionally exporting grain. The typical supermarket daily offers a wider selection than people of just a few generations past ate in a lifetime. Houses with running water, refrigerators, more bedrooms than people, and other commonplace miracles have replaced dirt-floored hovels shared by three or more generations. Improved health care has stretched life expectancies from less than fifty years in 1900 to more than seventy today. Before railroads, people rarely left their home counties. Many thousands now cross continents and oceans each day. In 1900, not one student in ten earned a high school diploma, the presumptive minimum for entry into the workplace since World War II. Telecommunication makes knowledge of events, still the dearest of commodities through the early nineteenth century, available worldwide, instantly, at little or no cost. Progress has been the only true status quo of the modern era.[44]

When the Prodigal Son started worshiping at the altar of perpetual progress, his self-identity became what Charlene Spretnak correctly identified as *homo economicus*, Economic Man.

Consequently, the arrangement of economic matters is believed to be the wellspring of contentment or discontent in all other areas of life. Economic expansion, through industrialism and computerization, is the Holy Grail of materialism, the unquestioned source from whence follows abundance, well-being, and the evolution of society. That evolution is understood to be decidedly directional: The human condition progresses toward increasingly optimal states as the past is continuously improved upon.[45]

Economics became the fundamental criterion of judging the success of everything and everyone in society. But although it was easy to become a true believer in "economism," it is never easy to be cognizant of the consequences of one's belief system. In fact, it is almost a truism: the more we worship something, the less we are able to be perceive its consequences.

If everything is viewed through an economic lens, we don't always see the psychological and spiritual price that is paid for such worship. When our head is spinning with the constantly new and newer, as well as the fast and faster, how do we read the moral compass? When our mantra is the motion of upward and onward, when is there time for contemplation? When the air is filled with the noise of the now, who listens to the still quiet voice of one's soul. Economism, suggests Neil Postman, is

> without a moral center. . . . It promises heaven on earth through the conveniences of technological progress. It casts aside all traditional narratives and symbols that suggest stability and orderliness, and tells, instead, of a life of . . . technical expertise, and the ecstasy of consumption.[46]

How many of us thoughtfully consider how the economic system views us as people, when it is addicted to constant expansion and perpetual progress? Plain and simply, we are consumers. Period. Exclamation point! We are no longer children of God. We are not primarily seen as incarnations of divine spirit. We are not even seen as complex persons with heart and soul. We are simply consumers. Do we stop and think about what is diminished when people are viewed in a utilitarian rather than in a sacred manner? Do we think about how our own soul is stifled by fitting into that identity?

If materialism is our god and perpetual progress is the altar at which we worship, then consumption is the messiah. Our economic system is judged a success only when we are "sold" on the idea of consuming more and more. Over three-thousand ads per day bombard the average American in the attempt to convince us that a frill is a want, that a want is a necessity, that we will be much happier and much more successful if only we but buy their product. Alan Durning has examined this problem:

> Even if [the ads] fail to sell a particular product, they sell consumerism itself by ceaselessly reiterating the idea that there is a product to solve each of life's problems, indeed that existence would be satisfying and complete if only we bought the right things. Advertisers thus cultivate needs by hitching their wares to the infinite yearnings of the human soul.[47]

The Prodigal Son's altar, however, is beginning to crumble. The gods of economism are being discovered to be gods with clay feet. And the messiah appears to be a false messiah. The always insightful and provocative Sam Keen writes that, "as the twentieth century draws to a close, we must write the obituary for the great god Progress. We are living in the last days of the myth of unlimited growth and technoutopia, and the religion of the Mall."[48]

The Prodigal Son, with all his ego needs and intellectual self-confidence, with his "religion of the Mall," whether he likes it or not, faces one more incarnation before he is really and truly "out-a-here"—that of being the final Epoch II caterpillar whose destiny is to die in the chrysalis and be transformed into the Epoch III butterfly of spiritual maturity.

Spirituality is not a voluntary accessory to life. It is organic, ontological, and essential to our very being-ness; it does not allow us to linger long within immaturity and self-centeredness, within the illusion of isolation and self-sufficiency, or to wallow long in despair and cynicism. We know intuitively that we are connected to larger wholes, to other people, to the rest of nature, and to the Spirit that creates, permeates, and sustains the universe. Most of all, we know that there are meaning and purpose within those relationships. We do not fully understand all those relationships, but we are beginning to know that they are crucial to a full and complete understanding of life. And we know that maturity and growth are necessary if life is to continue. There always comes the time to grow up and grow on, and that time appears to be now.

Questions for Those on a Quest

To quest is to question,
and the quality of the sacred quest
has more to do with the questions we ask today
than with answers entombed within past dogma.

1. What do you think about the Genesis creation story? What do you think about the scientific creation story? Do you think there is a conflict between the two? If so, how do you resolve that conflict? Do you think it needs any resolution?
2. How has the deep value of reductionism influenced your theology? How has it influenced your relationship with the

world? Are divinity and humanity, heaven and earth, spirit and matter, body-mind-spirit, separate and distinct? If not, how do you think about these things?

3. In what way has patriarchy influenced your self-image and your life experience?

4. How do you relate to issues of power and control?

5. What do you think are the root causes of violence, and what can be done about it?

6. To what extent has your view of the world been conditioned by the prism of isms—racism, sexism, sectarianism, nationalism, or anthropocentrism?

7. What was your most memorable act of asserting your developing ego or declaring your independence—an act of self-determination, self-definition, defiance, separation, divorce, or rebellion? When, literally or figuratively, did you "leave home?"

8. Did pathology change your path? Did tragedy change your trajectory? If so, how did that contribute meaning and purpose to your spiritual journey?

9. How do consumerism, economism, and progress affect your life?

Chapter Three

Crisis in the Chrysalis
The Current Transformation of Soul

We are privileged and condemned to live on the cusp between epochs reminiscent of the time when humankind switched from hunting and gathering to agriculture. . . . Old values, visions, worldviews, and ways of organizing social, economic, and political life are transmuting.

Sam Keen, *philosopher and theologian[1]*

I imagine that future generations will look back on these closing years of the twentieth century and call it the time of the Great Turning. It is an epochal shift . . . [and] I consider it an enormous privilege to be alive now, in this Turning, when all the wisdom and courage we ever harvested can be put to use and matter supremely.

Joanna Macy, *Buddhist, deep ecologist, and general systems theorist[2]*

All the tumult and seeming chaos, when viewed in the light of historical perspective, can be seen to represent not only the death agonies of an old order but also the birth pangs of a new epoch.

L. S. Stavrianos, *historian[3]*

The most important thing happening in the world right now is the transformation of humanity's Soul. Nothing else comes close, and that is not mere hyperbole.

None of the dramatic events and processes that the world experienced in the closing decades of the twentieth century, from the fall of the Berlin wall to the invention of the World Wide Web—and any that we will experience in the early decades of the twenty-first century—compares in profundity and long-term influence to the transformation of Soul. In fact, all the dramatic political and technological events are effects, not causes.

We are living right in the midst of another punctuation or transformation of Soul—only the second in humanity's entire evolutionary journey—and everything about how humanity thinks and acts, as well as every institution in mainstream human cultures, will be thoroughly and dramatically changed. What technology is developed and how it is utilized are determined by the state of the human Soul.

We have already examined the dramatic changes that took place when the human Soul moved from Epoch I to Epoch II, from hunting-and-gathering societies to civilization and all its technological advances, from one evolutionary purpose and deep-value system to an entirely new one, and from our species' childhood to adolescence. That previous transformation, however, will pale when compared to the long-term effects of this transformation, in part because of the content of the current changes, in part because of the pace of this transformation. The first punctuation of Soul took several millennia to complete, so the changes were relatively slow and imperceptible. Individual lifetimes could not experience the Soul's changes. Cultures had a long time in which to absorb the implications of that transformation. Not so this time.

The current transformation of Soul is not going to take millennia. It is not going to take centuries. The shift from Epoch II to Epoch III is probably going to complete itself within decades, experienced within a single lifetime. Consequently, we are experiencing chaos, radical dislocation of psychological and emotional habits, dramatic shifts of paradigms and value systems, the shaking of foundations of institutions, and crises within every faith that has given us comfort and solace in the past. It is not an easy time in which to be alive.

Marilyn Ferguson once told me that she often reflected on how living in these times makes us feel as if we are Linus with our blanket in the dryer—we miss our favorite security blankets. Or it is, she said, as if we were trapeze artists *between* trapezes—we are having to let go of what we have been holding onto, not at all sure if we will "catch" something else, or if there is an emotional and valuable safety net to catch us if we fall.

The chrysalis is the metaphor of death and rebirth we are using in this book, but the symbol is no longer simply an interesting intellectual consideration of something that happened ten-thousand years ago. It is now an expression of our current existential experience. We live in a chrysalis, albeit not always comfortably. It is the environment that defines our lives. We are the Epoch II caterpillar that is dying, dissolving, and disintegrating. We are experiencing the loss of identity. At the same time, whether we know it or not and whether we like it or not, within us and all about us, the butterfly of Epoch III is forming, reforming, and transforming as it prepares to experience a new birth and fly into totally uncharted territory.

After epochs of physical and psychological maturation, respectively, the evolutionary purpose for this next epoch, at least as implied by the evidence gleaned from Deep-value Research, appears to be that of our species' developing a more mature spirituality. It seems to be the time in humanity's evolutionary journey when our Soul is coming of age into a more holistic state of being, a new integrity of physical, mental, and spiritual maturation. In other words, it is time in our evolutionary and maturational journey to get our act together in body, mind, and spirit.

Because of the existential and ontological nature of a Soul's transformation and because it is happening so quickly, this is no easy process. There is no smooth buttery slide from yesterday into tomorrow. We are not adolescent humanity one day and adult humanity the next. With the escalating rate of change and the emotional, intellectual, institutional, and theological changes that are and will be taking place within our own lifetimes, *crisis* is an appropriate word for what is happening within the chrysalis. As has been frequently cited, the ancient Chinese were apparently aware of the mix of possibilities within a crisis—their very word for crisis, *wei-chi*, has two characters, one meaning "danger" and the other meaning "opportunity." Indeed!

We live in a dangerously opportune time, and virtually all of us know that we are in a crisis. We lack the level of sacred meaning and purpose that our souls want and need. We know that we are missing the ultimate spiritual nourishment we must have in order to live full and complete lives. It is a crisis time, in part, because the old religious answers are not nourishing for many of us, anymore. Our old theological and religious "security blankets" are in the dryer. One part of us feels the danger, while another part intuits the opportunity for a fresh, new, creative spiritual journey. It is, without question, a time filled with confusion, chaos, crisis, death, rebirth, danger, *and* opportunity.

We have learned to surf the new wave of cyberspace, but our spirits drown in the deluge of data. We wonder if the media-hyped "information highway" is taking us to any meaningful destination. We get high on high-tech, and "log on" with our modem to some "on-line" service. But where are we going with all this? Where is the meaning?

How do we make sense out of the fact that the Cold War is over, but our spiritual lives are as cold as ever? Why is it that when Communism is eliminated as our favorite scapegoat, we look for other scapegoats rather than teaching our own demons and angels to dance the dance of personal responsibility and integrity? Why did the de-structuring of the Berlin Wall and the Iron Curtain lead to the re-structuring of racial and ethnic hatred in the former Communist countries? Why does it feel as if, just as we diminish our concern over the international arms race, we have to increase our concern over the local arms race between official law enforcement and so-called "patriot," "militia," or "survivalist" gangs? Why has the terror of horrible nuclear bombs diminished only to find the horror of terrorist bombs increased? And why is there such a growth of fundamentalism all around the world, in both numbers and in ferocity, while the religious motivations fundamentalists espouse seem to make them less rather than more loving?

Welcome to the crisis in the chrysalis.

We have been living a life of overachievement regarding the "how's"—technology that elicits fascination, pride, excitement, and amazement. We have more and more data with faster and faster access. But we are beginning to awaken to the fact that we have been living a life of underachievement regarding the "why's."

Welcome to the crisis in the chrysalis.

There is nothing like a transformation of Soul to bring the "why's" into crisis. A characteristic of our time is an existential anguish about losing the clarity and certainty of the former why's. It is the anguish of a caterpillar crawling into claustrophobic dissolution, disintegration, and death. It is a natural, organic process, but that's not to say we caterpillars like it.

As we explore the crisis in the chrysalis, keep in mind that every one of us probably has both the dying caterpillar and the emerging butterfly within us—subpersonalities, if you will. Every one of us has an investment and a comfort level in some aspects of the past, while at the same time, every one of us can feel, at some level, the excitement of the future being born within. Every one of us has both fear of the dangers inherent in such a huge transformation, and hope for the opportunities for a deeper, more meaningful, life.

We would do well to keep this dualism in mind whenever we polarize and demonize—a favorite habit of adolescence. This transformational time of entry into adult maturity will be aided if we can be gentle with our own growth processes, as well as gentle with others who do not see the situation in the same way that we do. After all, the same imaginal cells that are the caterpillar become the butterfly, but it takes time. The transformation of Soul is a process. Collectively and individually, we are living a verb-like existence. Life, particularly in a transformational time, is an active verb, not a static noun.

In this chapter, we want to consider some of that verb-ness. What is it like to be living right in the midst of only the second transformation of Soul in humanity's entire evolutionary journey? We may prefer a stable and static noun-ness to our lives—after all, simple definitions, the certainty of dogma, and the clarity of either/or polarizations gave our adolescent Soul great comfort—but we no longer have that choice. The choices in our time are simply to spend a miserable life in negative resistance or learn to be a verb, either to dig in your heels or to learn to fly.

In this chapter, we will consider how the obituary of the Prodigal Son is being written on "post-it notes," we will examine the timing of when we entered the chrysalis, and we will look at how we might discern the direction of the future, what the personality of the caterpillar consists of, and how we might behold the essence of the butterfly.

The Obituary of the Prodigal Son—on "Post-it Notes"

There are good reasons for suggesting that the modern age has ended. Many things indicate that we are going through a transitional period, when it seems that something is on the way out and something else is painfully being born. It is as if something were crumbling, decaying and exhausting itself, while something else, still indistinct, were arising from the rubble. . . . Today, this state . . . of the human world is called post-modernism

Vaclav Havel[4]

William Shakespeare wrote, "What's past is prologue"—but prologue to what? When we are more familiar with the past than we are with the future, when we know where we have been but don't know where we are going, we tend to define the present in reference to what we are leaving rather than what we are entering. Thus, our moment in history has been defined by many with the prefix *post*.

The past six-hundred years, as we discussed in the last chapter, is referred to as the Modern Age—consequently, the present time in history is called the Post-modern Age. Post-modernity is the favorite label among academics who talk about the changes taking place in our time in history, changes that contrast sharply with the Modern Age. In addition, scholars write and talk extensively about numerous other "posts"—post-Cold War, post-structuralism, post-liberalism, post-Keynesian, post-Cartesian, post-Newtonian, post-Christian, post-menopausal, post-doctoral, and a seemingly perpetual plethora of other "posts." The point here is that, when we don't know the butterfly's name, we call it a post-caterpillar.

The importance and extent of this transformation, however, should not be described solely in academic jargon, jotted down on "post-it" notes, and passed around between scholars. The transformation of humanity's Soul happens from the inside out, from the bottom up. It is happening within you and me. It is a fundamental shift in humanity's collective depths, experienced in each one of us as a special-case scenario. Every one of our souls is participating in the transformation of humanity's Soul, and to be aware of it in our own lives, we need only awaken to our depths.

It is not a social program handed down from some "planner" sitting on the top of some bureaucratic ivory tower. It is not a religious program defined and described by a religious hierarchy. No leader of any kind needs to give permission to initiate these changes. This transformation of Soul is a natural and organic process within the deepest possible levels of human existence, and it works its way to the surface of our everyday lives and changes the way we experience the world. So, throw away the "post-it notes." Pay attention to your depths. Feel the caterpillar's disintegration down deep within your soul, as well as the faint fluttering of new wings.

Entering the Chrysalis

Given the complexity of the human family and the diversity of cultures, any attempt at identifying the most influential deep-value system is problematic enough. Even more difficult is the attempt to identify precisely when the Epoch II caterpillar entered the chrysalis for its transformation into the Epoch III butterfly. Generalizations carry the danger of oversimplification. Nevertheless, although recognizing inherent problems, we need to identify some of the general processes in that human journey, so that we can maintain our big picture overview of humanity's evolutionary journey.

Historians and cultural analysts will look back from a vantage point in the future and suggest that the latter half of the twentieth century was the time that humanity, in general, began the transformational process of leaving its adolescent epoch and began to grow an adult Soul. In fact, we can see by the quotes beginning this chapter that some visionaries have been describing this transformation right in the midst of it happening. I could fill an entire chapter with similar quotes from numerous people, experts in a variety of fields who have seen this transformation of Soul coming and who have, in a variety of ways, tried to describe its import—Lewis Mumford, George Leonard, Marilyn Ferguson, Albert Einstein, Jean Houston, Pierre Teilhard de Chardin, Willis Harman, Peter Russell, Charlene Spretnak, Fritjof Capra, and many others.

The tremors of a Soul-quake are not, however, felt everywhere at precisely the same time. Specific cultures and particular countries will point to different decades in the late twentieth and early twenty-first centuries as the defining period for them, the time of demarcation between their former Soul and their new one. Eastern Europe, for instance, will no doubt identify the 1980s as the time that the most visible signs of Epoch II's death and Epoch III's birth began to surface, given the dissolution of the Soviet Union, the loss of legitimacy for Communism, and the fall of the Berlin Wall.

South Africa, in contrast, will no doubt say that it entered the chrysalis in the 1990s. Consider how quickly, for instance, that Nelson Mandela went from prisoner to president. As the decade began, Mandela had been in prison for twenty-seven years, and the African National Party was outlawed. Most so-called international "experts" and all other self-proclaimed "realists" would have said— indeed, did say—that any hope of the ruling white minority voluntarily permitting democratic elections was both naive and unrealistic. It simply wasn't going to happen, they said. Yet, within a period of only five years, to the surprise of virtually all observers, South Africa was transformed.

We will not attempt to document every country's entry into the chrysalis, whether that has been in the past, is currently happening, or is about to happen. Nevertheless, as we examine the emergent Epoch III in the last half of this book, we will show how each and every deep value is being manifested throughout the world and will give some attention to the historical timing as well. In this chapter, however, we will concentrate specifically on some of the more subtle nuances of what took place in the womb/tomb of the American Soul as it experienced the transformational crisis in the chrysalis.

The United States of America began to experience the crisis of transformation in the 1960s. Generally speaking, we see a stark contrast between the placid surface and calm waters in the America of the 1950s and before, and the eruption of Soul that created the tsunami of the 1960s. A tidal wave of change created havoc throughout the American experience.

For all too many of us, life in the 1950s was unconsciously and unquestionably reflected in the *Ozzie and Harriet* television show and Norman Rockwell paintings. For those of us who just happened to be straight, white males, life was basically good, stable, safe, and serene. We gave little thought to the fact that since the culture favored us in so many ways, it must be disfavoring others. The shadow side of our culture, for many of us, was out of sight and out of mind. We had no idea of what was about to erupt from the cauldron of humanity's Soul and no clue regarding the radical changes that were about to occur.

Those of us who lived privileged lives in middle America gave little thought to the quarter of the people in our nation who lived in the artificiality of an American apartheid—racially separate eating facilities, drinking fountains, restrooms, and swimming pools. Most of us never gave serious consideration to the fact that a black man could be lynched if he was not appropriately humble in the presence of white people, if he did not shuffle in a certain way, or if he dared to look a white man, let alone a white woman, in the eyes.

Professional baseball was "integrated" in 1954, due to the extraordinary courage of both white executive Branch Rickey and black player Jackie Robinson. But "integration" is hardly the appropriate word for a spot of black in a sea of white. Consider how the burden of success was put squarely on the shoulders of the one black player, Jackie Robinson. Make no mistake about it—the entire experiment would have been considered a failure if Jackie Robinson had just once responded to the treatment he received in (un)kind. Or if he would have responded in simple, understandable self-defense, as most of us would have. If he would have retaliated for any of the excessively and extraordinarily ugly racism he confronted on a daily basis, our culture, in the 1950s, would have said, "See, it just won't work. It obviously is not meant to work. You simply cannot mix the races."

Many of us who were given praise for our athletic achievements in the 1950s rarely thought about the enormous number of talented black athletes who were never allowed to compete with or against us. Our pride in our own abilities was never tempered by the realization that our "success" was artificially protected because the competition was restricted. In hindsight, it boggles the mind to realize how oblivious we white athletes were to that bubble of privilege.

In the 1950s, the Professional Golfers Association (PGA) was explicitly "for golfers of the Caucasian race." The courageous and pioneering efforts by Lee Elder and Charlie Sifford, however, eventually enabled a young Tiger to come out of the Woods and show us a level of skill in golfing that took interest, amazement, and empowerment to a new level. Jack Nicklaus, voted the best golfer of the twentieth century, observed that the young Tiger Woods plays the game at a level "with which we are not familiar."

In the 1950s, most of us gave little thought to the ways in which we polluted our environment, how we contributed to the massive extinction of other species, or to the complex matter of animal rights. Most of us never considered how the patriarchal structures and assumptions of our culture were blatantly unfair, oppressive, and disempowering to women. We were seeing the world through the Epoch II prism of isms and the narrow-minded myopic blinders of an adolescent deep-value system.

There were no such things as rape crises centers, no attention to battered wives, no affirmative action, no equal opportunity employment. The terms *date rape* or *spousal rape* were not in our vocabulary and likely would have been considered contradictions in terms.

Most of us never questioned the education we were receiving in which we were being taught, by implication at least, that no human being of any worth lived in America prior to Columbus' "discovery of the New World" in 1492. Only animals and those slightly above the animal state, "savages," lived here. We were not informed that our celebrated forefathers engaged in massive genocide and trivialized the Native American culture and spirituality. Those savages would, of course, have to be Christianized—for their own good! Nor were we informed about the fact that our "founding fathers," and even some of our presidents, were slave-owners.

In the 1960s, however, the American Epoch II caterpillar entered the chrysalis and started to disintegrate—and quite loudly at that! It was not a voluntary act for many of us, but, after all, that is the way organic change takes place. An acorn doesn't become an oak tree because of a majority vote among the acorns; it is just the natural process.

Outside agitators, troublemakers, uppity blacks, and feminists disturbed America's Epoch II slumber, and Rachel Carson's *Silent Spring* was anything but silent. Racism, sexism, anthropocentrism, and authoritarianism were increasingly challenged. People, particularly the young and the disempowered, began to demand liberation from old conventions and traditional conformities. The free-speech movement on campuses, the so-called sexual revolution, and the more widespread feminist, environmentalist, and ecological movements, as well as the increased awareness of civil rights for blacks, women, gays and lesbians—all were and are part and parcel, indeed symptomatic, of the transformation of America's Soul that began in the 1960s. It all added up to loud, wrenching, despairing, death agonies of the "good old days." And it is still going on. The aftershocks of this Soul-quake will not stop until we are completely transformed into an Epoch III Soul.

A chrysalis time is a tough time for anyone who is deeply committed to the caterpillar identity and values. The loss of identity that a transformation of Soul involves is no small matter. A caterpillar is inherently unable to believe that any good can come out of this agony unto death, very certain that the destruction of Epoch II is tantamount to the world's going to hell in a hand basket. The caterpillar, after all, is convinced that caterpillar-ness was created in the image of God. Any dissolution of caterpillar-ness, therefore, must be explained away as either God's final act in human history— just before all "Right-believing" caterpillars are taken up into heaven—or as a terrible time when atheists, secular humanists, and liberals are taking the world directly to hell. It is not surprising, therefore, that caterpillars become a bit defensive and more than just a little preoccupied with the end of the world. After all, the caterpillar's world *is* ending!

What Direction Is the Future?

The caterpillar and the butterfly are both within the chrysalis. The past is dying right along side the birthing of the future. It can be a confusing time, unless we have some way of distinguishing between the two, some ability at discerning the difference. In a "both/and" time, one person can point to some evidence and say, "See, *that* is the future." Another person can point to other evidence and say, "No, you are wrong; *that* is the future."

What can make it even more confusing is the "supernova effect." A supernova is a dying star that gets bigger and brighter in the very process of its dying. Religious fundamentalism is a case in point. Fundamentalism is antihistorical and afraid of change. Intuitively, fundamentalists know the old deep-value system is dying; and, because of their fear, the movement is temporarily infused with a great deal of energy. It can be seen to be getting bigger, brighter, and certainly louder. Nevertheless, fundamentalism is not the future. It is not a butterfly. It is a caterpillar that is dying, albeit with a supernova flair.

Deep-value Research provides a particular perspective on the direction of the future. The metaphor of the chrysalis suggests an evolutionary, organic process, not a devolutionary one. The metaphor provides the large framework of the history of the human Soul—that of maturation—and clearly suggests that the future is not a return to the past. Humanity is moving from adolescence into adulthood, not back to its childhood. We are moving from Epoch II into Epoch III, not back to Epoch I. The metaphor of a chrysalis is an organic process with a clear and unmistakable direction—the caterpillar is about to die and to be transformed into a butterfly, like it or not. The caterpillar is the past; the caterpillar is dying. The butterfly is the future; the butterfly is "a-borning."

Nevertheless, it is a confusing, chaotic, and crisis-oriented time. There is a great deal of mystery involved any time we explore the realm of Soul—and that means there had better be a large dose of humility and a truckload of forgiveness. We will not understand the changes taking place within our depths, let alone be gentle with and forgiving of our fears and trepidations, unless we understand some of the dynamics of a both/and period of time.

Rabbi Zalman Schachter-Shalomi, a friend who occupies the Chair of World Wisdom at the Naropa Institute in Boulder, Colorado, came up with a marvelous image as we walked lazily around a lake in South Boulder one spring day, visiting about these very issues. Zalman spoke of what it might feel like if you were a pregnant woman with no concept of birth. Just consider *that* for a moment!

How confusing it would be for a woman to experience all the changes taking place within her body and how frightening the contractions would be when they got closer together and more severe, if she did not know of the impending birth. Imagine how she would feel if she were not able to anticipate the relief, the joy, and the celebration that birth would bring. She would, understandably, fear that she was dying, that the world was coming to an end. She would, understandably, wish that she could return to the time before all these painful and confusing changes began taking place. She would, understandably, very much like to see tomorrow in the rearview mirror.

That is exactly what the caterpillar part of us feels like. It is very difficult, perhaps impossible, for a caterpillar to imagine being a butterfly. Consequently, the caterpillar part of us fears the changes attacking us daily and prefers a strategy of retreat. We want to go back—back to when we were a healthy caterpillar, back before all these destructive changes started happening, back to when we had a clear sense of who we were, back to the basics of Epoch II.

The caterpillar part of us knows very well that our world is in crisis. All sorts of contractions and contradictions are going on in and around us, and our favorite traditional institutions are not working very well anymore. No wonder we want to retreat, to go back to a time before this damnable crisis in the chrysalis. Nostalgia for the stability, clarity, and certainty of the past is paramount in the caterpillar's soul. In terms of the two Chinese symbols that make up the word *crisis*, the caterpillar part of us—individually or collectively—feels the danger, whereas the butterfly part of us welcomes the opportunity.

Inevitably, it seems, we tend to be more attentive to that which is dying than to that which is being born. Even when we experience the birth-pangs of the new, our emphasis seems to be upon the pain and agony of the moment, rather than upon the identity or promise of the yet-to-be. Perhaps it is necessary to feel the loss of the old before we can welcome the new. We may need to experience existential hunger and thirst before we know that we want and need fresh spiritual nourishment. The consequence of focusing on the dying, however, is that it becomes a time of widespread and increasing pessimism, despair, cynicism, depression, and spiritual malaise. As Charlene Spretnak expressed it, "The disintegration in recent years of so much that previously seemed stable is disconcerting to anyone who has been paying attention."[5]

Another problem with paying attention to and becoming preoccupied with that which is disintegrating is that we often fail to see the changes that are coming. Consequently, we feel blindsided by the future, and that in and of itself leads to paranoia and a very fearful existence, as well as a frequent misunderstanding regarding the direction and content of the future.

Consider some of the personality traits of the caterpillar part of us, traits that lead us to misunderstand and misinterpret the future.

The Conservative Self-identity of the Caterpillar

The caterpillar tends to see its mission as that of conserving and preserving the neglected past. The caterpillar tends to feel that outside forces are leading us into a dangerous future and that it is only through vigilance that our religion, our nation, and our world can be saved from that fate.

One of the most amazing phenomena on the recent American political stage has been the ascension of the conservative self-identity and the demonization of anything deemed to be liberal. Most politicians, over the past couple of decades, have tried desperately to distance themselves from the liberal label, knowing that being "branded" a liberal is tantamount to political death. But let's consider what those labels really mean.

During this crisis in the chrysalis, the terms *conservative* and *liberal* have not been used in a dispassionate, analytical, or simply descriptive way. They are, rather, loaded terms, usually blazoned badges of pride and/or epithets of derision. But step outside the current highly charged atmosphere, and rise above the emotionally laden political and public discourse, and consider calmly and dispassionately the dictionary definition of those two words. *Webster's Encyclopedic Unabridged Dictionary* defines them as follows:

> *Conservative:* disposed to preserve existing conditions, institutions, etc. and to agree with gradual rather than abrupt change.

> *Liberal:* favorable to progress or reform, as in religious or political affairs.

No question about it, there are substantive differences between the two, certainly enough to warrant the use of two different words. The person or the part of each of us that is "conservative" has a greater interest in conserving and preserving the status quo and wants change to happen slowly, if at all. The person or the part of us that is "liberal" is clearly more attentive to that which needs to change and, therefore, favors progress and reform.

Why are we so prone to oversimplification, categorization, polarization, and the demonization of and/or pride in labels? Are we not all some mixture of the two? Doesn't every one of us treasure aspects of our own lives—our history, our traditions, and aspects of the body politic—that we want to savor, to preserve, to conserve, and to change slowly, if at all? At the same time, doesn't every one of us sense the need for change and reform in some areas of our individual or communal life? If something is disempowering us or taking away our treasured freedoms, are we not in favor of change? If we are ill, don't we prefer the transformation of pain and illness to wellness and well-being? If we have an awareness of or a sensitivity to people who are suffering torture, rape, or genocide, don't we prefer progress in human kindness and the reform of existing conditions? Don't we all want to heal the soul of violence in our culture? If we have a teenage son or daughter who is into some dangerous experiment of immaturity, don't we wish for, indeed pray for, maturation, growth, safety, change, and transformation?

Sometimes the overly simplistic use of labels to characterize a person, a political party, a profession, a religion, or a philosophy of life is simply not accurate and certainly not helpful in developing healthy relationships. In a larger sense, we can appreciate how the caterpillar part of us fears the death of its former self-identity that inevitably takes place within the chrysalis.

In the 1990s, probably no politicians were more representative of the "conservative" identity than President Ronald Reagan and former Speaker of the House Newt Gingrich. Gingrich gave voice to this identity in his 1995 book *To Renew America*:

> For the past thirty years, we have been influenced to abandon our culture and seem to have lost faith in the core values, traditions, and institutions of our civilization. The intellectual nonsense propagated since 1965—in the media, on university campuses, even among our religious and political leaders— now threatens to cripple our ability to teach the next generation to be Americans. . . .
>
> I believe we can revitalize American society, restore the greatness of American civilization, and reinvigorate the American economy while we remake the structure of American government. My optimism is based on the simple belief that we have seen enough of the decay and failure of the welfare state to be ready to restore our historic principles. Older Americans who grew up with the certainty and convictions of World War II and the Cold War are eager for a rebirth of American values. Baby Boomers who grew up with the counterculture are now sober and mature enough to see that many of its principles simply don't work. . . .
>
> We must reassert and renew American civilization. From the arrival of English-speaking colonists in 1607 until 1965, there was one continuous civilization built around a set of commonly accepted legal and cultural principles. From the Jamestown colony and the Pilgrims, through de Tocqueville's *Democracy in America*, up to the Norman Rockwell paintings of the 1940's and 1950's, there was a clear sense of what it meant to be an American. . . .
>
> Since 1965, however, there has been a calculated effort by cultural elites to discredit this civilization and replace it with a

culture of irresponsibility that is incompatible with American freedoms as we have known them. . . . Until we reestablish a legitimate moral-cultural standard, our civilization is at risk.[6]

Gingrich, evidenced by his following and his influence, gave voice to what the caterpillar in many throughout the culture felt. Life had gotten very confusing since the 1960s and the world we knew and were comfortable with was falling apart. We should always keep in mind, however, that there were muzzled minorities in this country— actually constituting a majority of Americans—who were neither comfortable with nor empowered by those "good old values."

When you think about it, you can see that today's conservatives do, in fact, desire change and reform on certain matters of culture— the direction of the change they want, however, is almost always to go backwards. The simple answer, for the conservative group, is to go back prior to the 1960s, back to when the Epoch II deep values still had vibrancy, back before the "calculated efforts by the cultural elites" began taking our culture straight to hell, back before we got into the chrysalis and the disintegration of a "cultural war" began to take place. Understandably, in times like these, a great deal of energy is invested in "back-to-basics" movements—in the institutions of education, politics, family, and religion.

When we face signs of a crumbling identity, the loss of preferred values, and an impending transformation of Soul, survival and preservation instincts kick in. The caterpillar thinks the Epoch II deep values are the only good ones and that we are in chaos precisely because we left the "good old values." The caterpillar's answer is to go back and to work at those values harder and more efficiently. The dying caterpillar is more interested in resuscitation of the old than in embracing death and rebirth. The past is the caterpillar's frame of reference, spiritual gears stuck in reverse and grinding against the evolutionary flow, trying desperately to return to yesteryear. It is understandable, therefore, that the caterpillar part of us likes the self-identity of being a conservative and feels that liberals out in left-field are ruining everything that is good and right.

Consider, however, the possibility that all the coziness with anything "conservative" and the lampooning of anything "liberal" are simply wrong about the Soul of America, past or future. Essayist Roger Rosenblatt points out that the United States actually has a national soul that is, in fact, liberal. The Declaration of Independence and the Constitution provide a liberal foundation for this country, and we have, generally speaking, liberal ideals and values:

> Liberalism dominates the [national] debate and defines the terms of the debate. The conservative assaults on the L word, which were made most effectively by President Reagan, have been so routine over the past 16 years that there is a whole generation of people under 35 who have never heard "liberal" uttered as anything other than a joke or an insult. Yet they live in a liberal country. Conservatives may have ruined the word but have adopted most of the content of liberalism. . . .
>
> [But] the triumph of liberalism is not a political victory. Rather it is a triumph of temperament and attitude; it reflects how America wishes to exist.[7]

Two experiences in my own life, thirty-two years apart, illustrate the point that Rosenblatt is making. The first experience was in 1959 in Nashville, Tennessee. I was a graduate student at Vanderbilt University and had just finished playing a handball game at the YMCA. While cooling down in the locker room, I became embroiled in a heated and definitely "uncool" discussion about the "Negro problem" in Nashville. Some of my fellow handball players began to rail against "those trouble-making niggers" who were trying to integrate lunch counters and other public facilities in Nashville at the time. The opinion was expressed by most of those in the locker room that racial integration was simply never going to happen—and it shouldn't. It was against God's will. It was unbiblical. All sorts of dastardly things would be the result of racial integration and of going against God's will, and they proceeded to enumerate them ad infinitum and ad nauseam. In their view, my protests to the contrary were advocating an anti-Christian "liberal agenda," and it was their job to make sure that their culture was protected against such "outside agitators"—after all, I was from Iowa, unquestionably a hot-bed of liberalism.

Fast forward to 1992. Another athletic club, another locker room, another discussion that followed a handball game—only this time it was in Boulder, Colorado. It was, as Yogi Berra would have put it, "deja vu, all over again," only on a slightly different topic.

This time the topic was "those trouble-making queers" who were trying to impose their "anti-Christian lifestyle" on Coloradans by passing laws for the equal protection of homosexuals. Some of my fellow handball players expressed the opinion that the "special rights for gays" were simply never going to happen—and they shouldn't. The gay lifestyle is against God's will. It is unbiblical. All sorts of dastardly things would be the result of protecting gay rights, and they proceeded to enumerate them ad infinitum and ad nauseam. In their view, my protests to the contrary were advocating an anti-Christian "liberal agenda," and they would do everything possible to keep perspectives like mine from prevailing. Since I lived in Boulder at the time, I guess I had to be considered an "inside agitator."

The important point in recalling these two experiences is this: not one of those guys in the Boulder locker room in 1992, every one of whom considered himself a "conservative," would have argued for racial segregation. I doubt that any of them would have openly defended racism, as did my handball buddies in Nashville some thirty-two years earlier. And it is not simply a matter of different cities and different subjects. What was called a "liberal agenda" in the 1950s is now accepted by most conservatives—*their* lives have moved from right to left.

How long has it been, for instance, since a conservative politician running for public office has advocated racial segregation—and been elected? Why are the conservative politicians today, politicians who advocate good, old traditional values, not advocating separate drinking, eating, swimming, and educational facilities for blacks and whites? Why are the conservative politicians who advocate "family values" not railing publicly against interracial marriage? Not so long ago and for a large number of people, those *were* the conservative values. Those *were* the values thought to be worthy of preservation. As a people, we move in a liberal direction, although sometimes at a very conservative pace. The natural organic process of growth and development within the chrysalis, like it or not, is through the death and disintegration of the caterpillar. The caterpillar simply cannot embalm and preserve the past, as much as it might want to. If there is to be life in the future at all, it will be through the process of death and rebirth, giving up caterpillar-ness and welcoming new life as a butterfly.

Bumper-Sticker Simplicity

Another caterpillar quality in a chrysalis time is the overwhelming desire for clear, simple answers to all this chaos and confusion. The caterpillar wants unambiguous answers, a simplistic bumper-sticker morality, one for which there is no room for the "but-on-the-other-hand" arguments. That caterpillar part of us exhibits the typical ego insecurity of adolescence, wanting a clear and rigid definition of who is "in" and who is "out," who are the good guys and who are the bad guys. Diversity is too confusing. Pluralism is too fuzzy at the edges. Consider two examples of this.

Race, Sex, and "Bible Libel"

As suggested above, there are many parallels between the way some people dealt with the racial issue in the 1950s and 1960s and the way some people today deal with the issue of homosexuality. The former has been and the latter will eventually be seen as the caterpillar's fear of diversity, pluralism, and the blurring of boundaries. The caterpillar wants clarity, simplicity, either/or, right or wrong.

When the issue of race was tearing at the fabric of American society and dominating the hurting hearts and controversial conversations, caterpillar entrenchment ensued, the wagons were circled, and the attempt was made at defining racial boundaries—absolutely, clearly, and simply. Ludicrous attempts were made to define what percentage of Negro blood made one a Negro. Whiteness, as well as marriage and family values, had to be protected from any "mixing." If due diligence was not given to protecting the values of separation, categorization, and compartmentalization, human society itself would crumble into moral decay. Of course, the fact that some white slaveowners had fathered children of mixed race was a fact kept in the closet and in the shadows.

The caterpillar's need for oversimplification, however, was not limited to definitions. Particularly revealing is the way the caterpillar used religion in general, and the Bible in particular, to lend bumper-sticker brevity, clarity, and simplicity to support its argument.

One of the ongoing miracles of the Bible is how it can perfectly mirror the person looking into it. The Bible can be recreated in the image of virtually any person who wants to justify him- or herself, and any subject can be rationalized by quoting the Bible. Many of us have used the Bible in the same way a drunk uses a light pole, for support rather than for enlightenment. Instead of studying the Bible with a willingness to have one's prejudices and close-mindedness challenged, those of us with some of the caterpillar within are tempted to use simplistic, out-of-context biblical texts for supporting our prejudices.

Part of what lends the Bible to this kind of pole-leaning, bumper-sticker bibliolatry and self-justifying religious sloganeering is that it is written in chapters and verses—an interesting manifestation of the Epoch II deep-value of reductionism, wherein we thereby become pre-occupied with parts and ignore the whole. Brief extracted verses can be used, irrespective of the larger context, to "prove" God's will on this or that subject. The only preface needed to assure the truth of a claim is "the Bible says." Renowned scholar of world religions Huston Smith wrote a song back in the days preceding the chrysalis period about the use and abuse of the Bible. He entitled the song "Bible Libel."

In the late 1940s and early 1950s, Smith had become tired of the radio airwaves' being inundated with preachers using the Bible to justify their belief in the inferiority of African-Americans, Jews and, if the preacher happened to be Protestant, Catholics. The Bible was being used to "prove" that the United Nations was the Antichrist. Smith was so galled by it all that he composed and sang the following song at a political rally on the capitol steps in Denver, Colorado, with Pete Seeger backing him up on the banjo:

> They make the Bible say the white race is supreme,
> but the Bible doesn't harp on any such theme.
> There's Bible Libel going around,
> Gonna tell it to the Lord 'til the heavens resound,
> Gonna sing and shout 'til that Judgment Day
> When the Lord tells some preachers they've got hell to pay.[8]

To bring that theme into today's biblical justification for the bigotry against homosexuals, consider the "Bible libel going around." First of all, one might presume that the Christians who proclaim Christ as Lord would give primacy in their faith to what Jesus actually said and did. But, as far as we know, Jesus never addressed the subject of homosexuality in his words or in his deeds, and he apparently did not consider sexual orientation as something terribly important. Jesus, it seems, was busy living, preaching, and emphasizing love and compassion, particularly towards those marginalized by mainstream society or excluded by the self-proclaimed protectors of religious orthodoxy.

"There's Bible Libel going around." St. Paul presumably had a problem with homosexuals, but he also had a problem with women's speaking up in church. Paul writes, in a letter to the church in I Corinthians 14:34–35:

> As in all congregations of God's people, women should not address the meeting. They have no license to speak, but should keep their place as the law directs. If there is something they want to know, they can ask their own husbands at home. It is a shocking thing that a woman should address the congregation.

So, why aren't the caterpillar's in mainstream Christian denominations bringing to trial any clergyperson who allows women to speak up in church? Or, for that matter, how can any Bible-believing Christian denomination ordain women who, presumably, are uppity enough to think that they actually have the right to preach to the congregation? The Bible (Paul, that is) says that they should not do such a thing.

"There's Bible Libel going around." If people can find one or two passages in the Bible that condemn homosexuality and consider it proof of God's will, why aren't they giving equal outrage to the fact that divorce is unbiblical? So is being clean-shaven, eating shellfish, or putting on a garment woven with two kinds of yarn. If we were to list all the passages in the Bible that could be lifted out to "prove" what God is against, well, it would be a very long list, and none of us would actually live our lives in accordance with it.

Perhaps the most obvious Bible libel regarding the homosexual issue, however, is the way in which the book of Leviticus is used for bumper-sticker simplistic support, rather than for enlightenment. Leviticus 18:21–23 is often used to show that God condemns homosexual activity. But why should any Bible-believing caterpillar who wants literal clarity about God's will stop with the eighteenth chapter? Why not take the nineteenth chapter just as seriously, and just as literally?

If we actually considered the nineteenth chapter of Leviticus as part of "God's Word," we would have to demonstrate against any business that keeps a hired man's wages until the next morning (there goes much of our system of business), and we would have to condemn anyone who takes sides against their neighbor on a capital charge (there go the lawyers). We would also have to be against anyone who seeks revenge (there goes the death penalty).

The caterpillar's need for simple categorization and clear distinction leads to all sorts of trouble, whether it be in terms of racial or sexual definitions. Absolute boundaries and unambiguous distinctions are impossible to establish and maintain—humanity is much more complex than that.

For instance, if we widen the sexual issue beyond homosexuality, we can see that even the biological boundary between male and female is often blurred through natural organic processes. About one child in every 2,000 births is biologically "intersexual," reports Emily Nussbaum, "about the same proportion as cystic fibrosis."[9] If we get further into the subject, we can see that it reveals the caterpillar's discomfort with any sexual ambiguity. If we are willing to think with a clear head about the very emotionally charged issue of homosexuality, we can see that it, too, has to do with our discomfort with sexual ambiguity.

The biological fact is that, for the first eight weeks, all of us are essentially the same. Most of us then develop towards either being male or female. But in some of us, development is less definite, less well defined, and more ambiguous—in those who are that one in two thousand.

A culture's prejudices begin to affect that intersexual baby at the moment of birth. With no intent at demonizing the medical profession—after all, everything in the medical area is conditioned by the same deep-value system and cultural paradigms as is the general public—consider what happens at the birth of a sexually ambiguous baby.

First of all, because there are many degrees of differences along the fuzzy boundary between male and female, it is a matter of judgment as to whether or not any "problem" exists, a judgment typically made by the doctor or doctors alone, only rarely in consultation with the parents. In one doctor's mind, an enlarged clitoris may be within the normal range, whereas another doctor may see it as an abnormally undersized penis.

Second, an intersexual baby is judged to be a social, psychological, and medical emergency, something that necessitates surgical correction. A culture that desperately needs, in virtually every area of life, separation into distinct categories, has not been able to assume that biological and sexual ambiguity is "normal." Thus, the abnormality needs to be corrected.

Third, practically all intersexual babies are "assigned" to be female, since the medical procedures and techniques are better for that assignment. Indeed, the surgical training videotape's very title reveals that bias: *Surgical Reconstruction of Ambiguous Genitalia in Female Children.*

The American medical protocols, established in the 1950s, guided physicians who were confronted with the birth of an intersexual baby to assign the sex, operate, and protect the family from any concern by telling them that their child simply had a "correctable deformity."

The day is coming when we will be more comfortable with the fact that real life is ambiguous in many ways. Racial mixing has gone so far that we can never return to "racial purity"—of course, it was a myth from the very beginning, for if you remember our discussion back in chapter one, we are all descendants from our African mothers. The day is also coming when we will be unafraid of biological and sexual ambiguity, including ambiguity and/or diversity in sexual orientation. We will grow up and grow beyond having to consider such diversity and ambiguity as a deformity that needs our "correction."

In spite of the caterpillar's discomfort with ambiguity, life has always been experienced in degrees, in varied shades, in nuanced tones, in a ubiquity of ambiguity. The process of living is not done in static nouns, in spite of our Epoch II desire to force life into dogmatic nouns of certainty and stability. Life, it turns out, is full of action verbs, and they just keep messing things up.

The future is not on the side of caterpillar entrenchment and resistance to the "liberal agenda." "Bible-libel" will not be tolerated. An Epoch III butterfly is emerging that will celebrate the rich diversity of life. I am happy to report one small bit of evidence—the American Academy of Pediatrics, in the fall of 1999, "convened its first official committee on changing intersex medical protocols."

The NRA and "Constitutional Libel"

The National Rifle Association's use of the Second Amendment to the Constitution of the United States is similar to the Religious Right's use of the Bible—more for support than for enlightenment. Because this kind of behavior is typical of the caterpillar in the chrysalis, we will examine it briefly here—not the larger issues of guns and violence in America that continues to baffle people around the world and not the growing concern for control and safety even in gun-loving America, but simply how the NRA uses the Second Amendment. The NRA leans heavily upon what it claims is a "constitutional right" to own any number and type of guns and to be free of any kind of constriction or restriction. It is, it proudly announces, protecting a fundamental American freedom. But is that a legitimate interpretation of the Constitution, or is it a spurious claim by a desperate caterpillar, trying by any means possible to conserve and preserve the Epoch II value system?

Let's return to the beginning, to when the Second Amendment was proposed by James Madison and adopted by the Constitutional Convention. Northwestern University professor Garry Wills has researched both the content of Madison's proposed Second Amendment and the context of the debate before final adoption, a history of content and context, by the way, which the NRA, in Wills' words, has "distorted in a wondrous way."[10]

The introduction and ratification of the Second Amendment primarily concerned the relationship between a national standing army and state militias, what today we call the National Guard, and the idea that the latter could be federalized in an emergency. It was about how best to guarantee a safe and secure country and how to define the relationship between the states and the federal government in doing so. It was also about not forcing conscientious objectors to participate in the military.

The initial proposal by Madison read as follows:

The right of the people to keep and bear arms shall not be infringed, a well armed and well regulated militia being the best security of a free country; but no person religiously scrupulous of bearing arms shall be compelled to render military service in person.[11]

As Wills points out, the context is clearly military and the term "bearing arms" had to do with military service, nothing at all to do with the personal ownership of guns. Notice that the clause protecting religious conscientious objectors from bearing arms and rendering military service never assumed that such people could not or would not use a gun in the act of hunting.

In the way the language was used at that time, one did not, in the singular, bear arm or bear an arm, because the word, etymologically, means the "equipment" or "equipage" of war. Wills reports:

What Madison and the Congress did was underline the independent action of the militias when they were not federalized, pledging that the new government would keep them equipped for that local purpose. The right to demand this service is the first and foremost meaning of "Second Amendment rights."[12]

The NRA ignores the actual history of the Second Amendment's introduction, its actual content and intent, and the context of the debate surrounding the amendment. It then takes the first line out of context and uses the Constitution in the same bumper-sticker, overly simplified way in which the Religious Right uses the Bible. This time, however, it is Constitution Libel.

Journalist Michael Gartner—another agitator from Iowa, that bastion of liberalism—has picked up on the notion that the Second Amendment was drafted and adopted primarily for the purpose of guaranteeing a safe and secure country. Gartner writes that, since the Second Amendment is about the "constitutional right" of safety and has nothing to do with the private ownership of guns, we the people have the right not to be shot. The NRA, Gartner argues, is infringing upon his constitutional right for a safe and secure country.

Gartner poses an appropriate question: "If the Second Amendment . . . really did guarantee all of us a right to go armed—as the NRA likes to claim—how come the gun people never test it in the Supreme Court?" "Because," Gartner answers, "the Supreme Court has twice said the Second Amendment is no guarantee of a right to have a gun." He reports how the Supreme Court ruled in 1980 that "the Second Amendment guarantees no right to keep and bear a firearm that does not have 'some reasonable relationship to the preservation or efficiency of a well-regulated militia.'" Gartner also reports that "lower federal courts have said the same thing at least 23 times since 1942."[13]

Garry Wills reports on the other Second Amendment case before the Supreme Court, which occurred in the 1939 case of the United States v. Miller. In this case, the Court ruled against a man "who claimed that the amendment allowed him to keep and bear a sawed-off shotgun. The Court declared that a sawed-off shotgun is not a militia weapon."[14]

Fortunately, the butterfly of Epoch III will not be swayed by either Bible libel or constitutional libel. The butterfly represents a more mature Soul, one that celebrates diversity and pluralism, that can tolerate ambiguity. Bumper stickers will not weigh it down, and the NRA cannot shoot it down.

It is now time for us to move beyond our analysis of the caterpillar and the post-caterpillar—it's time to name the butterfly.

Behold the Butterfly of Epoch III

What the caterpillar calls the end of the world, the master calls a butterfly.

Richard Bach[15]

It is the natural and organic time for humanity to leave adolescence behind and come of age into adult maturity. It is time for us to name the butterfly that is forming within the chrysalis, for it does, after all, have a name and an identity all its own. The emerging butterfly of humanity's new Soul is dramatically different from the caterpillar Soul of Epoch II, and the rest of this book will be our best attempt to name it, to describe it, and to understand its nature and content.

But before exploring the emerging DNA of the new Soul, before examining the deep values of Epoch III in some depth and detail, I want to offer three observations and pose one question that will accompany us throughout the rest of this book.

The Butterfly's Influence Will Be Global

The new science of chaos theory explains itself with what it calls "the butterfly effect," and it has a wonderful relevance to our discussion here. The phrase is credited to meteorologist Edward Lorenz, and it was his way of saying that the world is far more interrelated and far more sensitive to fluctuations than we used to think. Lorenz asked the question, "Does the flap of a butterfly wing in Tokyo affect a tornado in Texas?" His answer was "Yes!" Today's sciences are showing us a world wherein small and seemingly insignificant events help to create major changes half-a-world away.

In applying that analogy to Deep-value Research, we can trace how the faint flutters of the Epoch III butterfly's wings, observed and described by visionaries in virtually every field throughout the past half-century, will be increasingly felt by all of us around the world. Even a tornado that is experienced in one part of the world—the fierce winds of change that a Soul-level transformation can unleash—may have been observed previously elsewhere only as a whisper of a Spirit-breeze.

Similar to its findings in Epochs I and II, Deep-value Research suggests that, in spite of the exceptions that can be found in native and indigenous peoples and in the world's subcultures and counter-cultures, mainstream human cultures throughout the world will be dramatically influenced and changed by the emerging Epoch III evolutionary purpose of spiritual maturation. The visionaries of our time have looked through the eyes of the butterfly and have seen the future.

From the political realm we hear Vaclav Havel, president of the Czech Republic:

> The main task in the coming era is . . . a radical renewal of our sense of responsibility. Our conscience must catch up to our reason, otherwise we are lost. . . .
>
> It is my profound belief that there is only one way to achieve this: we must divest ourselves of our egotistical anthropocentrism, our habit of seeing ourselves as masters of the universe who can do whatever occurs to us. We must discover a new respect for what transcends us: for the universe, for the earth, for nature, for life, and for reality. . . .
>
> A better alternative for the future of humanity, therefore, clearly lies in imbuing our civilization with a spiritual dimension.[16]

The modern-day scientist may represent the purest incarnation of the Prodigal Son. Yet, from the visionary scientific genius Albert Einstein, we hear an affirmation of mysticism—"the sower of all true art and science"—even at a time when his colleagues were denigrating anything mystical:

> To know that what is impenetrable to us really exists, manifesting itself to us as the highest wisdom and the most radiant beauty, which our dull faculties can comprehend only in their most primitive forms—this knowledge, this feeling, is at the center of all true religiousness. In this sense, and in this sense only, I belong to the ranks of devoutly religious men.[17]

Anthropologist Loren Eiseley, one of my favorite visionary naturalists, spoke about the genius of the Epoch III spirit in science, when it "opens vaster mysteries to our gaze. Moreover, science frequently discovers that it must abandon or modify what it once believed. Sometimes it ends by accepting what it has previously scorned."[18]

The courage to accept "what it has previously scorned"—such as finding spiritual meaning and purpose within the scientific study of the material universe—is found increasingly throughout the burgeoning literature in which scientists reflect on how they embody both a zeal for science and religious faith, the Epoch III synthesis and synergy.

Even *homo economicus* is being awakened by the butterfly's wings, as well as by the tornado created half-a-world away. Duane Elgin, formerly a senior social scientist at SRI International, continues to be a careful observer of social trends throughout the world. He points out that the Trends Research Institute of New York identified "global simplicity" as one of the top ten trends of 1997:

The voluntary simplicity trend that originated in the United States is now spreading throughout the industrialized world. From Scotland to Australia and Finland to Canada, masses of people are beginning to embrace the belief that they can enhance the quality of their lives by cutting back on the quantity of products they consume. Never before in the Institute's 17 years of trend tracking has a societal trend grown so quickly, spread to broadly, and been embraced so eagerly.[19]

Elgin also reports that a study on consumption in America found that "without fanfare, a deep change is occurring in the culture and consciousness of the United States":

Twenty-eight percent of the survey respondents said that, in the last five years, they had voluntarily made changes in their lives that resulted in making less money, such as reducing work hours, changing to a lower-paying job, or even quitting work. This is an enormous shift. Extrapolating from the survey to the U.S. population, this suggests that in the last five years, more than 50 million Americans "downshifted," or made changes to simplify their lives.[20]

As stated at the beginning of this chapter, nothing happening in the world right now is more influential than the transformation of the human Soul. It is the nature of a new Soul, with its new evolutionary purpose and its entirely new deep-value system, to change everything about human culture—how we think, how we act, how we create and manage our institutions, how we train our professionals, what technology we develop, and how we use that new technology.

Ironically, the established religions may be the last to understand a transformation of Soul: that's why, in virtually every age, spiritual prophets have challenged the status quo in the religions of the time. Sometimes they have been crucified for doing so; sometimes they have been ignored until well after their time in history.

This raises concern for whether or not organized religion will be able to take this transformational trip with the rest of us. First of all, religion typically looks to the past and relies on previously developed answers, on its creeds, doctrine, and dogma. Second, humility is tough to come by if you feel that you are the receiver, perceiver, and possessor of revealed divine truth. If you believe there are no human fingerprints on that truth, that what you have is a direct, literal, uncontaminated "Word of God," then even personal arrogance can be denied with the claim that it is God's certainty, not ours. Such a stance makes it virtually impossible to become a butterfly.

But what if God is doing something new in our time? How do we hear that news if we are busy answering every question with a quick and automatic answer, shouted into the ears of anyone foolish enough as to wonder where God is taking us? How do we see the horizon if our eyes are focused on the rearview mirror? How do we feel those textures if our hands are tightly grasping the scriptures written many centuries ago? How do we inhale the fresh air of the Spirit, if we are holding our breath in fear?

If Deep-value Research is right, or even close to being right, then any religion that fails to consider this transformation of Soul will lose legitimacy among the seekers of Soul. The temporary brilliance of the fundamentalistic supernova flair will soon fade to darkness.

Any institution, whatever the field, is in for a rude awakening if it thinks it can stay the course, remain the same, or change only slightly and gradually. When we are in a relatively stable period during the middle millennia of an epoch, we may get away with a slow and conservative pace of change; but when we are living right in the midst of a Soul-level transformational crisis, change is at a liberal pace or faster. This is not a matter of the "liberal agenda" by some inside or outside agitators, and it is not the consequence of uppity minorities. It is the organic within-ness of the human Soul taking us into a whole new state of being.

The deep, powerful, and subterranean energies of change that we are experiencing at this time in history will cause disruptions, eruptions, paradigm shifts, and faith-quakes all across the human landscape. Just as an earthquake deep in the ocean triggers the massive tidal wave known as a tsunami, a Soul-quake deep within the collective human psyche will launch a spiritual tsunami that will drown all former assumptions about what a human is, what divinity is, how the divine-human relationship works, and how we structure and run our institutions, as well as how we train our professionals. Buckle your seat belts.

Epoch III Deep Values Will Emerge Suddenly Yet Gradually

As we have stated before, Soul-time, like geological or cosmological time, is different from our daily experience of clock or calendar time. In that regard, as far as the big picture is concerned, we have talked about our living within a "sudden" punctuation or transformation.

It might be helpful, however, to observe that, when we get down to the living of our days, the various Epoch III deep values will not emerge instantaneously or simultaneously. A transformation of Soul does not happen overnight, and the deep values meant to facilitate that Soul-level change do not appear in the culture all at the same time.

We should, in fact, be thankful that they don't, for we would be incapable of handling all that change all at once. As someone once quipped, "The purpose of time is so that everything doesn't happen all at once." We might say that the enlightenment of the Epoch III dawn is on a cosmic rheostat. The enlightenment is being turned up by degrees; otherwise, it would blow all our circuits. Our eyes, our minds, our hearts, and certainly our souls need a little time to adjust.

Earlier we mentioned that this epochal transformation is occurring at a much faster rate than did the first—within decades rather than millennia—and that is true. It is also true that, when we get inside this rather sudden—relatively speaking— transformation, we are confronted with new deep values on a gradual basis.

This "sudden gradualism" of the butterfly's emergence means two things. One is that the four new deep values of Epoch III did not all emerge at the same time, as will become clear as we go through the second half of this book. The first three all have decades, and in some cases, centuries of gradual emergence. The last one, however—the spirituality in and of time—is the most recent to emerge; for that reason, it will probably be experienced as the most controversial.

The second thing that this gradually emergent transformation means is that our understanding and experience of any and all the new deep values are only partial. If we think the changes have been profound so far, well, "we ain't seen nothing yet." There is much more to come. To date, we have only seen a portion of how these new deep values will radically change human existence. And that is why I offer the third observation.

Courage and Humility Are Necessary for This Quest

Only the naive think we have experienced all the changes and challenges that this transformation will present us. Only the arrogant think we understand how much we will be transformed. And only the cowardly try to hold onto yesteryear and to deny that God can do anything new.

I personally have been researching and attempting to live this transformation of Soul for over twenty years; and the deeper and further I go, the more I become aware of how stupid it would be for me to think that I really understand what is going on, in any final or complete way.

A burning desire to understand my life and the time of my life, in context, was what started me on this quest. And, indeed, I have learned a few things. The two primary things I have learned is that it will take all the courage I can muster to engage wholeheartedly in the sacred quest and that I had better have a backpack chocked-full of humility to accompany me on the journey.

I don't know where this phrase originally came from, but I remember my mother telling me many years ago, "The bigger the island of knowledge, the longer the shoreline of wonder." Indeed! The sacred quest is not easy, so it will take courage.

And the sacred quest is humbling. It is a journey into the Grand Mystery, and it is wonderfully wonder-filled. That is why hard, rigid dogma will have to be handled softly in the future, why the sacred quest has more to do with questions than with answers. And so, the question that I ask. . . .

How Does One Become a Butterfly?

Perhaps not surprisingly, a children's story brings us the wisdom we need. Trina Paulus, in her marvelous 1972 book that has become a classic, *Hope For The Flowers*, writes:

> "How does one become a butterfly?" she asked pensively.
> "You must want to fly so much that you are willing to give up being a caterpillar."
> "You mean to die?" asked Yellow.
> "Yes and no," he answered. "What looks like you will die, but what's really you will live."[21]

That's the kind of faith that will keep us company as we move into an unknown future, faith that the butterfly essence of who we really are and who we are called to be will live, if we just have the courage to die to what we have looked like in the past. We can participate in the death of the old and in the resurrection of the new, if we but welcome into our hearts the butterfly faith.

The crisis within the chrysalis does indeed have danger. But the opportunities are incredible if we look with sacred eyes into our future, listen with sacred ears to the whispers of God speaking to us about tomorrow, love the quest and the questions with a sacred heart, and fly out of the chrysalis on sacred wings. Eventually, the world will become a butterfly-friendly place in which to live.

Questions for Those on a Quest

To quest is to question,
and the quality of the sacred quest
has more to do with the questions we ask today
than with answers entombed within past dogma.

1. Does it feel to you as if you are living within one of history's major turning points? If so, what feels different? How are we moving away from the Prodigal Son's priorities?
2. In your own life, is there a shift from the "how" questions to the "why" questions? If so, what are the examples of that?
3. How do you perceive life in the United States to be different after the 1960s than before?

4. What are those parts of you that you would identify with the caterpillar? How are you dealing with their potential (inevitable?) demise?
5. What parts of you are already of the butterfly faith?
6. How are you dealing with the birth-pangs of our time in history?
7. How do you deal with other people who appear to be at different stages of the metamorphosis? To what extent are you judgmental? To what extent are you compassionate?
8. What do you believe are the primary dangers within this crisis time? What do you believe are the opportunities?
9. How do you understand the need for courage at this particular time in history?
10. How do you understand the need for humility at this particular time in history?

Part Two

The Future of the Human Soul

Chapter Four

Re-membering Human–Nature

A human being is part of the whole, called by us the universe. A part limited in time and space. He experiences himself, his thoughts and feelings, as something separate from the rest, a kind of optical delusion of his consciousness. This delusion is a kind of prison for us, restricting us to our personal desires and to affections for a few persons nearest to us. Our task must be to free ourselves from this prison by widening our circle of compassion to embrace all living creatures.

Albert Einstein[1]

It is almost unbelievable, in retrospect, how long it took us to become aware that the Epoch II value system as it relates to nature is an unnatural and unhealthy "optical delusion" and clearly unsustainable. The mainstream cultures of the world have been anthropocentric and short-sighted for a very long time. However, the paradigmatic nature of deep values is to be largely unconscious. Consequently, for most of Epoch II, we rarely questioned our ego-need assumption regarding the separation of humanity and nature, or rarely thought about our self-serving rationalization regarding the human "right" to dominate, use, misuse, and abuse the natural world. Like typical Epoch II adolescents, we have been self-centered and self-absorbed, so enamored of our recently developed mental capabilities and so preoccupied with our scientific achievements that we could not see beyond our own narrow self-interests. Nor did we ask the tough-minded questions about the consequences of such thinking and acting.

Rachel Carson woke us up with her 1962 book *Silent Spring*. She had researched the consequences of our massive use of pesticides, particularly DDT, and her book is usually credited with launching the environmental movement. Keep in mind that, prior to the 1960s, the word *environment* meant simply "surroundings." Carson expanded our understanding of an important word and transformed how we see the world and relate to it.

Few of us had the vision to see the big picture at the time, but Carson's courageous contribution coincided with and corresponded to the other Epoch III deep values that emerged in America in the 1960s. She, like other heroic pioneers and visionaries, was at first ignored, trivialized, even hated, and often considered to be just plain wrong, particularly by the scientific community. It is significant, therefore, that, for those not already awake by 1992, a group of prestigious scientists touched off the thirty-year "snooze-alarm." In a historic and unprecedented consensus among the world's leading scientists, a declaration of warning to humanity was signed by more than sixteen-hundred senior scientists from seventy-one nations, including over half of all Nobel Prize winners. Their statement read, in part:

> Human beings and the natural world are on a collision course. Human activities inflict harsh and often irreversible damage on the environment and on critical resources. If not checked, many of our current practices put at serious risk the future that we wish for human society and the plant and animal kingdoms, and may so alter the living world that it will be unable to sustain life in the manner that we know. Fundamental changes are urgent if we are to avoid the collision our present course will bring about. . . .
>
> No more than one or a few decades remain before the chance to avert the threats we now confront will be lost and the prospects for humanity immeasurably diminished. We the undersigned, senior members of the world's scientific community, hereby warn all humanity of what lies ahead. A great change in our stewardship of the Earth and life on it is required, if vast human misery is to be avoided and our global home on this planet is not to be irretrievably mutilated.[2]

There are now a vast literature and growing awareness regarding the consequences and unsustainability of humanity's Epoch II lifestyle. The *Silent Spring's* wake-up call has turned out to be anything but silent, and the scientist's "snooze-alarm" finally has us alarmed.

We have become alarmed, finally, about polluting our air, drinking water, lakes, and rivers. We have become alarmed, finally, about how some technology destroys the earth's protective ozone layer and the serious consequences of that destruction. We have become alarmed, finally, about the destruction of the planet's rain forests, as well as of the old-growth forests and the loss of rich and multidimensional benefits they provide to the planet's ecosystem and our own health and well-being. We have become alarmed, finally, about the extinction of species, but do we yet fully grasp the fact that extinction is irreversible?

We could go on and on, for the lamentable litany of our belated learning is expanding daily. We now know that to continue thinking in anthropocentric ways about our relationship with nature, combined with our adolescent addiction to consumption, is suicidal. We must change our minds about and change our way of relating to nature and to wild animals. We must repent—*repentance* being an appropriate word since the Greek root, *metanoia*, means to change one's mind.

Our purpose here, however, is not to rehash all the sorry statistics and scary scenarios regarding humanity's Epoch II estrangement from nature. It is, rather, to focus upon and attempt to understand the deeper causal level of why we separated from nature in the first place, why that human–nature estrangement is now being reconciled, how we who live at this time in history can resonate spiritually with the new and emerging Soul, and what some of the benefits will be of doing so.

A meaningful synergy and a purposeful synchronicity exists among much of what has been emerging over the past four decades—the environmental movement, the ecological movement, animal rights groups, the "second wave" of the woman's movement, the appreciation and appropriation of native and indigenous nature-based spiritualities, the "greening" of business, and the shift from mechanistic to organic metaphors—from Buckminster Fuller's "Spaceship Earth," for instance, to the living and breathing "Gaia hypothesis," suggested by James Lovelock and Lynn Margulis.

We will not explore any of the above in detail, but simply point out how they are all related in a bigger purpose and timing. They are all parts of a connected whole, like the separate dots in a picture: if we step back to get the big view, we can see that the larger picture reveals a Soul being transformed. We are, collectively, participating in the process of re-membering that which we dis-membered some ten-thousand years ago—humanity and the rest of nature.

The impact and import of the human–nature reunion is huge. It's enormous. It's gargantuan. This is no fad or temporary aberration, and no amount of backlash will prevent it. The current transformation of Soul is manifested in a plethora of social change movements, but the most significant change will be in this reconciliation and healing of the ten-thousand-year-long fracture of Soul.

It will change our notions regarding the nature of humanity. As we move through this growth-spurt from adolescence into adulthood, we will discover the true nature of being human and the appropriate relationship between humanity and nature. We will begin to sense the meaning and purpose of our participation in the big, wide, wonderful web of life.

Our discussion here will consider just four of the spiritual benefits of healing the human–nature rift: (1) being saved from the original sin of Soul, (2) becoming born-again pagans, (3) understanding that patriarchy is "history," and (4) discarding our ego-oriented spirituality and growing an ecologically oriented spirituality.

Being Saved from the Original Sin of Soul

The natural world is the maternal source of our being as earthlings and the life-giving nourishment of our physical, emotional, aesthetic, moral, and religious existence. The natural world is the larger sacred community to which we belong. To be alienated from this community is to become destitute in all that makes us human.

Thomas Berry[3]

In earlier chapters, we considered the human Soul's "punctuation" ten-thousand years ago from childhood into adolescence, from Epoch I into Epoch II. The reason for that growth-spurt was the emergence of a new evolutionary purpose—ego and mental development. We discussed how, just as an individual human develops an ego by learning to distinguish "self" from "other," humanity as a species followed the same process, separating and distinguishing humanity from the rest of nature. If sin means separation, and the presumption here is that it does, then that demarcation ten-thousand years ago was humanity's original sin of Soul.

In nontheological language, the separation of human–nature was what Morris Berman calls our "basic fault," what ecologist Challis Glendinning calls our "original trauma" and our state of "homelessness," and what psychiatrist Robert Jay Lifton refers to as "the broken connection." Paul Shepard, in his book *Nature and Madness*, is accurate, even though maddingly obscure, when he suggests that we suffer from "an epidemic of the psychopathic mutilation of ontogeny" or "ontogenetic crippling." Geneticist David Suzuki, in *The Sacred Balance*, says that when we separated ourselves from nature, we gave ourselves permission to "act on it, abstract from it, use it, take it apart; we can wreck it, because it is *another*, it is *alien*." Of such is the alienation of human-nature—the original sin of Soul.[4]

One of the more interesting analogies of the human–nature separation comes from theologian-turned-"geologian" Thomas Berry, who says that we have become "autistic" in relationship to the natural world. We have so insulated and isolated ourselves from our Mother the Earth that we cannot hear, see, or feel her presence.

Our adolescent epoch fits those various descriptions. It may have been a necessary stage of human growth and development, but there was a huge price to pay. We are now becoming aware of that price, and the awareness itself is part of the Soul's preparation for change. Now is the time for change, the time for a Soul-level reunion, reconciliation, healing, and whole-making. It is the time for us to grow up and remember our innate connection with nature and to remember the essential nature of humanity.

We never were, of course, physically separated from nature— it was a psychological and egoistical illusion. Actual separation would be impossible, for we *are* nature and inextricably *in* nature. We are made of nature and live every moment of our lives in an intimate dance of change and exchange with nature. Fundamental distinction and separation was and is, as Einstein said in our opening quote, an "optical delusion." We are made of spiritualized matter, and that matters spiritually!

To begin to see our sacred unity with nature accurately and clearly, to begin to save our Soul from its original sin, to heal the pathologies that a fractured Soul inevitably leads to, we must become born-again pagans.

Becoming a Born-again Pagan

Humans are tuned for relationship. The eyes, the skin, the tongue, ears, and nostrils—all are gates where our body receives the nourishment of otherness. . . . . For the largest part of our species' existence, humans have negotiated relationships with every aspect of the sensuous surroundings . . . and from all of these relationships our collective sensibilities were nourished.

Today we participate almost exclusively with other humans and with our own human-made technologies. It is a precarious situation, given our age-old reciprocity with the many-voiced landscape. We still need that which is other than ourselves and our own creations . . . [for] we are human only in contact, and conviviality, with what is not human.

David Abram[5]

The word *pagan* has been misunderstood; even *Webster's Encyclopedic Unabridged Dictionary* gets it wrong. The dictionary identifies a pagan as "a person who is not a Christian, Jew, or Muslim . . . an irreligious or hedonistic person." The original meaning of *pagan*, however, was simply "to be a country dweller." In order to re-member the human–nature division, we need to spend more time in the country. We need to return to an experience of the wilderness if we are to become fully human. In other words, for the spiritual maturation of Epoch III, we need to become born-again pagans.

The "born-again" reference is, of course, because we have all been pagans before. We have been in the wilderness of the heavens, where the stuff of our body was created and where, presumably, we spent several billions of years. We have also dwelled in the wild country-ness of this planet, throughout many incarnations, during the some four-and-a-half billion years of our Mother Earth's existence.

In contrast, humanity's non-pagan history is very brief. Only in the past few thousand years has it occurred to us to denigrate someone who lived in the countryside as an irreligious or uncivilized person. Civilization itself has been around for only a few millennia, and cities for even less time than that. In fact, most of us did not live in cities until very recently: England did not become predominantly urban until 1850 and the United States not until 1910. Humanity has been pagan for most of its existence, becoming urbanized and "civilized" only recently.

Many Epoch II religions, manifesting the deep values of reductionism and hierarchy, separated divine and human, heaven and earth, and spirit and matter, and then established the hierarchical power arrangement of divine over human, heaven over earth, and spirit over matter. Such arrangements inevitably led to thinking that matter, nature, and the body are profane rather than sacred, that country dwellers are different from those of us in the cities, and that persons who are just a bit too earthy, too natural, and too sensual are downright dangerous.

It is critical for us, at this time in our spiritual journey, to become familiar again with our essential pagan nature and to experience, to the extent that our individual circumstances allow, the more-than-human world. It is time when the salvation of our Soul depends upon shifting our attention to creation and creatures and away from the manufactured. To do so, we need to spend more time outside the city and become just a bit more uncivilized.

Most of us have grown up citified and civilized, and that has influenced us more than we know—not always positively. Consider, for instance, the bias revealed in the dictionary definitions of the word *civilization*, which include "living in cities," an "advanced state of human society," and a "high level of culture." To be "civilized" is to be elevated "out of a savage, uneducated, or rude state." The dictionary also suggests that to become civilized is to become "enlightened."

The time has come when we need to question those definitions and to consider how our Soul becomes truncated when we limit our lives to only human and human-made relationships. The Soul's enlightenment as we approach Epoch III is brighter and clearer when we are removed from the "pollution" and the "smog" of civilization.

Consider the consequences of being exposed too much to the tame and too little to the wild. One consequence is that we become confused between the wild and the not-wild. How many of us think that we are witnessing "wild" animals in the artificial context of a zoo? How many of us experience "nature" only at youth camps, on hiking trips, or in camping experiences that we make as "civilized" and "cultured" as possible, while exterminating the insects that "bug" us. When we relate to nature and wild animals like that, what is it that we miss in our understanding of nature and of the wild? What is it that we miss in understanding the nature of humanity? Charlene Spretnak, in *The Resurgence of the Real*, tells about being in a conference and listening to two of the finest writers on the natural world, Barry Lopez and Richard Nelson:

> A love of language and nature—and a humility before both—permeated their comments, but one observation in particular lodged vividly in my memory. After speaking about the ways in which wild animals are so acutely aware of minute events in their considerable range of attention that their consciousness extends far beyond their fur into the sensate forest, Lopez observed that a bear taken out of its habitat and put into a zoo is still a form of mammalian life, but it's not a bear. *It's not a bear.* . . .

Spretnak then elaborated:

> *It's not a human* if its felt connections with the unfolding story of the bioregion, the Earth community, and the cosmos are atrophied, denied, and replaced. *It's not a human* if it can no longer experience awe and wonder at the beauty and mystery of life, seeing nothing but resources and restraints. *It's not a human* if it is socialized to be oblivious to the unity of life, so lonely that it is vulnerable to all compensatory snares.[6]

For us to become fully human we must remember our essential pagan nature. Alice Walker, one of our most wonderful articulators of conscience, in both her writing and in her personal activism, has said that, if we lose our connection with wild animals, "we will lose the spiritual equivalent of oxygen."[7]

We became spiritually deprived and unable to breathe in the full nature of humanity during the epoch of developing our sense of "self." That is rather paradoxical, don't you think? To become fully human, we had to live temporarily within a restricted sense of being human. But then, is that not precisely what we all do individually—living through childhood and adolescent self-centeredness before growing into a more mature sense of the larger world within which we live, move, and have our being?

For several millennia, we became amnesic about the magnificent, magical magnanimity of the human–nature relationship. We lived within an artificial self-image, an illusion of separation, and a deluded sense of independence. We created self-serving rationalizations that we had a God-given right to dominate, manipulate, use, abuse, and control the other-than-human world.

Consider what we miss when we spend all of our time within human-constructed environments dealing only with human-made things. Stop for a moment and think about your typical day—how much nature, wild animals, or wilderness is there in your day? And how often do you think about the important difference between natural creation and creatures vis-a-vis the constructed or manufactured?

We should not conclude a discussion such as this, however, without acknowledging the fact that some people have very little choice regarding where they live, very little freedom to choose habitation alternatives, and very little "disposal income" with which to venture out of the inner cities and into the more-than-human world. But the inner cities and those places we have allowed to become slums would not have to be hostile and lack natural green space and vegetation if public policymakers, city planners, educators, and employers were of a whole-souled mind to give financial priority to "greening" the living, educational, and working environments of the inner city.

When our educational, religious, medical, business, and financial priorities are developed out of Epoch III spiritual maturity, we will make room in our budgets for frequent and extended experiences in the more-than-human world. We will make wilderness experiences central to our business, educational, religious, and healing activities.

Robert Greenway was a professor of psychology at Sonoma State University for many years. Greenway was among the first to develop "ecopsychology" courses at the collegiate level. He led many wilderness experiences for his students and created a graduate training program for wilderness leaders. He also conducted research on the effects that spending time in the wilderness had upon his students. Greenway found that among those who had wilderness experiences:

- 90% described an increased sense of aliveness, well-being, and energy.
- 90% stated that the experience allowed them to break an addiction (defined broadly, such as from nicotine, chocolate, other foods, etc.).

- 92% cited time alone to contemplate the wonders of nature as the single most important benefit.
- 76% reported dramatic changes in the quantity, vividness, and context of their dreams, after about three days in the wilderness.
- 77% said that, upon return, they made major lifestyle changes.

Particularly relevant to our upcoming discussion on patriarchy is the fact that Greenway found remarkably different experiences between men and women on a couple of key points. First of all, the transition from the city into the wilderness was easier for women, and the transition back into the urban world was easier for men. Second, when it came to stating their major reason for going into the wilderness,

- 60% of men and only 20% of women said that it was to conquer fear, to challenge themselves, and to expand their limits.
- 57% of women and only 27 percent of men said that their purpose was to "come home" to nature.[8]

Patriarchy Is "History"

As stated before, nature is virtually synonymous with the organic feminine principle, so when humanity separated itself from nature, it split the Soul along gender lines. We then brought the masculine side of Soul into prominence and sublimated the feminine. The inevitable result was a humanity that operated out of a patriarchal deep value. The assumptions of male dominance and female submission conditioned virtually everything and everybody throughout Epoch II. All our major world religions and all our mainstream cultures, developed as they were in Epoch II, were patriarchal. Consider, for instance, the implications of the statement by biblical scholar Marcus Borg: "So far as we know, all the biblical authors were men."[9] Do we really want to claim, by implication, that "God's word" could only be spoken through men?

Patriarchy is incompatible with the spiritual maturity of an adult Soul. It is "history" precisely because its time in history is over. Patriarchy was a deep value of Epoch II, and as Epoch II dies, patriarchy will die. As we will see in chapter six when we explore more thoroughly the maturation of power, any system of domination will lose its legitimacy as we grow into spiritual maturity. Any institution that hopes to survive long into Epoch III, including religion, will have to move beyond any form of patriarchal domination and control.

The impact of this deep-value shift, however, will not be limited to institutions. We probably cannot even imagine how much ten-thousand years of patriarchy has influenced the way we individually think and act—for women as well as for men. Patriarchy defined for most of us what it meant to be a man or a woman. Patriarchy has conditioned, perhaps more than we know, the ways in which we think about education, health-care, business, athletic competition, sexual orientation, diversity in all categories of human experience—and on and on and on. A deep value such as patriarchy permeated all of our personal and cultural life, and we can only begin to guess how much its demise will change all of us.

From Ego-Spirituality to Eco-Spirituality

As we become conscious of the unseen depths that surround us, the inwardness or interiority that we have come to associate with the personal psyche begins to be encountered in the world at large: we feel ourselves enveloped, immersed, caught up *within* the sensuous world. This breathing landscape is no longer just a passive backdrop against which human history unfolds, but a potentized field of intelligence in which our actions participate. As the regime of self-reference begins to break down, as we awaken to the air, and to the multiplicitous Others that are implicated, with us, in its generative depths, the shapes around us seem to awaken, to come alive.

David Abram[10]

What David Abram says so beautifully and so poetically is that the time has come for the disposal of an ego-oriented spirituality and the growth and development of an ecologically oriented spirituality. The dawn of Epoch III awakens us from the narrow, self-serving, and self-centered ego-spirituality of our collective adolescence to the new epoch of exploring a liberating big-picture and expansive eco-spirituality. We are part of something much bigger than ourselves, something much bigger than humanity. We will not fully understand what it is to be human—indeed, to use the central metaphor of this book, we will not mature as a species—until we understand our participation in that larger context.

The Expansion of "Self"

In Epoch II, we were preoccupied with a very small sense of "self,"defining ourselves primarily in contrast to an "other." After all, that was our evolutionary purpose in Epoch II. We are human; they are animals. We are human; that is inanimate and desouled nature.

Then, consider how even in recent years when we started to become aware of our dependence upon the environment, most of the attention was self-centered. The cry went out that we needed to stop polluting and overusing, degrading, and abusing the environment because it was not in *our* self-interest to do so. We needed to stop damaging *our* life-support system. We needed to stop exterminating species because *we don't know what we may gain from them in the future.* We needed to stop destroying the ozone layer so that *we* won't get skin cancer. Our motivations for changes, so far, have been extraordinarily self-centered and anthropocentric.

One of the most amazing examples of a self-centered Epoch II ecological-economic link, however, was a recent study, reported in the journal *Nature*, that determined that nature is worth $33 trillion a year! As Dave Berry would say, "I'm not making this up." This was an actual ostensibly serious scholarly study![11]

Ecologists, economists, and geographers, representing twelve prestigious universities from three countries, calculated the world economic output as averaging $3,000 per year for every person on the planet. Nature, they figured provided goods and services worth somewhere between $2,600 and $9,000 per person annually. Thus, $33 trillion is a medium estimate: it could be as low as $16 trillion or as high as $54 trillion. The obnoxious absurdity is in putting a price, any price, on the value of nature. Donella H. Meadows, a professor of environmental studies at Dartmouth College, reflected on such human valuation of nature in financial terms and said it "is like calculating the rent you owe your mother while you're still in her womb."[12]

While all the above may very well be true, they reveal an immature spirituality, a spirituality of "shallow ecology." The "deep ecologists" have been calling us to the greater compassion that is representative of the emerging Epoch III deep value.

Epoch III spiritual maturity is not a shallow and self-centered ecological and economic perspective of life. It is more akin to "Deep Ecology," so named in the early 1970s by the Norwegian philosopher Arne Naess. Deep Ecology points us toward the Epoch III expansion of "self," a self fundamentally interconnected to and interdependent upon the entire web of life. It is a sense of self that knows there is intrinsic value in all aspects of creation, a sense of self that knows that we humans are participants and companions, not spoiled adolescents who are served by everything and everyone else.

The maturation of humanity from adolescence into adulthood will move us from a preoccupation with an isolated, atomistic, hard-and-fast, skin-encapsulated ego sense of self into a softer, more expansive, more permeable sense of self. In other words, we will come to know a larger self in Epoch III.

Historian Theodore Roszak points out that traditional psychology thought our task was to know more about the self, whereas the current task is to realize that there is *more self* to get to know. Deep Ecologist Joanna Macy talks about "greening the self." And psychologist Chellis Glendinning tells of visiting with anthropologist Frances Harwood who said, after spending time on the Solomon Islands, living in Bali, and trekking through Nepal, that what is learned is "a transparency of psyche, a wide-openness that emanates a space and time far beyond what we associate with the individual."[13]

Self or other, ecology or cosmology—it is only a matter of scale and the sensitivity of our imaginations. We are interrelated with everything in the cosmos. Our "self" and the universe are one. As Charlene Spretnak put it, we are "an unbroken continuity of cosmos/Earth/continent/nation/bioregion/community/neighborhood/family/person. These are the extended boundaries of the self."[14] As one philosopher suggested, our true identities do not stop at the city limits. Our being and the Ground of our Being are one—and unlimited.

Bernard Campbell sums it up well:

> The components of the natural world are myriad but they constitute a single living system. There is no escape from our interdependence with nature; we are woven into the closest relationship with the Earth, the sea, the air, the seasons, the animals and all the fruits of the Earth. What affects one affects all—we are part of a greater whole—the body of the planet.[15]

Native Keepers of the Vision

Native and indigenous peoples, certainly more than mainstream cultures, have held the vision of an ecological spirituality, while mainstream cultures have been preoccupied with an ego-based spirituality. The extent of that difference was tragically demonstrated throughout Epoch II when mainstream cultures encountered native cultures.

In North America, for instance, when Europeans first colonized what they called the "New World" and what the Native Americans called "Turtle Island," the native nature-based spiritualities were seen as inferior, subhuman, savage, and pagan. They were trivialized, trampled upon, and eliminated in favor of "civilized" Christianity. European-Americans continued that presumption for a very long time, with Eurocentric and Christocentric myopic self-centered exclusivistic arrogance. As a result, the foreigners who invaded the American continent not only claimed the land to be theirs and engaged in massive genocide—generally without any sense of collective injustice or personal shame—but also turned a deaf ear to the spiritual wisdom native to the people who had lived in harmony on and with this land for upwards to thirty-thousand years.[16]

Consider how tragic it was for the Native Americans—for their traditions, their spiritual concept of the human–nature cooperation, and their very lives—when wave upon wave of Europeans invaded their homeland and destroyed their spirituality. As Epoch III dawns in our Soul, we are just beginning to appreciate the spiritual wisdom that had been held in trust by the Native Americans. In fact, as hinted earlier, the awakening of mainstream consciousness to native spiritualities, at this time in history, is evidence of the current transformation of humanity's mainstream Soul.

Once again, our purpose here is not to explore each of these emergent Epoch III subtexts in great detail. Our purpose is the big picture, the larger context to which the subtexts contribute and in which they fit. It might be helpful, however, to be reminded, with just a few illustrations, of the nature-based spiritual wisdom that has been held in trust by our Native American brothers and sisters, until the dominant culture was ready to hear, see, feel, and receive.

Lakota Chief Standing Bear sums up the difference between the indigenous nature-based spirituality, an eco-spirituality, and the ego-spirituality of Epoch II dominant cultures:

The Indian and the white man sense things differently because the white man has put distance between himself and nature; and assuming a lofty place in the scheme of order of things has lost for him both reverence and understanding.

Kinship with all creatures of the earth, sky, and water was a real and active principle. For the animal and bird world there existed a brotherly feeling that kept the Lakota safe among them. And so close did some of the Lakotas come to their feathered and furred friends that in true brotherhood they spoke a common tongue. . . .

The animal had rights—the right of man's protection, the right to live, the right to multiply, the right to freedom, and the right to man's indebtedness—and in recognition of these rights the Lakota never enslaved the animal, and spared all life that was not needed for food and clothing.

This concept of life and its relations was humanizing and gave to the Lakota an abiding love. It filled his being with the joy and mystery of living; it gave him reverence for all life; it made a place for all things in the scheme of existence with equal importance to all. The Lakota could despise no creature, for all were of one blood, made by the same hand, and filled with the essence of the Great Mystery.[17]

I have long been fascinated with Black Elk, the keeper of the sacred pipe for the Oglala Sioux and a medicine man whose entire life was influenced by what he called his "power vision" that he had on Harney Peak in South Dakota when he was a nine-year-old boy. Most of what we know about Black Elk, his famous vision and even his life, was preserved by "Nebraska's Poet Laureate In Perpetuity" John Neihardt.

Neihardt had heard about Black Elk's vision and wanted to learn more. It was in August of 1930 that Neihardt arranged to visit Black Elk where he lived, about two miles west of Manderson, South Dakota. They sat together for an entire afternoon with long periods of silence. Finally, late in the day, Black Elk spoke: "What I know was given to me for men and it is true and it is beautiful. Soon I shall be under the grass and it will be lost. You were sent to save it, and you must come back so that I can teach you."[18]

Neihardt did return, and he listened carefully and at length as Black Elk shared his visionary experience regarding the future of his people, the white man, and this land. The result was Neihardt's now-celebrated book *Black Elk Speaks*.

In another interview, Black Elk said that a person is awakened to spiritual wisdom "when they realize their relationship, their oneness, with the universe and all its powers, and when they realize that at the center of the universe dwells *Wakan-Tanka*, and that this center is really everywhere; it is within each of us."[19]

Chellis Glendinning recounts a story that was passed on to her by the Haudenosaunee statesman Leon Shenandoah. As the story goes, all the creatures of the world gathered in council to clarify the special tasks each was to perform in the service of Creation:

> One by one, they step forward. The beaver is here to look after the wetlands and to monitor how the streams flow through the mountains. The worm is here to burrow through the earth so that the roots of plants may find air and nutrients. The deer is here to slip through the woodlands, to watch what is happening. The council is progressing well—but one poor creature stands in the background, uncertain of his role. This is the human. At last a man steps forward and haltingly addresses the assembly. "We are confused," he says. "What is the purpose of human beings?" The animals and the plants, the insects and the trees—all are surprised. "*Don't you know?!* It's so . . . obvious!" "No," replies the man, "we need you to tell us." And the other creatures of the world responded, "Your purpose is to glory in it all. Your job is to praise Creation."

Shenandoah added, "Our religion is all about thanking the Creator."[20]

Lame Deer, from the Sioux people, addressed a conference inside the grand cathedral of John the Divine in New York. Thomas Berry recalls the event:

> When Lame Deer spoke, he stood with the sacred pipe in his hands and bowed in turn to the four directions. Then, after lifting his eyes to survey the vast cathedral, he turned to the audience and remarked on how over-powering a setting it was for communication with divine reality. Then he added that his own people had a different setting for communion with the Great Spirit, a setting out under the open sky, with the mountains in the distance and the winds blowing through the trees, with the earth under their feet, surrounded by the living sounds of the birds and

insects. It was a setting . . . so profound that he doubted that his people would ever . . . be able to experience the divine adequately in any other setting.[21]

Consider the difference between intentionally experiencing the Divine in a more-than-human setting and our constructed sanctuaries that presume it is best to worship God in as artificial and closed environment as possible. An Absaroke (Crow) woman, Vera Jane He Did It Half says, "Everything we do is a prayer. Our religion is a way of life." Charlene Spretnak points out that "there is no word in Native American languages for 'religion,' the closest concept usually being 'the way you live.'"[22]

Do you suppose that, someday, we could actually change the way we live—from the presumption of consumption into an attitude of gratitude? At this time in history, that may sound like naive, fanciful, and wishful thinking. But what if, as Deep-value Research is suggesting, humanity is in the process of being transformed at the Soul level? If that is the case, then we should not be surprised if we are moving toward a lifestyle, mind-style, and soul-style that are unimaginable within the Epoch II mind.

A Personal Quest for the Sacred

There is a familiar fable in which a hunter asks a woodcutter if he has seen any lion tracks in the area. "Matter of fact," replies the woodcutter, "I can lead you right to the lion himself." The hunter, surprised at the possibility, finds it quite frightening. "It's . . . it's the tracks I'm looking for," he stammers, "not the lion."

One of the pitfalls of traditional sacred quests is settling for tracks, of fearing an actual encounter with power itself. It is easier, and safer, to study somebody else's sacred quest than personally to trod the actual, trudging, sometimes scary and disturbing journey itself. There is even the temptation to study, think, and talk about something or someone far in the past—the more ancient, the more revered—rather than to engage in the quest here and now. We are more comfortable with a map than with the actual territory, sometimes even confusing the two. Religion often acts as if worshiping the sacred experiences of others were more important than doing the work ourselves—sacredness by proxy rather than by personal experience.

In stark contrast, the sacred quest we are talking about is not a spectator sport. It cannot be experienced vicariously. Although it can be informed by the experience of others and can be enriched by communion with other questers, in the final analysis, it is a deeply personal experience. It is a personal dance of integrity within our own depths—a dance between the philosophical and the practical, the cosmic and the personal, the big context of history and the textual immediacy of the present. That is why we talked about courage in the previous chapter.

Because of this, in the process of considering how each emergent Epoch III deep value is currently transforming human culture, we will also consider how we individually might live a life that resonates within that larger transformation. By sharing some of my own quest for growing an Epoch III soul, my hope is that it will aid in some small way, perhaps even enrich, your own quest for spiritual growth.

The Multistoried Mountain

Run to the mountain
Shed those scales on your eyes
That hinder you from seeing God.

Dante Alighieri, *Purgatorio, canto 2*

For my wife Diana and me, the celebration of "Interdependence Day" came on July 4, 1995, when we moved out of Boulder and into our new home on the gentle top of Stone Mountain along the Front Range of the Colorado Rockies. It was the time in our lives when it was important to live within the more-than-human world, to listen attentively to the sounds of the wild, to feel the rhythms of nature, and to attempt to see the sacred and the ensouled world with new eyes.

It is said that seventy percent of the body's sense receptors are found in the eyes; but, for me, for my experience of the world, the percentage seems to be even higher. So much so, that my earlier book was entitled *Sacred Eyes*, and I feel a special kinship with Dante's words quoted above—I came to the mountain to shed the scales that hindered me from seeing God.

Since becoming a born-again pagan, my life has been blessed with a perpetual epiphany of mountaintop experiences. There is something awe-inspiring for me, something meditative, when my view is uninterrupted for great distances. Living on the top of a mountain, on what we call "Winged Spirit Mesa," we have the glorious panorama of viewing both the plains to the east and the snow-capped Continental Divide to the west.

Writing days for me usually begin early in the morning when the world is quiet and dark. The craft of writing is periodically interfused with a meditative appreciation of the special visual delight of the gradual process by which our daytime star brings the enlightenment of a new day.

The privilege of the panoramic view enables me to sit at my desk, writing and watching while welcoming the dawning enlightenment. The eastern horizon is asleep at first, symbolizing the human darkness of sleep and inwardness. But gradually, at a pace that is gentle enough for an observer to be able to feel the awakening deeply, the blackness starts changing to shades of red and yellow, fading almost imperceptively into the morning blue.

Then there is that magical moment when the west answers back with its own color of the dawn—the alpenglow—that beautiful lavender hue that splashes across the snowcapped Continental Divide, just as our planet Earth rotates towards our home star enabling it to become visible above the eastern horizon. The gift of the alpenglow is brief, but, for that wonder-filled few moments, the balance of color between the east on my left and the west on my right frames Pikes Peak directly ahead, that majestic mountain over one-hundred miles away that defines the southern horizon as well as divides the mountains and the plains.

That beauty is infused with additional meaning when I remember that it was on that very mountain, in 1893, that the poet Katharine Lee Bates gave praise to the alpenglow as she penned the words to *America the Beautiful*. I often find myself, in that musical, magical, mystical moment, singing her words: "for purple mountain majesty, above the fruited plains."

The beginning of every day seems to nourish the wilderness of my soul, and my attempts at thinking and writing are invoked by the spirit of such magnificent, marvelous, and miraculous beauty.

What I feel every day on this mountaintop was given voice by the worth-full words of William Wordsworth in *Tintern Abbey*:

And I have felt
A presence that disturbs me with the joy
Of elevated thoughts; a sense sublime
Of something far more deeply interfused,
Whose dwelling is the light of setting suns,
And the round ocean and the living air,
And the blue sky, and in the mind of man.

Central to the thinking of the eighteenth-century Swedish visionary, scientist, and theologian Emanuel Swedenborg was that every appearance in nature corresponds to a state of our mind, and that both speak of Spirit. I have found that insight to be true for me, for in my experience of becoming a born-again pagan, I have experienced a myriad of mirrored states of nature and mind, correspondences between landscapes, air-scapes, mind-scapes, and soul-scapes.

A very different but equally wonderful correspondence greeted me on another morning, when the flickering flames of the candles on my desk prior to the dawn seemed an appropriate participatory juxtaposition to the sparkling city lights below and the twinkling starlights above. Flickering, sparkling, and twinkling—quiet correspondences to my soul's daily awakening.

Then, as the dawn caressed our mountaintop, clouds rolled in from the east and covered the plains and the cities below. Amazingly enough, the top layer of the clouds remained below our 7000-foot perspective. Our home became an island just a few feet above a sea of soft billowy clouds, and I felt like an isolated and solitary observer on top of the world. I could imagine walking out across that blanket of white all the way to the eastern horizon. To the west and the south were other mountaintop islands with no visible evidence of civilization. It was a private communion and correspondence with the mountaintops, the sunrise, the clouds, and the art-show-in-progress—an extraordinary outer dawning that seemed to call forth a more than ordinary inner awakening to how, in a certain sense, we are creatures alone in a solitary relationship with our Creator. It was a time when the outer world was hiding distractions from sensing that private pagan passion of participation, in the wonderful process of sacred questing.

Mountains have long held a very special spiritual power and enticement for humanity. The building of pyramids may have been an attempt to duplicate mountain mystique on lands where there were no mountains. The special spiritual significance of Machu Picchu, the ancient Inca city in Peru, may be linked to the fact that it is high in the Andes. Black Elk had his famous "power vision" on Harney Peak in the Black Hills of South Dakota. Moses was called by God to go to the top of Mount Sinai to receive the Ten Commandments. There are many stories linking Jesus and mountains—from his initial forty days in the wilderness to his frequent retreats into the mountains to pray, as well as his transfiguration and his crucifixion.

In the theology of Epoch II, heaven is up and earth is down, so being on a mountaintop, in Epoch II logic, is being closer to God. I do not resonate with that hierarchical theology, but, for different reasons, the mountain is a very special spiritual catalyst for me. There is something about a "Rocky Mountain High" that lifts my spirit into lofty realms. My mind and soul seem to soar into great heights and on to great distances. For me, the mountain's mystique lies in the grand view and the correspondences of nature and mind. My eyesight's being unencumbered for great distances seems to free my insight from blocks and constriction.

The Limitless Sky

In 1605, Miguel de Cervantes published *Don Quixote*, in which he expressed the belief that there are "no limits but the sky." The modern phrase that owes its heritage to Cervantes is "the sky's the limit." The word *sky* comes from an ancient word meaning covering, so it is understandable that Cervantes thought it was the ultimate limit. The sky was thought to be a cover for the earth, a rather low cover at that.

Recently, however, our minds and spirits have been liberated from small spatial limitations. Astronomy and cosmology have removed the cover and have expanded our awareness of a sky of seemingly limitless grandeur. The sky, as we now know it, is not a cover or restriction for our imagination, hanging low overhead. It is, rather, a mind-boggling and spirit-stretching window into an awe-inspiring, miraculous, and wonder-filled universe. Clearly, one needs to get in pretty good spiritual shape not to have such soul-stretching result in a bit of pain. Uptight soul fibers, after all, get ripped apart by such awesome high-mindedness, whereas flexible souls can stretch to such lengths, heights, depths, and gargantuan periods of time.

I have always been fascinated with the night sky, when the blue dominated by one very bright star turns to the black sprinkled with billions of tiny star-dots, when the relatively near turns to the unbelievably far away.

In an economically oriented culture, being "in the black" has the financial connotation of having more money coming in than going out, having more income than expenses. Consider, however, being spiritually oriented and experiencing the correspondence of being in the cosmic blackness where in-coming awe far exceeds any meager personal outgo. We cannot compute the economics of that difference.

One of my favorite soul-stretchers these days, stretching my soul-fibers out into astronomical dimensions, is the mathematical cosmologist Brian Swimme, a man who swims through the oceanic concepts of the universe with Olympian skill and grace. Swimme reminds us that the native and indigenous peoples of South America believe that to become human "one must make room in oneself for the immensities of the universe."[23] Now, that is really a room with a view!

From that soul-room with a view, I had communion last night with the light coming from the Andromeda Galaxy. I find it awe-inspiring to consider that the light photons entering my eye, and the enlightenment entering my soul, left that galaxy some two-and-one-half-million years ago. I find it mind-boggling to think that that enlightenment has been traveling for that gigantic period of time, over that enormous distance, at the prodigious speed of over 186,000 miles per second. And I consider the fact that each of several billions of stars in the Andromeda Galaxy sacrificed several tons of itself every second in order to give that light. The soul-warming enlightenment has entered my eyes and is now part of me— physically, mentally, and spiritually.

Diane Ackerman put it well: "There is a way of beholding nature that is itself a form of prayer."[24] And I do, indeed, feel that it is a prayerful beholding of that which we do not know—a sacred communion with distant places, with vast ranges of time, and, probably, with other living beings coming to us from long ago and far away. My spirit can soar into that realm, into and out of the black, for the rest of this lifetime and for many more. It is hard to imagine how one could not be excited about waking up each morning to participate in this incredible universe, how one could not feel blessed to live another day, another month, another year. I am energized by the anticipation of how much there is yet to learn and to experience.

Our Familiars and Not-so-familiars

Novelist Alice Walker, another marvelous soul-stretcher to grace our time, writes of "familiars," what we usually call pets. Diana and I currently have three familiars who share our lives and with whom we have had the privilege of becoming increasingly familiar. There is "Feather," a canary who will commune with us for only so long, exchanging simple tweets with our simple whistles, until its spirit can be contained no longer and he humbles us by launching off on a musical, magical, melody of song. Then there is "Raven," our feline companion whose life's purpose seems to be *not* to become very familiar or, perhaps more accurately, familiar only on his terms. He tries to maintain the persona of independence and care-lessness, but his "act" is betrayed by the fact that he chooses to express his independence all day by sleeping within three or four feet of where I am writing, and by caring— no, demanding— to have Diana hold him when she comes home at night.

Our most familiar, however, is a wonderful Belgian Sheepdog "Gypsy-Bear." She is a passionate participant in our home and in our lives. In fact, she responds so strongly to passion that she becomes a real nuisance wherever Diana and I engage in any passionate sexual activity—but I don't plan on sharing the rest of that story!

Since entering the more-time-at-home-writing phase of my life, I have tried to observe Gypsy-Bear more closely, to pay more attention to her nature and her nurture—a permeable membrane for her, to be sure. She is as familiar with and at-home in the out-of-doors environment as well as indoors. She relishes being in nature as much as being within our nurture. And the latter is clearly a two-way experience, for she nourishes our souls in so many ways.

Gypsy-Bear, Diana, and I hike around the mountaintop virtually every morning. Initially, I thought that the purpose was to take the dog for a walk, along with some good exercise for Diana and me. But the more I paid attention the more I realized that, while I was walk-ing and exercising, Diana and Gypsy-Bear were being in and com-muning with nature. Diana seems to have never forgotten her essential pagan nature. She, unlike me, never had to be born-again into an at-home-ness in nature— it is just who she is, an incredible personification of feminine-nature. It is not an overstatement to say that she has been the midwife for my pagan birthing process.

Returning to Gypsy-Bear, it is interesting how she uses very different barking sounds to communicate with us, and only under very unusual circumstances. She almost never barks at the many animals that inhabit this wilderness. Whether it is deer, elk, bear, bobcat, or coyote, I have watched her and them observe each other carefully and seem to have a very thoughtful live-and-let-live tolerance and respect for each other's "space."

I have watched Gypsy-Bear and a big black bear stand about twenty feet from each other just studying one another. And, then, in a surprising move—what seemed to be almost a gesture of peace— Gypsy-Bear sat down, while still watching the big black bear very intently. In actuality, the bear was less interested in Gypsy-Bear than she in it, which gave me some sense of relief, as it was busy raiding the bird-feeders in its autumnal preoccupation with food.

On three occasions, however, Gypsy-Bear has barked, and the barks are so specific and so different that I know precisely what is the focus of her attention. If hikers come within one hundred yards or so of the house, she gives one kind of bark. On another occasion, Gypsy-Bear and Raven were out on our front porch, and I was reading on the top deck. A unique bark from Gypsy-Bear, however, let me know immediately that there was a dangerous situation. I ran downstairs to find Raven face to face with a rattlesnake that was about to strike. Gypsy-Bear unquestionably saved Raven's life. And she repeated the exact same saving act another time with the same unusual bark, saving Raven's life again from an impending rattlesnake strike.

A third very different and very distinctive bark, however, involves a longer story. It is a story involving the not-so-familiar mountain lion. The story has three "chapters," as of this writing— one occurred before we had Gypsy-Bear and, in fact, before we actually built our home, and the last two involved Gypsy-Bear's versatility in her bark-announcements regarding visitors.

The mountain lion is probably the most powerful animal inhabiting this mountain wilderness—this continent's "big cat,"what wildlife experts call "the Rolls Royce of North American predators."[25] "Mountain lion," "panther," "puma," and "cougar" are simply different names for the same animal. "Cougar" is what it is known by in South America, and the name "puma" is of Inca origin. But there is an even more interesting story behind the naming of the mountain lion.

Early Dutch traders apparently mistook the cougar for a female lion and asked the Native Americans why they did not bring in the skins of the male lion. As Ted Andrews relates, "The Indians relishing a joke on the ignorant white traders told them that all the males lived in a distant range of mountains and were so fierce that no one dared hunt them. Thus the name mountain lion came to be."[26] The Native Americans, thereafter, frequently called this magnificent animal the "Spirit of the Mountain."

Tragically, after two hundred years of vigorous hunting, the once-plentiful mountain lion who roamed throughout the United States is now found only in the western states. The last one in Vermont, for instance, was shot more than a hundred years ago. No wonder this animal generally stays clear of human beings! It is almost impossible to observe a mountain lion in nature. Pulitzer-Prize-winning author Wallace Stegner beautifully expressed this elusiveness in his *Memo to the Mountain Lion*:

> Solitary and shy, you lived beyond, always beyond. Your comings and goings defined the boundaries of the unpeopled. If seen at all, you were only a tawny glimpse flowing toward disappearance among the trees or along the ridges and ledges of your wilderness.[27]

That rarity of human sighting is part of what makes our experiences with the mountain lion so remarkable. Our first experience with the mountain lion took place in the late spring of 1995, before our home on Winged Spirit Mesa was completed. I was in Boulder, and Diana was up on our property alone.

For this story to make sense, it is helpful to know that one of the first things Diana did after we bought the property was to walk the mountaintop until the energy of the mountain "told" her where her medicine wheel should go, that special, sacred place on which she conducts her rituals of connecting with Spirit in general and nature and the animal world in particular. Only then did she decide where to build it, which she proceeded to do by herself.

On one particular day, with our home nearing completion, Diana was performing a ritual of blessing for this wilderness, the animals, and our new home. As is her custom, she called in the four directions, blessed the land, and blessed the animals who call this mountain their home. She then asked Spirit if we might share this mountain wilderness with the animals in peace and mutual respect.

Diana—who combines within her being a gentle feminine soul and the toughness of a construction worker—then started hauling stone. The little excavation needed for our home turned up a lot of stone, and she was building a rock wall simply to store the rock until we had other use for it. She was about fifteen yards to the east of her medicine wheel when she became aware of an unusual sound emanating from the pine trees just to the north of the medicine wheel. At first, the sound was peripheral to her awareness because she was focused on hauling the stone. But the sound persisted and grew louder, gradually demanding her attention. It sounded like a strange growling, snarling, and hissing, unlike anything she had ever heard before. She stopped the stone work and looked carefully into the trees.

There, in the pine trees immediately to the north of her medicine wheel, not more than twenty yards from where she was standing, was a magnificent mountain lion in full profile with its head turned and looking directly at her.

Keep in mind that mountain lions are usually silent and rarely heard by humans unless cornered or its cubs threatened. In this case, the mountain lion was not cornered and had no cubs with it. Diana was not making any threatening moves in its direction. It could have remained hidden, silent, and anonymous, the usual behavior for a mountain lion. Yet, it seemed, inexplicably, to be drawing Diana's attention intentionally.

Later, Diana wondered about the possible meaning of such an appearance and such unusual behavior. Why was the mountain lion seeming to draw attention to itself? Was there meaning in that? Was there meaning in the fact that it was precisely north of the north spoke of the medicine wheel? Was it in some way responding to Diana's ritual blessing? Was it answering Diana's request that we live in harmony and mutual respect in this wilderness?

The Native American traditions that Diana uses in her medicine wheel rituals have the snake as the totem animal to the west, the coyote to the south, the eagle to the east, and the white buffalo to the north. In each ritual, she calls in the power of those respective animals and directions. She has often joked that, since we have snakes, coyotes, and eagles atop Winged Spirit Mesa, if a white buffalo ever showed up, then we would know this is *really* powerful land.

Diana came down to our home in Boulder, shared the excitement of the experience with me, and then went into our library to research the meaning and power of the mountain lion. Her attention was drawn to a book by Sun Bear, a Chippewa medicine man, who had a great vision of the medicine wheel's meaning wherein the mountain lion was seen as the animal totem for the north, for those born between February 19 and March 20. Diana's birthday is February 20th!

Is that just a coincidence? Or could it be that the mountain lion came to inform Diana that it, not the white buffalo, was her appropriate totem animal to the north? Could it be that the mountain lion, who knew this mountain better than we and for a much longer time, was responding to Diana's ritual blessing with a blessing of its own? Could it be that the mountain lion was reciprocating her prayer that we might live in harmony with all the other creatures on this mountain?

My left brain prefers to be cautious about drawing conclusions that might not be warranted, careful not to be taken in or swayed by the appearance of the moment. All the rest of my being, however, wants to tell the left brain to lighten up, to expand its sense of reality, to get with Shakespeare's realization that there is more to this world than is "dreamt of in our philosophy," and to welcome the magical, mysterious, magnificent connections between humans and the more-than-human world.

Let's face it: this old left brain has spent more than sixty years of training in Epoch II "boot-camp." It has been taught in academic educational settings to analyze, distinguish, separate, and categorize. It has been acculturated into an Epoch II notion of being a manly left brain, a genetic gnosis of "guy-ness" that understands the world. As a result, it takes a while to become a born-again pagan. A left-brained, half-brained cripple takes some time to learn how to let nature walk him, to allow nature to teach him how to see with sacred eyes and feel with a sacred heart.

My custom is to begin each day of writing with a meditation on the subject matter for that day and a prayer that I will be receptive to what God wants to come through from my soul on that particular day. We had not seen the mountain lion again for a year and a half, in spite of the fact that we hike around this mountaintop almost daily. Yet, eighteen months after the first sighting, I was at the point in my writing of this book where I was telling about Diana's original experience. Consequently, before I began writing, I was in prayer and meditation about what the mountain lion, and the Holy Spirit—the Spirit of the Whole—wanted my soul to express through my mind and my fingers on the computer.

It was in that context that the mountain lion blessed our lives with a second appearance. And this is where Gypsy-Bear's "voice" also comes back into the story.

I was upstairs just shortly after noon, engrossed in writing about our experiences on Winged Spirit Mesa in general and Diana's first encounter with the mountain lion in particular. Diana had gone to her psychotherapy office in Boulder. Gypsy-Bear was downstairs, on the ground floor in the library. The quiet and solitary focus upon my writing was punctuated when Gypsy-Bear let out a kind of bark that I had never heard before. She communicated immediately that something very different was outside the library. I ran downstairs to investigate and was greeted, face to face, by the mountain lion who was right outside our front door looking in at us. Then, slowly, it turned and walked away, periodically looking back at us over its shoulder.

There was a feeling of time shifting into slow-motion—seemingly, so that I could fully absorb the awe and wonder of that magnificent animal. The mountain lion left via the southern ridge and down the side of the mountain and out of sight, but it was the most calm and relaxed leaving that you can imagine. Looking into the eyes of that magnificent and mysterious animal and the very processes of its being there and its leaving there—all seemed to have my heart overflowing with meaning and purpose.

Diana worked late that evening; by the time she arrived home, we had only a little time to share that event before bed. The next morning, however, I was up early, meditating on the subject matter of this very chapter once again and starting to include the latest story about the mountain lion. When Diana got up, she again went down to our library to research the mountain lion further. In a few moments, Diana came upstairs with her arms full of books, laid them out in front of the fireplace and expressed her frustration. "It makes no sense, but I cannot find the mountain lion in these books. I know its here, but I just can't find it."

At that precise moment, Gypsy-Bear "spoke" in a voice that I had heard only once before—yesterday, when the mountain lion visited us the first time—and she came running upstairs leading us to the sliding glass doors looking out to the West. And there, having just walked across our patio outside the library where Diana had been just moments before trying to find the mountain lion in our books, and still within just a few feet of the house, meandering to the west while periodically looking back at us over its shoulder, was the mountain lion. And, again, it was in a calm mode of behavior and with a confident manner that seemed to be calling forth meaning and purpose out of our hearts. It slowly moved to the western ridge, down the mountain side, and out of sight.

Is all of that just meaningless coincidence? Or is there something within those experiences that a born-again pagan needs to listen to and learn from? Consider the timing, for instance. Three times in an eighteen-month period we had been visited by the mountain lion. The first time was when Diana had just performed a ritual blessing on her medicine wheel, asking that we might live on this mountaintop in harmony and mutual respect with the animals who call this place their home. The second time was when I was meditating on and writing this very chapter, attempting to feel, hear, see, and sense what we are to learn from the more-than-human world—even more specifically, I was writing about the first experience with the mountain lion. The third time was the very next day when Diana was trying to find the mountain lion in our books, and I, again, was attempting to write about our mountain lion experiences.

Those experiences leave me with the feeling of wanting to express to the universe, with as loud a voice and as big a spirit as I can muster, one great big *Wow!* I want to sing its praises. What a privilege it is to be alive and to witness and participate in this awesome, wonder-filled world.

I trust that, as we reconnect with nature, as we re-member that which we dis-membered, and as we develop a new union with our soul-full communion with the more-than-human world, we will begin to see the deeper meaning in the timing of events and in our encounters with the natural world. Carl Jung observed many such meaning-full coincidences and called such occurrences "synchronicity." Perhaps the synergy (*syn*) of re-membering human–nature at this particular time in history (*chronos*) provides the syn-chron-icity of spiritual magic. And, just perhaps, it will enable us to grow an integrity of becoming whole-brained and whole-bodied at the same time we are becoming whole-souled.

Conspiring with Heaven's Breath

The human intuition regarding the link between God, wind, breath, and spirit permeates virtually all of history and every religious tradition. In almost every language the word for soul—*psyche, atman, prana, spiritus, geist, nephesh, ruwach, anima*— also means wind and breath. We aspire to be soul-full. We get inspired with Spirit. When we breathe together or when we are of one soul, we literally conspire. And when we die, we expire. The Latin word *anima*, for instance, not only means wind and spirit, but it leads to *animus* (soul), *animare* (to fill with breath), and, eventually, to *animal*.

My life is animated, inspirited, and ensouled with the opportunity to participate in the big sky and the clean, fresh air. To breathe deeply up here on the mountaintop is to participate not only in the most immediate and necessary act for our very life than anything else—breathing is more important than food or water, for we cannot survive more than a few minutes without it—but to participate in the act that links us to the world, past as well as present and future.

With every breath, I am transcending the Epoch II limited notion of "self." With every breath, I take in millions of molecules that were previously not me, but are now in and a part of me. The eminent Harvard astronomer Harlow Shapley calculated that with each breath we take in about 30,000,000,000,000,000,000 atoms of argon, an inert gas. Shapley then speculated about how that breath links us with life before ours:

> Your next breath will contain more than 400,000 of the argon atoms that Gandhi breathed in his long life. Argon atoms are here from the conversations at the Last Supper, from the arguments of diplomats at Yalta, and from the recitations of the classic poets.[28]

As highly acclaimed geneticist David Suzuki suggests, "Air is a matrix that joins all life together":

> Every breath is a sacrament, an affirmation of our connection with all other living things, a renewal of our link with our ancestors and a contribution to generations yet to come. Our breath is a part of

life's breath, the ocean of air that envelops Earth. Unique in the solar system, air is both the creator and the creation of life itself.[29]

What a wonderful symbol of forgiveness. Consider the fact that I am literally taking into me, becoming a part of me, that which inspired the person who betrayed me, the person who feels foreign to me, the person whom I don't like. Like it or not, we are conspiring in life. It is fore-given that we are one. The spiritual attitude of forgiveness is but one way of recognizing and manifesting that oneness.

I am breathing and participating in that oneness about ten-million times a year—a constant coming into union, a sacred communion, exchanging and interchanging with virtually everything on Earth. Nor is our inspiration limited to what we might think of as earthly: Lyall Watson estimates that one-hundred tons of extraterrestrial material enters our atmosphere every day. We have been listening for radio signals from outer space, while we may have been physically becoming extraterrestrials with every breath. ET "R" us. Cosmos "R" us. To "phone home," we need only engage in deep prayer and meditation.

Breathing is one way we commune with the heavenly Spirit, and wind is another. The two are closely linked. According to Genesis, God breathed life into human beings. Later, God spoke to Job "out of the whirlwind." Among Native American traditions, breathe and wind have holy connotations as well. For the Lakota, for instance, the peace pipe, among the most sacred of all possessions, is smoked in ritual fashion in order to make the breath visible. By so doing, it makes visible the usually unseen connections between those who smoke the pipe and all the other two-legged, four-legged, winged, walking, and crawling spirits of the world. Also participating in the interconnectedness are the rooted spirits of the trees, grasses, shrubs, and mosses. David Abram tells us that "the rising smoke carries the prayers of the Lakota people to the sky beings—to the sun and the moon, to the stars, to the thunder beings and the clouds, to all those powers embraced by *woniya wakan*, the holy air."[30]

Jesus, interestingly enough, was speaking directly to those of us trying to become born-again pagans when he linked wind and being born-again: "You ought not to be astonished, when I tell you that you must be born over again. The wind blows where it wills; you hear the sound of it, but you do not know where it comes from, or where it is going" (John 3:7–8). And, "while the day of Pentecost was running its course," the day Christians consider to be the birth of the church, "suddenly there came from the sky a noise like that of a fierce wind blowing. . . . And they were all filled with the Holy Spirit" (Acts 2:1–2).

If one lives on a mountaintop along the front range of the Colorado Rockies, one becomes very familiar with—whether one wants to or not—wind. I mean *wind*! A Pentacostal-type *fierce wind*: Winds at 60, 70, and 80 miles per hour are quite common, and it is not at all unusual to have winds exceed 100 miles per hour. The air at 7000 feet is not as "heavy" as at sea level, so it doesn't do the same kind of damage as it does in a hurricane or a tornado; but even the rarefied air at 7000 feet, when it is fiercely blowing, gets your attention.

On Winged Spirit Mesa, we sometimes get more wind than we ask for, and, if a fierce wind's blowing has something to do with the Holy Spirit, we've got plenty of the holy. As with the Spirit, we don't see the wind. We only see, hear, or feel its effects, effects that can be quite powerful. Sometimes, usually at night, the wind-spirit can blow so hard, the fierce wind can make so much noise, that one literally has difficulty sleeping. Some nights when the fierceness of the wind keeps me from sleeping, and I wonder if we'll still be in Colorado in the morning, I also wonder about Psalm 104: "O Lord my God . . . riding on the wings of the wind; who makest the winds thy messengers."

Okay, God, you've got my attention. What's the message?

One message that we understood early on was that, if we are to live in harmony with the spirit-wind on Winged Spirit Mesa, we have to be thoughtful about what we leave outside—if it is not nailed down! Anything that the wind can move just might have to be retrieved from Kansas in the morning.

The applicable phrase is "anything that the wind can move." One night the spirit-wind had more than its usual sound and fury, and, as we were soon to discover, it was definitely signifying something—a quite unusual message, as it turned out. The next morning Diana and I were out for our usual hike. We started out to the north, but circled back around and returned to our home via our driveway on the east. At the entrance to our driveway, we had erected a stone slab, with letters and numbers glued on the stone slab that announced "Winged Spirit Mesa" along with our address, a total of thirty letters and numbers. But on this particular morning, following the night of messenger winds, there were two letters missing, the *g* and the *e* out of "Winged." Only two of thirty letters were blown off the sign—but the sign now read "Win—d Spirit Mesa." Was it a coincidence? Was it a message?

But the story is not over. Several months later, we invested in a larger and heavier stone slab, and a friend offered to etch "Winged Spirit Mesa" and our address into the stone. No more letters that could be blown off! In fact, the stone slab must weigh about two-hundred pounds, and it is tilted back against a pile of rocks. Next to immovable by any wind, right? Wrong!

I've got to admit that my left brain *really* has difficulty with this one. But, a few mornings ago, after another night of fierce winds, we discovered that the entire slab had been blown over! Could it be that God wants this place to be called, at least once in a while, "*Wind* Spirit Mesa?" As of this writing, we're still stubbornly insisting on "Winged" Spirit Mesa, but stay tuned!

Questions for Those on a Quest

To quest is to question,
and the quality of the sacred quest
has more to do with the questions we ask today
than with answers entombed within past dogma.

1. What has been your journey of awakening regarding the human– nature relationship?
2. What do you do to create a more sustainable relationship between humanity and nature?
3. How has your inner life—your self-image and your spiritual practice—been influenced by an epoch of patriarchy? Do you think that needs changing? If so, how will you change?
4. Do you think it is important for you to become a born-again pagan? If so, what are you doing to facilitate that birthing?
5. To what extent has your spirituality, your theology, and your religious experience been Epoch II ego based? If you were to grow an Epoch III soul, what would your eco-spirituality, your eco-theology, and your eco-religion look like?

6. What have you learned from your "familiars?"
7. How do you avail yourself of the not-so-familiar animal world.
8. What does the wild, external world correspond to in your inner world?
9. When in the wilderness, what do you hear, see, feel, touch, and intuit?
10. When experiencing the more-than-human world, what kind of dialogue do you have between your left brain and your right brain?

Chapter Five

The Ubiquity of Wholeness

The classical idea of the separability of the world into distinct but interacting parts is no longer valid or relevant. Rather, we have to regard the universe as an undivided and unbroken whole. . . . Science itself is demanding a non-fragmentary world-view.

David Bohm, *Wholeness and the Implicate Order*[1]

Wholeness, as the second emergent deep value of Epoch III, is a natural and logical extension of the first. Reconnecting humanity and nature was the first step in becoming whole and the first act of healing the fractured Soul of Epoch II. The discoveries of science, as well as the emergent energy of healing, wholeness, and holiness, have now taken us far beyond the reconnection of humanity and nature. The enlightenment of the Epoch III dawn reveals the ubiquity of wholeness: *everything* is interconnected and interrelated.

Science Discovers Wholeness

One of the marvelous ironies in the evolutionary journey of humanity's Soul is that science, the Prodigal Son's crowning intellectual achievement that took reductionism to the maximum, would be the primary catalyst at the dawn of Epoch III for our discovery of how wholeness permeates the entire universe. As physics professor Paul Davies observes,

> For three centuries, science has been dominated by the Newtonian and thermodynamic paradigms, which present the universe

either as a sterile machine, or in a state of degeneration and decay. Now there is a new paradigm of the creative universe, which . . . emphasizes the collective, cooperative and organizational aspects of nature; its perspective is synthetic and holistic rather than analytic and reductionistic.[2]

Classical science, in attempting to understand the universe, reduced the big picture to a lot of little pieces. In a manner of speaking, science reduced the universe to a plethora of multiverses. Then, after we gave separate names to the pieces, we came to believe that the pieces were fundamentally different and distinct from one another. We proceeded to train generations of scholars and professionals in the specialized expertise of parts, constantly reducing the parts into smaller parts, creating even more specialties. As someone once cleverly remarked, we have experts who learn more and more about less and less.

No doubt, we have benefitted from reductionism. However, while assuming that the world was a collection of separate pieces and parts, we ignored an understanding of the whole. Or we assumed that the whole was simply the sum of the parts, thus misunderstanding the whole. Our method of knowing was to learn as much about the parts as we could, add up that knowledge, have the specialists collaborate, and then issue a dictum on what the whole is all about.

Sounds logical, doesn't it? Sounds reasonable. Start with the smallest part, learn more and more about the details, add up knowledge of the details, and we will eventually understand everything. It was the Prodigal Son's mantra. But the Prodigal Son was wrong.

The genius of science is its refusal to become static, its irreverence, if you will, regarding answers from the past. Answers from the past always have to stand up to questions and challenges of the present, frequently giving way to new insight. Science keeps exploring the creative edges, keeps pushing the envelop, keeps learning, keeps discovering. Science at its best is even willing to learn something that contradicts what had previously been thought to be "true." In science new discovery can overthrow previous dogma. And so, the courageous scientific community left the Epoch II deep value of reductionism and leads the way in accepting the Epoch III deep value of wholeness, as the quotation from David Bohm, which opens this chapter, attests.

Prior to the mid-nineteenth century, electricity and magnetism were thought to be two completely separate entities, but James Clerk Maxwell showed us that they were, in fact, unified. Classical science thought of the universe as a machine, comprised of separate, albeit interacting, parts. Space, time, energy, mass, and gravity were thought to be distinctly different elements of the universe. All this changed dramatically in the early decades of the twentieth century with the emergence of relativity and quantum physics, as well as the other "new sciences" of chaos and complexity theories. Collectively, they constitute dramatic and revolutionary changes in the scientific worldview.

Albert Einstein almost singlehandedly started the revolution. Believing intuitively in an inherent harmony to the universe, Einstein looked for wholeness and found it, explaining how space and time were actually space-time, how mass was actually just pent up energy, and how gravity was included in the holistic mix.

Quantum theory was more of a team effort, beginning in the 1920s but no less revolutionary. Although relativity and quantum theories are different in many respects, they share the critical common insight that "the primary emphasis is now on *undivided wholeness.*"[3] This insight was such a radical departure from previous thinking that many of the physicists involved in creating the revolution often admitted that they were not at all sure they understood it. One story involves Einstein's declaring enthusiastically that he had never completely understood quantum theory until he read Bohm's 1951 textbook on the subject, some three decades after the revolution began.[4]

Einstein, in fact, never gave up his intuition that the universe is whole. He started the holistic revolution when he published his "special theory of relativity" as a twenty-six-year old clerk in the Swiss patent office, and he devoted the last half of his life searching for what he felt sure was the next step in scientific discovery, a theory that would show how everything is interrelated and interconnected. His search for a Grand Unifying Theory (GUT) has led many scientists to find their priority in trying to discover a Theory of Everything (TOE). "The search for such a TOE," writes Paul Davies, "has become something of a holy grail for physicists."[5]

Another indication of how the deep value of wholeness was emerging from the human Soul is how "systems theory," although pioneered primarily by biologists, erupted almost simultaneously from several scientific disciplines in the early decades of the twentieth century. The central discovery of systems theory is that the essential qualities of a living system are found only in the whole, not in the parts, and that the nature of the whole is destroyed when it is dissected into parts. Systems theory claims that we cannot know the whole by analyzing the parts. As physicist Fritjof Capra put it, "Ultimately . . . there are no parts at all. What we call a part is merely a pattern in an inseparable web of relationships."[6]

Then there is the seminal contribution from cosmology, theology's materialistic twin in considering the Big Picture. The etymology of the word suggests that wholeness was in our intuition from early on—*cosmos*, as the Greeks used it meant a single, harmonious system and the Latin root for "universe" means "all things turned into one."

Some analysts of the twentieth century claim that the single most important scientific contribution in the past one-hundred years was made by astronomer Edwin Hubble. Previous to Hubble's discoveries, we thought that our galaxy, the Milky Way, was the totality of the universe. But Hubble discovered that one of those "stars" we were looking at was actually another galaxy—our closest neighbor, the Andromeda Galaxy—with billions of stars of its own. Then he discovered that there are actually billions of other galaxies and that they are all speeding away from each other. Hubble's notion of an expanding universe eventually led to the dramatic understanding that, if the expanding universe were thought of as a movie played in reverse, it meant that, about fifteen-billion years ago, the entire universe was in a single point and an explosion called the "Big Bang" started the expansion. Thus, in spite of the great distances involved, everything in the universe was fundamentally and intimately related. Everything in the universe apparently started in a unity, is one indivisible whole, and the whole is simply expanding. We participate, it seems, in a pregnant universe, growing and expanding. We are kin to everything in the universe—the kin-dom of a universal God.

The Astronomical Point of View

Moving from scientific theory to human experience, consider how the view of the planet Earth from the outside changed the astronauts from reductionistic scientists to holistic humanitarians and how pictures of space taken by those astronauts have changed the rest of us:

American astronaut Edgar Mitchell: "We went to the moon as technicians; we returned as humanitarians. . . .

"My view of our planet was a glimpse of divinity." (Mitchell, in fact, was so moved by the astronomical point of view that he returned to earth and founded The Institute of Noetic Sciences, an effort devoted to the exploration of consciousness in a completely holistic universe.)

Soviet cosmonaut Vladimir Kovalyonok: "After an orange cloud—formed as a result of a dust storm over the Sahara and caught up by air currents—reached the Philippines and settled there with rain, I understood that we are all sailing in the same boat."

Syrian Muhammad Ahmad Faris: "From space I saw Earth—indescribably beautiful with the scars of national boundaries gone."

American John-David Bartoe: "As I looked down, I saw a large river meandering slowly along for miles, passing from one country to another without stopping. I also saw huge forests, extending across several borders. And I watched the extent of one ocean touch the shores of separate continents. Two words leaped to mind as I looked down on all this: commonality and interdependence. We are one world."

Indian Rakesh Sharma: "My mental boundaries expanded when I viewed the Earth against a black and uninviting vacuum, yet my country's rich traditions had conditioned me to look beyond man-made boundaries and prejudices. One does not have to undertake a space flight to come by this feeling."[7]

Astronauts were transformed by the astronomical point of view. But, as the astronaut from India put it so aptly, we do not have to travel physically into space to imagine that astronomical point of view and to have that imagination expand our souls.

"Once a photograph of the Earth, taken from the outside is available . . . a new idea as powerful as any in history will be let loose." That prophetic observation has been attributed to Fred Hoyle, ostensibly uttered in 1948. We were provided with that powerful image in the revolutionary 1960s. The mythologist Joseph Campbell grasped its significance when he suggested that the pictures of Earth from outer space would probably provide the new mythology for the future.

The image of the whole Earth had an enormous spiritual impact upon us precisely because the human Soul was at the time in its evolutionary growth and development receptive to that image—the soil of the human Soul was ready for accepting the seed of the heavenly point of view. We now know that we are made of star-stuff and that every cell in our body has within it the memory of the astronaut's perspective—*astro* meaning star and *naut* meaning to navigate or to travel.

Like many other important scientific discoveries and spiritual epiphanies, the powerful impact of seeing the whole Earth from space was serendipitous. It was not planned that way. Soul growth was not the intention of the space program. President John F. Kennedy did not have spiritual maturity in mind when he challenged America to beat the Soviet Union in the race to the moon. The National Aeronautics and Space Administration (NASA) did not have an emergent Epoch III Soul in mind when it trained astronauts or installed cameras on the spacecraft. Nevertheless, intention notwithstanding, the United States concluded the 1960s, the decade in which the volcanic and transformative fire of the emergent Epoch III Soul erupted onto the surface of the American cultural landscape, by providing the world with a powerful and unforgettable image of wholeness—an image that, perhaps more than any other single image, has inspired us with Epoch III's heavenly breath.

With that breath of fresh air, with that inspiration of Spirit, we know that it is time to grow beyond exclusivistic religions, sovereign national boundaries, and sexist or racial discrimination. It is time to transcend in-groups and out-groups and to appreciate the one group that celebrates both its diversity and its commonality. We live as one beautiful Earth family, within one profoundly interconnected web of life.

Ironically, what started out as a nationalistic goal of winning the space race led to the realization of an interdependent human race. What began as a great competitive challenge ended up teaching us something about the necessity for cooperation. What started out as a total materialistic and technological venture ended up in spiritual territory, transforming all of us. Those who had received the best of Epoch II training in "The Right Stuff" ended up with their star-stuff transformed into Soul-stuff.

What a marvelous precursor to the Epoch III synergy between science and spirituality: science enabled us to "reach for the stars" and provided the technology to photograph that astronomical point of view for the earthbound, yet Spirit had the deepest and most profound impact on the human psyche. In fact, interest in a dialogue between science and spirituality, which is substantial and widespread, is one more confirmation that Epoch III is emerging from the human Soul.

We are intuiting that wholeness is, indeed, ubiquitous. It is not just in the astronomical point of view that we see it. The transformation of the human Soul, and the emergence of a new deep value of wholeness is evident throughout human cultures—in the development of the World Wide Web and the "dot-com" technologies, in business practices, in national and international relations, in economic and environmental forecasting, in education, in health care, in education, and even in religion, which sometimes, ironically, seems to be the most reluctant institution to change and the slowest to awaken to Soul-level changes.

We see the isolation and insulation of "sovereign nations" dissolving with the advent of weapons that can reach anywhere in the world and wipe out entire populations. We see that communication technology provides us with almost instantaneous awareness of and direct contact with anything happening virtually anywhere on the planet. We have become aware of how the temperature of water in the Pacific Ocean can impact skiing in Colorado, farming in the country's heartland, floods in the northwest United States and in Texas, crops in Florida, and plane schedules all over the planet. We have a global economy wherein a company operating in one country can affect wages half a world away and where a stock market spasm in a small far-eastern country can have reverberations throughout the entire world.

The big Epoch III picture of wholeness often reveals the foolishness of our former Epoch II parochial perspectives. Throughout our adolescent epoch, we invested in developing weapons and defending "national security." We engaged in an enormously expensive arms race with our enemies. Eventually, however, it made all of us downright M.A.D.—realizing that we had reached a point of Mutually Assured Destruction. What a disgusting development that turned out to be! We reached the point that, if we ever used the weapons in which we had invested so much of our brain power and financial resources, none of us would survive. Reaching for the goal of national security we discovered a mutual, total, and complete insecurity. Hardly seems fair. Certainly redefines our adolescent notion of "winning," doesn't it?

We have also been shocked into realizing our global interdependence by the population explosion and by ecological disasters such as oil spills, acid rain, and nuclear accidents. The proliferation of nuclear waste materials and the depletion of the protective ozone layer also contributed to our awareness. Many factors have shattered any illusions we had of national or individual atomistic isolation or insulation. The transportation revolution has made it a small world, and the communications revolution has made it virtually an instantaneous world. An economically interrelated world put the lie to the lingering notions of anything resembling a "sovereign" nation, and it is not coincidental that virtually every field of human activity has picked up on the concepts of systems theory.

The Hologram: A Metaphor for Epoch III

As suggested earlier, David Bohm was perhaps the clearest and strongest scientific voice articulating the new understanding of the universe as that of an "undivided wholeness, in which analysis into distinct and well-defined parts is no longer relevant."[8] Precisely because the idea of undivided wholeness was such a radical departure from Epoch II science and the deep value of reductionism, Bohm searched for a metaphor that would help us understand this new and profoundly important idea. He realized that the hologram, a photographic image in which the whole is found in every part, provided the perfect metaphor.

The word *hologram* is a combination of the Greek words *holos*, which means whole, and *gramma*, which means message. We might translate it as meaning the message of the whole, the message *is* the whole, or that the message is *in* the whole. Not only in the etymology and meaning of holography do we find a meaningful Epoch III metaphor, however, but also in the very process of its discovery.

Although the theory of holography was developed in 1947 by Dennis Gabor, eventually winning him a Nobel Prize, the full realization of its potential was stymied because the light sources needed to illuminate the image were not "coherent." Only in 1960, with the invention of the laser, a form of nearly coherent light, could clear holographic images be created.

A holographic image differs from our usual photographic images in that, with the latter, you look at it and see the image you photographed. With a holographic image, however, you see only fine irregular ripples, what are called "interference fringes." Only when the photograph is illuminated with a laser can you see the image, and the image then appears in three dimensions, not like the flat two-dimensional picture that we are accustomed to in regular photographs.

Without getting into all the technical details about how a holographic image is created, the metaphorical meaning for our purposes is that, if you break a piece of the image off and shine a laser light through it, you still see the entire image. The smaller the piece that you cut off, the fuzzier the image, but you still have the entire image. In other words, every part contains the whole.

Consider how a regular photograph illustrates Epoch II reductionism and how a holographic photo illustrates Epoch III wholeness. Imagine that you have in your hand a regular photograph of your family. Cut the picture into pieces so that each piece contains the image of one member of your family: this piece is the picture of your mother, that piece shows your father, and separate pieces picture you and each of your siblings. Now imagine that a stranger came upon some or all of those pieces. Holding the piece of the picture that contains your mother's image, the stranger would assume they would be "seeing" your mother. If the stranger wanted to see your entire family, all the pieces would need to be found and put together, as one would a jigsaw puzzle. That was the world view of Epoch II reductionism: looking at a piece, we thought we were seeing all that was necessary to understand that piece. To know the whole, put the separate pieces together.

Imagine, in contrast, that there was a holographic photo of you and your family, and that it, too, was cut up into pieces. Now, imagine that a stranger came along and picked up the piece that contained the image of your mother. Illuminating that piece with laser light, the stranger would not see your mother in isolation—the supposedly "separated" image of your mother would actually contain the entire family. In an Epoch III way, the photo would be showing that, in a real sense, you cannot completely isolate one member of the family. Every person is seen *in relationship* to the whole. Every person is viewed *in the context of* the entire family. We exist within a web of relationships. The whole consists not only of our parts, but our relationships.

Interestingly enough, shortly after the holographic metaphor became available, and virtually simultaneous to the time that Bohm, at the University of London, began to apply this metaphor to the macrocosm of the entire universe, Stanford University neurophysiologist Karl Pribram was exploring it as a metaphor for the microcosm of the human brain. Two great scientists at the same time, in a very holographic manner although half a world away from each other, intuited the richness of the hologram as a metaphor for science's new understanding of the world in which we live.

The holographic photo turns out to be a marvelous metaphor not only for the new and emerging scientific understanding of the physical universe, it is also a wonderful metaphor for the spiritual appropriation of the metaphysical universe.

The Spiritual Intuition of Wholeness

If we imagine that the laser light that illuminates the hologram represents the love of God, it is the coherent light of Epoch III enlightenment that enables us to see the ubiquity of wholeness. Think about that: the love of God shining through each individual enabling us to see and feel the image of the whole. Gives new meaning to the biblical phrase of being "created in the image of God," doesn't it?

Panentheism: The Holographic Theology

The word that expresses the holographic metaphor theologically is panentheism. Panentheism (*pan* meaning all, *en* meaning in, and *theos* meaning God) suggests that God is in everything and everything is in God. In other words, instead of the reductionistic theology of Epoch II, wherein an external God, heaven, and Spirit contain all goodness but are thought to be distinct and separate from humanity, earth, and matter that contain all evil, the Epoch III holistic theology suggests a more integrated reality.

Panentheism expresses a holistic vision that unifies the physical and the metaphysical, the transcendent and the immanent qualities of God, the correspondence of the out-there and the in-here, the up-there and the down-here, the material and the spiritual. It brings God down to earth, as it were, and elevates humanity up into heaven. Once again—we are spiritualized matter and materialized spirit, and that matters spiritually!

The word *panentheism* was first introduced by K.F.C. Krause in the nineteenth century, but, as a theological insight, it has been around for a long time. The concept is found in the scriptures and has been expressed by prophets of the major world religions for millennia. But, until recently, most of us just did not see its holistic truth because we were reading the scriptures with Epoch II reductionistic eyes.

If, however, we read the scriptures with the acuity of Epoch III sacred eyes, what do we see? We see an example of panentheism in the Hebrew Bible, for instance, when Moses asks God, "What is your name?" Hebraic scholars say that the answer God gave to that question is difficult to translate into English. The most common translation that most of us have been familiar with is, "I am who I am." But, as Marcus Borg tells us, Martin Buber, certainly one of the best known Jewish scholars of the twentieth century, explained that the phrase should be translated, "I will be present as I will be present" and indicated it means that God "is present in every now and every here."[9]

We also find a panentheistic view expressed in Psalm 139:

Where can I go from your Spirit?
Or where can I flee from your presence?
If I ascend to heaven, you are there;
If I make my bed in Sheol, you are there.
If I take the wings of the morning and settle
at the farthest limits of the sea,
even there your hand shall lead me,
and your right hand shall hold me fast.

We find it in the words of Jesus in the Gospel of John 14:10: "Believe me that I am in the Father and the Father in me." And we find it in Paul's letter to the Ephesians 4:6, when he speaks of "one God who is Father of all, over all, through all and within all."

A holistic and panentheistic perspective is found in other religions as well. In Buddhism, enlightenment is seen as the realization that everything is Buddha nature. In Islam, the Koran suggests that all things reside in God and God is in all things. In esoteric literature, we find it expressed in the phrase "as above, so below." And from almost anyone who has ever had a mystical experience and who has struggled to explain that experience in words, we hear a basic expression of panentheism in their use of words like *wholeness*, *unity*, and *oneness*.

So why are we not more familiar with a holistic theology? Why do most of us, and most of our traditional religions, continue to project God out and up? Why are most of us in mainstream cultures more theists than panentheists? Theists believe in God but consider God to be separate from humanity, up in heaven, a separate and distinct place. Theists believe that God is "up there" whereas we are "down here." In a typical Epoch II either/or approach to the transcendent-immanent tension, theists have overemphasized the transcendent nature of God.

Others of us have emphasized the other side of that tension, the immanent nature of God—*pantheism*. Pantheism holds that God is virtually identical with nature. God *is* the tree, God *is* the rock, etc. Pantheism is different from pan*en*theism, in that it ignores the transcendent dimension of God. Theism and pantheism are either/or choices regarding the tension or balance between immanence and transcendence. Pan*en*theism is a holistic both/and perspective. Rejecting any notion of God is atheism, but that is not the focus of our discussion here, nor is the more humble agnosticism, although we will see much of the latter's spirit throughout these pages.

When people do believe in God—a figure that, in the United States, is reported to be greater than nine out of ten people—why is it that most understand the God/human relationship in such limited either/or ways? Why is it that so many traditional expressions of religious orthodoxy, and the professionals who consider themselves to be the guardians of that orthodoxy, consider panentheism to be heretical?

The Deep-value Research answer to all those questions is simple: humanity has had a ten-thousand-year-long adolescent epoch in which our thought and actions have been shaped by the deep values of reductionism and the hierarchal and imperialistic need of institutions to exert power and control over people. Epoch II religious institutions tended to see themselves as the protector of that patriarchal and hierarchal reductionistic theological orthodoxy. The method of protection was an imperialistic notion of dictatorial power and control.

Hierarchical theology and dictatorial imperialism worked well together. After all, anyone who wants to have power and control over your spiritual destiny would do well to maintain a clear distinction between God and humanity, as well as heaven and earth and this life and the next one. Only then can an institution claim exclusive salvic power and believe that it possesses the only legitimate conduit by which we can escape from the "down here" and get into the "up there," controlling the access, as it were.

To the Epoch II deep-value system and to the institutions built upon those premises, a holistic theology and an empowered populace are understandably a threat. Panentheism must necessarily be deemed heretical and dangerous, for the clear implication of panentheism is that everyone has democratic access to divine grace and power. Within a panentheistic theology and worldview, atonement permeates the entire universe. Atonement does not have to be conferred upon us by some institution, or earned via conformity to a particular belief system. Atonement—"at-one-ment"—is freely given, by the love and grace of God so to speak, because that is the way the universe has been created. God is in everything and everything is in God. Loving at-one-ment, therefore, is ubiquitous: it is the essential nature of God's relationship to the world. Panentheism just happens to be the best theological term for describing that wholeness.

Only now, as Epoch III begins to dawn, are most of us ready to discover the ubiquity of wholeness. Only now are most of us ready to see the world through Epoch III eyes. It is not, however, as if we have never had incarnations of that spiritual maturity in our midst, models of Epoch III right before our eyes, as it were. Name your favorite spiritual giant from the past—Siddhartha as the Buddha, Jesus as the Christ, Muhammad as the Prophet—and you may be identifying God's hints regarding the direction in which human evolution is moving. For those who had eyes to see and ears to hear, incarnational models of spiritual maturity were here long before the general Epoch III Soul was ready to awaken to its personal relevance.

It is a fascinating subject in and of itself to consider the combination of factors that enabled certain people to be seers, visionaries, and prophets. Why and how do they incarnate the Spirit of the future long before most of us? Why is it that some spiritual prophets become well know, even having followers create religions based upon their life and teachings, although usually they themselves had no intention of starting a new religion? And why are other Epoch III visionaries not so well known?

Emanuel Swedenborg

The eighteenth-century Swedish scientist and mystic Emanuel Swedenborg was one of the latter, relatively speaking. Although most of the general public has perhaps never even heard of Swedenborg, this extraordinary prophet of Epoch III was clearly one of the most remarkable persons to ever grace this planet. What is particularly relevant for our discussion is that Swedenborg incarnated an Epoch III synthesis of science and spirituality in general and understood the deep value of the ubiquity of wholeness in particular, in ways that far preceded what the world was ready to understand during his lifetime and for the following two-hundred-plus years.

He was born in Stockholm on January 29, 1688, and spent much of his adult life in developing Sweden's mining industry, but he possessed an intellect of incredible reach and depth, making significant contributions to many fields. Scholar James Lawrence summarizes Swedenborg's many accomplishments:

> In the natural sciences alone, for instance, he formulated an atomic theory of matter, was the first to correctly identify the function of the cerebral cortex and the ductless glands, introduced the first Swedish textbooks on algebra and calculus, founded the science of crystallography, and designed and oversaw the construction of what is still the world's largest drydock. Other more personal accomplishments such as playing the organ and speaking nine languages also clearly point to the prophet's broad intellectual genius.[10]

Nevertheless, in his mid-fifties, when he was "arguably Europe's most brilliant thinker," Swedenborg's life was interrupted by powerful mystical experiences. His life was suddenly and dramatically changed, from one dedicated to science to one committed to spirituality. George Dole, a well-known Swedenborgian scholar and translator, explains that Swedenborg was awakened at night with a vision of a figure "who identified himself as the Lord Jesus Christ and informed him that he was being commissioned to disclose the inner, spiritual meaning of the Bible."[11]

As time went on, Swedenborg did not limit himself to explaining only the Bible. Nevertheless, for the rest of his life—twenty-eight years until he died in 1772 at the age of eighty-four—he singlemindedly dedicated his considerable abilities to experiencing, understanding, and writing about spiritual realities.[12]

Although many have never heard of Swedenborg, or at least have read and know very little of his work, he has not been completely hidden over these past two-hundred years. An impressive list of extraordinary souls along the way recognized Swedenborg and what he contributed to the understanding of spiritual realms. In fact, the list of those who credited Swedenborg with having a great influence on their own lives constitutes a virtual Who's Who of Remarkable Persons.

In *Representative Men,* Ralph Waldo Emerson wrote, for instance, that, "the most remarkable step in the religious history of recent ages is that made by the genius of Swedenborg." Others who admired him include Blake, Goethe, Balzac, Dostoevsky, Yeats, Coleridge, Poe, George Washington, Abraham Lincoln, Carl Jung, Robert and Elizabeth Barrett Browning, and Helen Keller.

Could Swedenborg have been the most intelligent person ever? Obviously, any attempt to identify the greatest IQ in history is an attempt fraught with a plethora of pitfalls and a great many theoretical problems. Nevertheless, it is interesting to note an attempt at that daunting task by one prestigious university. Stanford University developed the Terman Standard Intelligence Test, a test that is used to determine IQ's. Based upon that test, "a group of Stanford researchers put together a massive data program to see if the computer could reasonably calculate the IQ of history's great minds. The test placed three titans in a fuzzy tie for first place: John Stuart Mill, Goethe, and Emanuel Swedenborg."[13]

The admiration for Swedenborg has been truly remarkable among a few perceptive people, and it has been international and transreligious in scope. Jorge Luis Borges, the extraordinary South American literary giant, wrote that "no one accepted life more fully, no one investigated it with a passion so great, with the same intellectual love, or with such impatience to learn about it," as did Swedenborg.[14] Borges even composed a sonnet entitled "Swedenborg."

And Czeslaw Milosz, the Lithuanian novelist who was awarded the 1980 Nobel Prize in Literature, wrote:

> Swedenborg's destiny was extraordinary. A scientist of wide reputation who pursued researches in various disciplines from geology to anatomy . . . he had a sudden moment of illumination, abandoned his scientific pursuits, and produced a voluminous oeuvre in which he described his travels through heaven and hell and his conversations with spirits.[15]

D. T. Suzuki, the Zen master credited with introducing Zen Buddhism to the western world, thought that Swedenborg was so theologically compatible with Buddhism that he referred to him as the "Buddha of the North," this, despite that fact Swedenborg's father was a Lutheran bishop, and that Swedenborg's own spiritual commitment was to interpret the Bible and serve as an apologist for the Christian faith. Nevertheless, Suzuki wrote, in admiration:

> Theological revolutionary, traveler of heaven and hell, expert on the spiritual world, great king of the mystical realm, seer unique throughout history, scholar of incomparable energy, clear-minded scientist, gentleman free from worldly desires—all of these make Swedenborg.[16]

Our purpose here, however, is not an extensive or a thorough analysis of Swedenborg's life and thought, but only to illustrate briefly how he was, in some amazing ways, a prophetic visionary of Epoch III spirituality, a man about whom the time has come for us to learn more, as our individual souls grow into that maturity. If we touch lightly and visit briefly, just a few of the peaks of the enormous mountain range of his contributions, we find an amazing similarity with some of what we are now beginning to understand as the emergent spiritual maturity of Epoch III and the deep-value system that will transform human cultures.

First of all, Swedenborg thought that simplistic and literal interpretations of the Bible completely missed the important spiritual meaning. The Bible, for Swedenborg, was a rich symbolic and metaphorical treasure trove for understanding spiritual realms. True to his initial mystical calling, Swedenborg emphasized the inner meaning of biblical passages rather than the literal words.

Second, Swedenborg was profoundly holistic in his own life, encompassing a scientific mind and brilliant intellect that has already been well documented with an esoteric mysticism that the highly rational "Prodigal Son era" had a difficult time in understanding. He was a rigorous scientific thinker who personally experienced and highly valued mystical enlightenment. Long before the so-called "split-brain" metaphor became popular, Swedenborg had an extraordinary level of skill and balance between the left and right hemispheres of his brain, between intellect and intuition, between rationality and mysticism. His spiritual use of dreams, for instance, was both extensive and impressive. As James Lawrence writes,

> More than a century before Freud, Swedenborg is the first person known to keep a journal of dreams, and to interpret them symbolically in a fashion akin to Jung's archetypal approach.[17]

Colin Wilson, the bestselling British writer and an expert on spiritual and esoteric literature, wrote, "No one who has read both Jung and Swedenborg can doubt that it was the mystic, not the psychologist, who ventured further into the depths of this alien world that lies inside us."[18]

Third, Swedenborg eventually grew into an intellectual humility that was quite remarkable, particularly given his extraordinarily able intellect. The more he moved into the spiritual phase of his life, the more he developed a humble theology, aware of the profound mystery that inhabits the spiritual realms, putting great limitations on our ability to "know." This is a quality which we have mentioned already in this book, and will continue to emphasize, as an emergent Epoch III "uncertainty principle." Swedenborg emphasized over two hundred years ago, and we are just beginning to understand today, that spiritual wisdom lies in appreciating mystery, creativity, uncertainty, humility, seeking, searching, questing, and questioning, more than it does in dogmatic formulations and the arrogance of assuming that we can really know the spiritual realms with any degree of absolute certainty.

That wisdom led Swedenborg to be a religious maverick, able to be open to new, different, and creative spiritual revelation, and impatient with a Christianity that he felt had been distorted to suit institutional purposes, a Christianity that had lost sight of its original purpose of helping people become more fully human.

Swedenborg's special relevance to this particular chapter is his profound belief in the ubiquity of wholeness and his powerful bias in favor of love as being the most important quality of the spiritual life. Our discussion of these topics will not be an attempt at an exegesis of Swedenborg's writing, nor limited to his particular expressions, but it will most certainly be compatible with his priorities. Swedenborg's understanding of a holistic universe scooped, as it were, both quantum physics and the holographic metaphor, as well as the theology that came to be known as panentheism.[19]

Because Swedenborg was ahead of his time, he provides us with an interesting prophetic and visionary understanding of the time into which we are now moving—the dawning of Epoch III. It is an emergent time of realizing that everything participates in one grand, magnificent, mysterious, magnanimous whole. Yet, within that wholeness, we are gaining a greater appreciation of diversity and pluralism, and learning that the part does not lose its identity in the whole. Wholeness does not mean that everything is homogenized into one bland soup of sameness. Rather, as we leave our adolescent epoch's ego insecurities and grow into adult maturity, we will be able to appreciate the benefits of diversity, each part enriched even further by participation in the whole. Swedenborg had a marvelous phrase by which to consider this diversity within wholeness: "distinguishable oneness."

"Distinguishable Oneness"

In any discussion of wholeness, it is important to understand how individuality, distinction, specialization, differentiation, and other manifestations of the Epoch II evolutionary agenda play into the "undivided wholeness of the entire universe." Differences do not simply fade away in a holistic universe. Individual identity is not lost once we transcend the ego development of our adolescent epoch. Specialization is not a mistake.

The only mistake of reductionism is in believing in the primacy or exclusive authority of the part, the individual, the specialization. The emerging deep value of wholeness has no need to deny the benefits from Epoch II reductionism; rather, it enriches those benefits by showing how they participate in the whole.

The maturational metaphor we are using as the lens through which to view the entire evolutionary history of the human species does not suggest that a particular phase of growth and development is a mistake or unimportant, and should, therefore, be discarded when we grow into another phase of development. Quite the contrary, each epoch's evolutionary purpose and its facilitative deep-value system are important developments along the journey, preparing us for the next development. We do not have to demean one particular step, in order to take the next step. We would not even be ready for that next step, were it not for the previous one.

How then are we to understand the Epoch II twin emphases of ego and mental development as we enter the Epoch III emphasis of spiritual maturation? What happens to the human ego, now so virile and strong? What happens to our sense of individuality, if we are connected and interrelated with everything in the universe? What happens to all the distinctively unique religions of the world, for the differences are real even though we are now aware of the many deep commonalities? What happens to the scientific, medical, and educational specialties?

This happens: we *celebrate* and *utilize* the diversity that is naturally part of the human species and the specialized knowledge that has been accomplished throughout Epoch II. Simply adding spiritual maturity—which, of course, is no simple matter—changes the mind and heart. Instead of insisting on an either/or, right-or-wrong, my-way-or-no-way division, the mind and heart become ensouled into an appreciation of both/and. Instead of being preoccupied with exclusivity and superiority, needing an "other" we can define as below us, not as good as us, people we can control, manipulate, use, abuse, and enslave, we will have greater appreciation of how diversity adds to our understanding, appreciation, and appropriation of the world. Instead of one claim to the "Truth," we will begin to understand that God "speaks" many different "languages" and that, by listening carefully to how others have "heard" that divinity, our own spirituality grows and develops.

No one race, gender, nation, ethnic group, or religion is able to understand and express all there is in life. And, clearly, no one theology, philosophy, or set of doctrines can encompass all there is to know about divinity. God is incognito in many guises. The incognito, holographic, panentheistic God is such a big picture that, even as we strive for understanding the large context, we can barely understand the small pieces—and even then, in a rather fuzzy fashion.

Particularity is a meaningful part of our concept of God. As Harvard theologian Gordon Kaufman put it:

> Every religious (or secular) understanding and way of life we might uncover is a *particular* one, that has grown up in a particular history, makes particular claims, is accompanied by particular practices and injunctions, and hence is to be distinguished from all other particular religious and secular orientations.[20]

Nevertheless, and wonderfully so, God is not only the whole, but is present in the small pieces as well. Consequently, "distinguishable oneness" is also applicable to the ethics of our everyday living. We are distinguishable from one another, yet it is our sense of oneness that undergirds the living of a loving and ethical life. Virtually every religion has some prophet expressing the ethics of spiritual maturity, and saying something akin to what Jesus said: "What you do to the least of my brothers and sisters, you do to me." And, we might add, you do to yourself.

Werner Heisenberg, one of the founders of quantum theory, saw this dynamic as so central to his conceptual revolution that he titled his autobiography *Der Teil und das Ganze* (The Part and the Whole). Arthur Koestler coined the word *holon* for explaining that what is a whole in one context is simultaneously part of a larger whole. Every entity, he is saying, is both a whole and a part. Ken Wilber amplifies Koestler's concept by saying, "Because every holon is a whole/part, it has two 'tendencies' or two 'drives,' we might say—it has to maintain both its wholeness and its partness."[21]

Similarly, Matthew Fox speaks of "deep ecumenism" as a movement "that will unleash the wisdom of *all* world religions."[22] But, perhaps the crowning thought on this matter should come from Archbishop Desmond Tutu, chair of South Africa's historic Truth and Reconciliation Commission (TCR) and winner of the 1984 Nobel Peace Prize. The concept of *ubuntu* was the stated goal when the TRC was created, and Bishop Tutu explains the concept:

> The Act says that the thing you're striving after should be "ubuntu," rather than revenge. It comes from the root of a Zulu-Xhosa word which means "a person." So it is the essence of being a person. And in our experience, in our understanding, a person is a person through other persons. You can't be a solitary human

being. It's all linked. We have this communal sense, and because of this deep sense of community, the harmony of the group is a prime attribute.

And so you realize, in this world view, that anything that undermines the harmony is to be avoided as much as possible. And anger and jealousy and revenge are particularly corrosive, so you try and do everything to try and enhance the humanity of the other, because . . . you are bound up with each other.[23]

Anyone who has seriously plumbed the depths of his or her own soul knows that the search eventually leads into a mystical, marvelous mystery and an intellectual paradox: the deeper we go into our own soul, the more we realize that we are communing with everybody, with the human Soul-at-large, with the God who looks like us but is also incognito in everybody. In the spiritual maturity of Epoch III is the profound realization of how the individual, fully developed, is in communion with the All.

We will continue to develop a spiritual ego. After all, how else can we discover our individual soul's purpose? At the same time, we are being called to transcend a narrow and insecure experience of ego, for that maturation is precisely how we discover how profoundly interrelated we all are. We will live the dynamic process of distinguishing and becoming one—"distinguishable oneness."

Baby Boomers: A Generation Manifesting Epoch III

In the United States, we have a generation that has been extraordinarily influential and, therefore, one that has been widely studied, the so-called "Baby Boomer" generation. "Boomers" are those born between 1946 and 1964, numbering some seventy-six million people and comprising fully one-third of all Americans.[24] They have already demonstrated a powerful capacity to influence culture and, if we look carefully, we can see how their spirituality both confirms the emergence of Epoch III and virtually guarantees its transformative power for the culture at large.

First of all, consider the "track record" of cultural influence that the boomers have had throughout their history. As researcher Ken Dychtwald points out,

At each stage of their lives, the needs and desires of the baby boomers have become the dominant concerns of . . . popular culture. . . .

If you can anticipate the movement of the baby boom generation . . . you can see the future. . . . The boomers redefine whatever stage of life they inhabit.[25]

Described by some as "a pig moving through a python," baby boomers, as they move through the human life span, are impossible to miss. At every stage of their lives, they have caused enormous change. At first, it was the diaper industry that was transformed. Then it was the baby-food industry: 270 million jars were sold in 1940, but that figure grew to 1.5 billion jars in 1953. As the boomers moved into our public school systems, they created a construction boom—"more elementary schools were built in America in 1957 than in any year before or since," and a similar record was set in the construction of high schools a decade later.[26] When the boomers went off to college, the collegiate student population rose from 3.2 million in 1965 to 9 million in 1975, and 743 new colleges were opened.[27] The influence of the baby boomers on culture, at whatever stage of their lives, has been enormous.

With the boomers now in their late-thirties to mid-fifties, they are beginning to give more attention to spiritual values, and there is no reason to believe that their historic and gargantuan influence will be any less in the area of spirituality. The nature of their spirituality will exert a profound influence on all of culture, including religious institutions, for they are now in the position of pastoring churches, running school boards, managing businesses, raising children, funding colleges and universities, going through mid-life crises, and, in general, running or about to run virtually everything in mainstream culture.

Perhaps the first thing that research identifies about boomer spirituality is that, instead of being comfortable with conformity to old institutional and dogmatic answers, boomers are independent questers and questioners. They are a "generation of seekers," which is precisely what Wade Clark Roof entitled his book, probably the single most influential and considered study of the baby-boomer value system. His research is so seminal, in fact, that it is usually referred to simply as "The Roof Report."[28] His follow-up 1999 book, *Spiritual Marketplace*, is subtitled, significantly enough, "Baby Boomers and the Remaking of American Religion." Let's be clear, however, about the causal influences: boomers are remaking American religion precisely because they are a large influential generation who are manifesting the Epoch III Soul. Epoch III is not happening simply because of the boomers.

Roof found that, in terms of religious involvement, the boomers started out in the 1950s as involved in religious institutions as any generation before them. But, in the 1960s and 1970s, they turned their back on the religious establishment in record numbers.

The boomers exemplified the emergent Epoch III interest in things spiritual, but had the general feeling that the institutional religions of Epoch II no longer facilitated or enabled their spiritual search. Consequently, they walked out, and most mainline denominations experienced thirty years of diminishing memberships. Nevertheless, in spite of their leaving the institutional church in droves, Roof found among the boomers a "greater attention to the spiritual quest." It was, and is, however, a new and a different kind of sacred quest.

One very prominent quality of the boomers spirituality is the deep value that we will turn to in the next chapter: a self-empowered and self-determined quest, with a distrust of any institution or leader who tries to dictate their spirituality from "on high." The boomers have felt an increasing gap between their spiritualities and the traditional religions. Their "locus of authority" is more internal than external.

But, even before we get to the deep value of empowerment, we find that the boomers are incarnating, from the soil of their souls to the flowering of their everyday lives, the deep value of wholeness. They demonstrate, Roof points out, a growing appreciation for "overcoming old dualisms . . . and [a belief] in the interrelatedness of all things."[29] The boomers tune-out the old religious claims of exclusivity and tune-in to the commonalities of people throughout the world and across all the parochial boundaries. As Roof reports, "Boomers have not just known pluralism, they deeply value it." They "value experience over beliefs, distrust institutions and leaders, stress personal fulfillment yet yearn for community, and are fluid in their allegiances."[30]

When a population as influential as the boomer generation begins to sense and manifest the deep value of wholeness—valuing the interrelatedness of everything, rejecting narrow exclusivity while affirming diversity—we see one more sign that Epoch III is emerging from the Soul of humanity-at-large, and attempts by institutions to stop the movement are doomed to failure.

Love: The Spiritual Power and Energy of Wholeness

Our discussion of wholeness would be incomplete if we were only to look at scientific evidence and spiritual intuition from the outside. Wholeness is not fully understood without understanding and living the internal power and energy of what makes everything whole—love.

Love is the spiritual "within-ness" to the entire universe, the healing power for all the fractures and estrangements within and between us. Love is the dynamic power that reunites all that has been separated in Epoch II. Nothing is more central to our discussion of wholeness, for love creates wholeness, and nothing is more important in our discussion about the sacred quest.

Generally speaking, we have trivialized the word *love*. We have robbed it of its power. Vietnamese Zen Master Thich Nhat Hanh suggests that we rob some words of their power so much that we make them "sick" and that we have to heal them. Love is just such a word, for its power is ontological, it is the very essence of the universe, and we need to heal our understanding of it in order to restore its meaning in our spiritual lives.

The true nature of love is enormously important to understand if we are to grow beyond the materialistic paradigm of Epoch II. It is not simply that the world is dead inert matter with religious people merely wanting love to be at the center of reality. It is not that, if religious people had the opportunity to remake the universe, they would like love to be essential. The point here is that love *is* the core essence of the world. Wholeness is ubiquitous and the power of that wholeness is love.

Love, however, is not just a passive essence of reality. Love is an active power that holds the universe in an embrace. Although religions in Epoch II all too often acted in unloving ways, the traditional scriptures, throughout the world, have often spoken of love's priority—in fact, most traditions have at least given lip-service to the notion that God is love.

169

Pierre Teilhard de Chardin, the French Jesuit priest and world-renown paleontologist, was another wonderful personification of our emerging Epoch III synthesis of science and spirituality and the growing awareness that the universe is spiritualized matter. Teilhard perceived during the first half of the twentieth century the spiritual-material integration, as well as the role of love. He saw love as the fundamental impulse of life and "a universal form of attraction linked to the inwardness of things."[31]

A more contemporary scientific voice, similar in spirit to Teilhard's and contributing another step in our awakening journey, is that of Brian Swimme, the mathematical cosmologist whom we referred to earlier. Swimme points out how the word *gravity* is the Epoch II scientific term for the essential spiritual allurement and attraction of the universe:

> Gravity is the word used by scientists and the rest of us in the modern era to *point* to this primary attraction. We do not understand the attracting activity itself. . . . The attracting activity is a stupendous and mysterious fact of existence. Primal. We awake and discover that this alluring activity is *the* basic reality of the macrocosmic universe. . . . I'm speaking precisely of the basic binding energy found everywhere in reality. I'm speaking of the primary allurement that all galaxies experience for all other galaxies. . . . [This is] love in its cosmic dimension.[32]

Entrainment

Another way of thinking about the ontological nature of love is through exploring the concept of entrainment. Take a brief ride aboard the train of entrainment for another view of how love is ontological and not simply an emotional feeling.

Entrainment is the word for the scientific discovery that, when two or more oscillators are near each other and are pulsing at *almost* the same rate, they invariably end up pulsing at *exactly* the same rate. They seem to "want" to harmonize. There is a mutual "sympathy" for attunement and at-one-ment.

Dutch scientist Christian Huygens, in 1665, noticed that two pendulum clocks placed near each other would eventually synchronize at precisely the same rhythm. The scientific explanation was called a "mutual phase-locking of two oscillators," but the simpler term is entrainment.

George Leonard describes how, in the film *The Incredible Machine*,

two individual muscle cells from the heart are seen through a microscope. Each is pulsing with its own separate rhythm. Then they move closer together. Even before they touch, there is a sudden shift in the rhythm, and they are pulsing together, perfectly synchronized.[33]

There is now substantial evidence that entrainment is at the core—at the heart, if you will—of human-to-human communication. Before I realized it had been scientifically proven, I had gradually come to that realization out of my own experience.

After forty years of public speaking, I finally awakened to the fact that my connection with my audience was always enhanced when I focused upon connecting to heart energy rather than strictly to intellectual and mental energy. When I am preoccupied with the ideas that I want to communicate, I never feel quite the same synchronization with an audience as when I meditate ahead of time and energize the communication link between my heart and the hearts of those in the audience. In other words, the best communication takes place when I emphasize the spiritual connection with my audience, a spiritual entrainment, if you will, rather than simply focusing on the explanation of intellectual ideas.

Eventually I was to discover, again thanks to George Leonard, that Dr. William S. Condon, when at Boston University School of Medicine back in the 1970s, had conducted pioneering work that appears to explain my experience. Condon engaged in what he called microanalysis of film taken of the conversation between two people. Slowing the film down so as to analyze every micromovment, Condon discovered that

Listeners were observed to move in precise shared synchrony with the speaker's speech. This appears to be a form of entrainment since there is no discernible lag even at 1/48 second. . . . It also appears to be a universal characteristic of human communication, and perhaps characterizes much of animal behavior in general.[34]

This kind of analysis, broken down into fractions of a second, proves that the listener is not *reacting* to the speaker's words or actions, but is entrained with the speaker, is *at-one* with, and fundamentally *part of*, the speaker. My experience would suggest that this is not only a reality, but can be enhanced through our intentionality.

Think of how the same phenomenon may be at work when we observe, as we did in the previous chapter, correspondences between the animal world and the human observer, the outer and the inner dimensions of reality. Or consider a different example of what may be the same attraction at the heart of reality—athletes who, in a team sport, know not only when they personally are "in the zone" of seemingly perfect performance but also when they are so synchronized with a teammate, that they that they are in that performance "zone" together. It is not uncommon at all for a quarterback and a receiver, who have devoted many hours together, to find themselves so entrained in the midst of a game that they intuitively "know" precisely what the other is going to do, even before the action takes place.

Is this not a form of "falling in love?" If we consider the larger ontological nature of love and not simply its emotional component, does this not confirm the fact that when two people get in close proximity—through investing long hours together, or through what feels like an immediate and natural "chemistry"—they "fall" into a synchronized entrainment?

Consider the now-well-known fact about women college roommates whose menstrual cycles become entrained. Or consider this as a possible explanation for the reason Diana and I, after being deeply in love for over twenty-five years, seem to constantly "know" what the other is thinking or wanting. Consider your own examples of that entrainment power of love.

M. Mitchell Waldrop, with a doctorate in elementary particle physics, explains the new science of "complexity." Complex systems, he says, are ones in which "a great many independent agents are interacting with each other in a great many ways," such as, for instance, "the quadrillions of chemically reacting proteins, lipids, and nucleic acids that make up a living cell, or the billions of interconnected neurons that make up the brain, or the millions of mutually interdependent individuals who make up a human society." But it is the very richness of these interactions, he says, that "allows the system as a whole to undergo *spontaneous self-organization*."[35] Of such are the scientific descriptions of the core essence of life that we can now call love.

What Is the Significance of One Foot Transforming?

You have heard, no doubt, about the spiritual significance of contemplating a Zen koan, a nonsensical phrase that does not lend itself to simple intellectual analysis? For example, "What is the sound of one hand clapping?" Or "What did your face look like before your parents met?"

With tongue firmly planted in cheek, I would suggest that the koan for our time in history is the following: What is the significance of one foot transforming? What this refers to, however, is not the appendage upon which you put socks and shoes. The foot in this koan is the twelve inches that separate our head from our heart. And the transformation of those twelve inches, in terms of priority, is extraordinarily significant in understanding the spiritual maturation of Epoch III.

Precisely because the evolutionary purpose for Epoch II was that of ego and mental development, our pride and joy became how good we were at thinking. The head of our anatomy was at the head of our priorities. We have all heard Rene Descartes' marvelously appropriate Epoch II mantra, "I think; therefore, I am." The reason this statement became so famous and so familiar is that it accurately states Epoch II humanity's self-identity, what we proudly stated, over and over again, as that which made us superior to all the other animals.

Consider, for instance, how we, the species that dubbed ourselves the doubly wise, *Homo sapiens sapiens*, believe that we are the pinnacle of evolution, simply because the human intellect has become so developed, in spite of how many other species surpass us on a great many other abilities.

Or consider how many people who, when finding the traditional term *God* unappealing, replace it with terms like *Universal Mind* or *Cosmic Consciousness*—the Ultimate must be the ultimate in mental powers. And think about Hollywood's frequent depictions of the human being of the future with an enlarged head (or the drawings of space creatures by those who believe they had been abducted by aliens) or the science fiction that envisions the future's being ruled by disembodied brains under glass.

Mike Davis, in his powerful 1998 bestseller *Ecology of Fear: Los Angeles and the Imagination of Disaster* documented how a disaster fiction, utilizing comets, blizzards, fire storms, volcanoes, and, the California favorite, earthquakes played up the image of doomsday Los Angeles. "Like the San Fernando quake 22 years before, the January 1994 Northridge earthquake was immediately followed by literary and cinematic aftershocks."[36]

One such novel places the ultimate disaster in 2024, with the lead character being the world's greatest seismologist, Lewis Crane, who lost his family thirty years earlier in the Northridge quake. Crane awaits the apocalypse on top of a Wilshire Boulevard skyscraper; as Los Angeles is destroyed by the greatest of all earthquakes, he downloads the contents of his brain into a computer, so as to be reincarnated instantly in a utopian colony on the far side of the moon.

Whereas the evolutionary purpose of Epoch II has been mental and ego development, and the symbol of identity has been the thinking brain, the evolutionary purpose of Epoch III is spiritual maturation, and that shifts the symbol of identity twelve inches to the "south,"to a loving heart. To update and paraphrase an Epoch III Descartes, "We love; therefore, we are human."

Theologian Rita Nakashima Brock's call for a "reclamation of heart" is both timely and appropriate:

> Heart, as a metaphor for the human self and our capacity for intimacy, involves the union of body, spirit, reason, and passion through heart knowledge, the deepest and fullest knowing. For we know best "by heart." Heart, the center of all vital functions, is the seat of self, of energy, of loving, of compassion, of conscience, of tenderness, and of courage—the Latin *cor* means heart. To take heart is to gain courage. Our lives bloom in fullness from the heart, the core of our being, which is created and sustained by interconnection.[37]

A Personal Quest for the Sacred

That transformation of priorities from head to heart constitutes a rather significant part of my own life story, as I attempt to live my life in tune with the time of my life and to have my spiritual autobiography resonate with humanity's biography of Soul at this great transformational time in history.

It is an obvious oversimplification, yet not far from the truth, to say that there have been three major passions in my life: sports, knowledge, and love. Although my spiritual heritage emphasized the latter two, my personal choices during the first twenty-two years of my life were clearly based on a passion for sports.

Nevertheless, my propensity for an eventual spiritual life had its roots in a significant event shared by my mother and father just minutes before I was born. They had a numinous experience with divinity, a powerful mystical moment within which they made a very particular commitment to God. It was a moment filled with a particular intensity and intentionality for them since their previous child had died soon after birth—in fact, they had had two children die soon after birth. Their physicians presumed that the cause of those deaths had something to do with an undiagnosed medical condition of my mother's and could, consequently, offer no optimism regarding my survival. They were prepared for the worst outcome, but were praying for the best.

My parents recounted the experience to me twenty-two years later. Their numinous moment with divine power occurred, they said, while they were in prayer regarding my impending birth. In the midst of the prayer, my mother and my father felt an unusually clear and powerful presence of God. And, in a moment of spiritual entrainment, they shared the commitment that, if I survived, they would do everything in their power to raise me in such a way that I would know the love of God deeply and thoroughly, so that I would eventually dedicate my own life in loving service to the world.

What astonishes me most about my parents, their wonder-filled experience and their commitment regarding my life, is that they held all of that secretly in their hearts for twenty-two years, loving me unconditionally, just as they did equally with all of their children, but never imposing their hoped-for direction for my own life. I guess that is what unconditional love means!

To understand the extent of their love and faith, however, one would need to know the challenges I threw their way as I was trying to grow up. My adolescent temper tantrums and excessive preoccupation with sports would have tried the patience of saints. To be more accurate, I was flat-out obsessed with sports, to an extent that might be hard to believe. As early as I have any memories regarding fashioning life's goals, they were all sports related. Images of policemen, firemen, doctors, or lawyers could not compete with images of professional athletes, in my childhood and adolescent imagination.

There just had to be many occasions when my parent's hearts would have cried out, "Where did we go wrong?" or "How did we fail so miserably?" or "Did we misunderstand that original experience?" If I were to reveal all that I did during those years, you would understand how severe their agony must have been at times. Yet, amazingly, they never told me about that experience, and never, ever, tried to make me feel guilty for not becoming what they had wanted, what they had been so profoundly committed to. What saintly patience on the part of my mother and father, and what an incredible ability to live and give unconditional love!

Needless to say, the eventual passions of knowing and loving were subsumed under that total and absolute passion for sports. I was very slow to respond or awaken to the efforts of the loving priorities exemplified by my parents or the desire for knowledge exemplified primarily by my mother. As parents, they gave me a wonderful head-start and heart-start to life, but my priority was still, "When do we start the game?"

Regarding my mother, it is hard to believe that there have been very many people to ever grace this earth who combined any greater degree and balance of intellectual ability and the ability to love as did my mother. Sam Keen makes the distinction between our preoccupation with IQ (Intelligence Quotient) and our failure to give importance to LQ (Loving Quotient). I was blessed by a mother who was extraordinarily gifted in both!

In one sense, however, it is not accurate to say that I was late in developing a passion for knowing per se, only for knowing anything outside the realm of athletics. Throughout high school, when I would steadfastly and rebelliously refuse to do any academic homework, I spent virtually every waking hour studying and practicing how to think and perform better in whatever sport I was involved in at the time. I was totally and completely a baseball player in the spring and summer, only to be transformed instantaneously into a football player at summer's end. That persona was just as total and complete, until it was time for the sudden transformation into being a basketball player. Round and round every year went—baseball, football, basketball, and then back to baseball—but my passion for knowing was limited to sports.

My parents were understandably nonplused when my only interest in academics, even throughout my college years, was to do the absolute minimum that was necessary to remain eligible to compete in intercollegiate athletics. They were not impressed when, as a college senior, I devoted all my study time to a one-credit course in "football theory," devising new and creative ways at designing an offensive strategy that would outsmart the best defenses of the day. As a consequence, I received an "A," turning in a term paper for a one-credit course which the professor said was superior to any master's thesis in football theory that he had ever seen, while at the same time I was devoting absolutely no study-time to and getting a "D" in the only religion course I ever took while in college. As it is popular to say nowadays, "Duh"!

As far as I was concerned, I knew exactly what I was doing. I had it all planned out, and my dreams were coming to fruition. I was about to be graduated from college, and I had reached the pinnacle of my life path. I had the opportunities lying before me that would be the fulfillment of all my hopes and dreams: on my desk was one contract to play professional baseball with the New York Yankees and another to play professional football with the Baltimore Colts. I was on top of the world, with only one question on my mind: would I devote my professional energies, totally and completely, to baseball or to football?

God, however, was evidently not very impressed with my "A" in football theory, nor with my dreams and goals of professional athletics. Instead, before I could get either contract signed, God reached down deep into my soul, quaked it real good, and completely redirected my life!

The night before that soul-quake, my first wife and I were asked to host a dinner for other Cornell College married couples, so that they and we could have an opportunity to meet and visit with the college's Religion-in-Life guest speaker, Dr. James S. Thomas. Thomas was at that time an executive with the Methodist Board of Education in Nashville, eventually to be elected an Methodist bishop, and later to become a good personal friend, the man to whom I co-dedicated this book.

I remember being very impressed that evening with the intellectual and spiritual power of Jim Thomas, but still had no idea of the role he would play in my life the following day. Nor did I have a clue the next day as we went into the worship service, mostly out of courtesy to our dinner guest. I certainly had no anticipation of anything meaningful about to happen, for my mind was totally preoccupied with my impending professional decision, and a delightful choice it would be: football or baseball, baseball or football?

The mystical, magical, and mysterious soul-quake occurred without warning and definitely without my permission. Jim Thomas was preaching, but I am not at all sure my experience had anything to do with the content of what he was saying. I do not even remember anything he said. Nevertheless, in an instant I was transformed, my life changed, my commitments totally redirected. I walked into that chapel thinking that I was an athlete who was about to accomplish his lifelong dream—I stumbled out of the chapel, somewhat dazed, yet knowing that I had experienced something more powerful than anything else in my life, and that my life was totally and completely redirected. I went into that moment as a twenty-two-year-old jock; I came out knowing that my life was dedicated to the service of humanity.

Because this was such a radical change for me and a completely unexpected turn by those who knew me—my coaches just about had brain-spasms when hearing the news—I felt that I needed to go home and explain it to my parents, in person.

When I arrived home and sat with them in the living room, I told them what had happened. I explained that, as strange as it may sound, I was not going to sign to play either baseball or football professionally, I was going to pursue a graduate degree in theology, what seemed to be the logical first step in following my new life path.

Because of the love I had come to expect from my parents, I certainly expected them to affirm my experience and to accept my decision to pass on professional athletics. But I also expected them to, at the least, be shocked and surprised. Not so! They simply smiled at each other, expressed their delight, and then told me of their experience just before my birth some twenty-two years earlier.

Anyone who has had a powerful, life-changing, mystical experience knows how difficult it is to find words to explain it. Any attempt at explanation has the feel of trivialization. Words seem inadequate compared to the power of the experience. Nevertheless, one just has to try. There is one particular aspect to that experience that has long interested me, and only recently have I felt that I understood it.

One often hears others speak of such experiences with specificity—either they saw something in particular or they heard something in particular. As in our earlier discussion of Swedenborg, he saw an image of Christ and heard a commission to reveal the inner meaning of the Bible.

My son Jim provides a more contemporary example, and one that has both interesting similarities as well as differences with my own experience. He, like me, had never considered a spiritual calling until he was twenty-two years of age. He, like me, had a powerful mystical experience that led him into pursuing a graduate degree in theology and then on into the Christian ministry. Jim Keck, by the way, was named after and baptized by Bishop Jim Thomas.

In turns out that, as adults, my son and I share a great deal in common—theologically, ethically, philosophically and, I might add, athletically. We have often discussed, however, one particular difference in our respective life-changing mystical experiences at age twenty-two. Jim had specific visions of Christ, while I did not. In fact, just after I had had my initial experience and tried to explain it to my parent's minister, the minister said, in the form of a question that reveals he already assumes he knows the answer: "Oh, so Jesus Christ called you to his ministry?" He just about passed out when I answered with a simple, "No." I was not trying to shock him; I simply was trying to answer honestly. There was just not that kind of specificity to my "call."

Jim and I have often speculated about how the specificity of his mystical experience may be precisely why his theology and ministry developed along more Christocentric lines than did mine. Although my initial response to the experience was to pursue a graduate degree in theology and to enter the Christian ministry, the experience itself contained no specificity or clarity of image, only the deep and profound realization that my life had been directed to the service of humanity. Only recently has the reason for that lack of specificity become clear to me.

As I mentioned previously, I begin each writing day with a meditation and prayer that I might be receptive to how I am to live the spirituality of Epoch III in general and what needs to be expressed through my soul into my writing on that particular day. One morning recently, I was meditating on this deep value of wholeness, but not in any way thinking about my "call" many years ago. Nevertheless, out of the meditation emerged an insight, with some considerable clarity and power. I realized that I did not envision a specific religious image in my initial mystical experience because I was being called to think about, and attempt to live and communicate, the way a holistic reality will transform all our religions and spiritualities. Although my faith path was and still is primarily Christian, I had a larger and more holistic calling. Specific religious images or symbols, at that seminal moment of awakening, would have narrowed my focus. That narrow focus was evidently not what God had in mind for me.

Head First

It was only in graduate school, after that powerful mystical "Great Turning," that I was motivated to become a student of something other than athletics. And, if I am to be perfectly honest, it was only after attaining my formal academic degrees—only after four years of earning a master's degree in theology and four more years in earning a doctorate in the philosophy of health—that I really learned to love learning. I am forever grateful that my mother lived to see that day.

Even when working on a graduate degree in theology, it was "head" over "heart" for me, intellectual learning over learning to love. That *should* be incredibly absurd, but it isn't. Advanced academic programs in theology are still head over heart, knowing over loving, and few of us even sense the absurdity involved when a graduate degree in theology emphasizes head-tripping rather than heart-expanding. But that is true for most graduate programs.

I certainly do not want to sound as if I am denigrating the passion for knowledge. Far from it. It was, and continues to be, one of the primary passions that gives my life meaning. It grew out of my life turn-around, and it continues to be one of the primary aspects in my soul's purpose.

Perhaps my first nonathletic immersion into the passion for knowing came after my second year in graduate school. I had spent two years learning how to become a student. In that process, I had been studying intensely the subjects of theology, Bible, church history, comparative religions, preaching, etc. I was learning what many of the great Christian thinkers throughout the ages had thought and how the church as an institution decided what it collectively wanted as its orthodox belief system. But, increasingly it became clear to me that I was spending a lot of time learning what *others* thought and believed, but very little time discovering what *I* thought and believed about religion and spirituality in general or Christianity in particular. What, I wondered, was my own faith? What did *I* believe?

If my ministry was to have integrity, I needed to know where I stood, more than I needed to know where Moses, Jesus, Paul, Augustine, Luther, or Wesley stood. Too often we look outside to saints or saviors to determine what is "revealed" or "right" regarding religion or spirituality. But my "calling" to ministry was so personal and so powerful that it seemed to me to be trivializing it unless I looked deeply inside to find out what God was calling me to be and to do.

I decided to interrupt my graduate program and to take an entire year off, free of the conventional academic focus upon the giants, history, and doctrine of Christendom, to discover what I thought and believed. The process of doubt would be my intellectual methodology. Ever since that year, spent at Hamline University in St. Paul, Minnesota, with Dr. George Ball as mentor, I have had a profound appreciation for the role that doubt can play in our growth and development, and most importantly, in our integrity— if we treat doubt seriously and with respect.

I proceeded to experiment with doubting everything that I could intellectually doubt. To make a year-long, complex process rather short and simple, I found that the only thing I could not doubt was the primacy and power of love. Nothing was more integral and true to my depths than love. Nothing, I felt, was more central to reality itself, as best as I could understand it.

I "got it"—but, in a very real sense, I got it only partially. I continued to be a slow learner regarding love. For the next fifteen to twenty years, my passions were primarily those of recreational and competitive amateur athletics; activism against racial injustice, poverty, and inadequate housing, and in favor of improving public education; the search for a solution to a personal health challenge; and the enjoyment of intellectual curiosity and learning. I continued to lead my life primarily head-first. I am embarrassed at what an inadequate and immature lover I was during those years—for my children as well as for my first wife.

Heart First

The dramatic shift for me was to come at age forty. My love life received the catalyst, the companion, the teacher, and the enabler I needed when Diana entered my life. I was awakened to the depths and mystery, the wonder and wonder-full-ness of love.

But love is not like a goal that can be achieved. It is not a win-this-game-then-move-on-to-the-next situation. It is not a *part* of life; it is life itself, a mystery to be lived, a process of continuing discovery, a wonder of perpetual celebration. And, for me, the mystery has been far more incredible, the process of discovery far more fun, and the wonder far more filled now that Diana is my partner in life.

Precisely because love is the primary energy within wholeness and precisely because love is, therefore, ontological, there is no end-game. One can take a lifetime, or more, to understand the substance of what Martin Buber was getting at in his famous distinction between "I–It" and "I–Thou" relationships. Every single day we can learn more about how we objectify others into an "it" and how we can discover and honor their "thou-ness."

One can take a lifetime, or more, to understand how to live a compassionate life. The only difference between an individual who is able to be kind to friends and family—which includes most of us—and one who sees through to the pervasive prejudice and systemic injustice is imagination. A compassionate life that is expanded by imagination would simply not tolerate sexism, racism, or economic injustice. A large imagination empowered by compassion would not stand for prejudice and discrimination because of the superficial differences of religion, nationality, race, or sexual orientation. So, you can see why it can take a lifetime, or more.

Joseph Campbell once said that the toughest thing Jesus ever said was to love our enemies. Indeed! Love, in all its dimensions, is flat-out the most important quality of life for us to learn. And, sometimes, the toughest.

One of these days, we Epoch II guys will awaken to the fact that the biggest "macho" challenge we can face is not physical or mental: it is the spiritual challenge of learning how to live, give, and receive love. To "be a man" in Epoch III will be to "have a heart." That is the heart of it all. (That, of course, is also the primary challenge for women. The nuances of the challenge may be different for men and women, but the essential challenge is still the same—the priority and maturation of love.)

I still have a passion for knowing. I would not have devoted over twenty years of my life in attempting to understand the history of the human Soul and the future into which God is now calling us, if I did not have a passion for understanding. I want a mind that can make sense out of my life in the context of the time of my life. I want a mind that can make sense out of the flow of history and the history of spiritual evolution.

The issue is priority. For a long time, I gave priority to that passion for intellectually making sense out of life (not to overlook or ignore my continuing passion for sports). I want to live as full a life as possible, with a head that has a passion for learning, a body that has a passion for athletic expression, and a heart that knows how to live, give, and receive passionate loving.

We can want all of that—the fullness of body, mind, and spirit, as well as both the head and the heart. But the priority is clear.

It is better to have a heart that makes love than a mind that makes sense!

Questions for Those on a Quest

To quest is to question,
and sometimes the quality of our spiritual quest
has more to do with the questions we ask today
than with answers entombed within past dogma.

1. How would you identify the benefits and limitations of reductionism vis-a-vis wholeness?
2. How would you compare science's propensity for openness and learning new things with the way religion deals with innovation and change?
3. Has the view of Earth from space affected you spiritually? If so, how?

4. Do you think the word *God* is still the best word for the Ultimate Divinity? If so, why? If not, why not? What other words do you think are better?
5. To what extent is your own theology reductionistic or holistic?
6. What word best describes your theological stance? Atheism, theism, pantheism, or panentheism? Is there another word that best describes how you think about God?
7. Have you ever had what you would call a mystical experience? If so, how would you describe it?
8. How do you deal with the issue of "distinguishable oneness?"
9. Can you tell your love story?
10. What aspect of love remains the greatest area of challenge for your own spiritual growth? Compassion? Forgiveness? Love as a healing force?

Chapter Six

The Maturation of Power

The separation of goodness from power made goodness powerless and licensed power to be evil. Many of us, whatever our behavior in the world, think about goodness and power in this way, so that when we are good we feel powerless and when we exercise power we feel evil and defend ourselves against guilt by claiming that's the way the world is, dog eat dog. But that is not the whole truth about the world, where we find nourishment and love as well as contest; and the exercise of power is not intrinsically evil.

Marilyn French, *Beyond Power*[1]

The issue of power is one of the central and most fascinating of all the issues involved in human existence. It is also one of the most complex. Thus, the maturation of power is a crucial and extremely influential ingredient in the transformation from Epoch II into Epoch III.

Two specific kinds of power dominated the human landscape throughout humanity's adolescent epoch. First of all, there was the projection of power externally and hierarchically—theologically, as well as in all human realms—to that which was ostensibly "above us." For most people, this meant denying one's own power, while acquiescing to the external source of presumed power and control. The second kind of power was manifested in the immature ego's need to exert power and control over those "below"—nature, animals, women, as well as other races, nationalities, cultures, and religions.

Those two notions of power permeated virtually all of the causal and influential Epoch II deep-value system—from patriarchal and hierarchal institutions to cultural traditions with majorities dominating minorities, to the political manifestations of imperialism, colonialism, and totalitarianism, and to the various theological understandings of the divine/human relationship. Consequently, it is understandable that a major change in our understanding and use of power in the future will impact virtually all aspects of human experience.

Although the transformation from Epoch II to Epoch III is not complete—plenty of the old manifestations of power are still "in power," if you will—what this chapter will make clear is that the trend toward the transformation and maturation of power is unmistakable. The direction in which the human Soul is growing is evident. Our very notions of power are changing in a manner and degree that are irreversible.

We will, first of all, examine the maturation of power in the political realm: the worldwide movement away from political imperialism, colonialism, and various forms of totalitarianism, and the trend towards the democratization of political power. Involved in, related to, and illustrative of this discussion will be brief explorations of the changes taking place in the institutions of warfare and slavery. We will consider how the United States of America illustrates "the chrysalis phenomenon," the time that the transformational process takes. And we will also consider briefly how communication and computer technology, although not the fundamental cause of this new deep value regarding power, drives the final nail into the coffin of Epoch II notions of centralized and hierarchal power.

Second, we will examine how the maturation of power will inevitably change the religions and spiritualities of the world. Theologies of hierarchical power that disempower the common person and patriarchal institutions that attempt to exert power and control over the individual soul will be delegitimated—we can already see it happening—because the human Soul simply won't acquiesce to it anymore. We are singing a "song of the Soul" with a new and different tune of personal power.

Finally, as with all the emergent deep values, I will share some of my personal quest for empowerment, with the hope that it might in some small way help to stimulate and facilitate your own journey toward and discovery of your innate spiritual power.

Political Power

All of the Epoch II versions of power developed, as we considered earlier, as the inevitable result of humanity's separation from nature and the fracture of the human Soul, with the masculine side elevated and the feminine side sublimated. The patriarchal and hierarchal manifestations of power began to show up politically, as humanity developed larger and larger political entities.

It is important to keep in mind that, throughout Epoch II, precisely because of the influence of the DNA of humanity's adolescent Soul, it was assumed by virtually everybody that the best if not the only way to achieve efficiency in the development and maintenance of civilizations was to concentrate power and control in the hands of a few at the top coupled with the acquiescence of the many below. Unless we keep that historic assumption in mind, we will not appreciate how substantial the change is that we are living through at this time in history.

Also assumed, virtually without question, was that larger and more powerful entities would, could, and should conquer smaller and less powerful ones. Consequently, city-states, which began to emerge in about 5500 BC, were eventually overrun by the larger and more powerful nation-states, the first of which apparently emerged in Mesopotamia about 2300 BC. Nation-states, in turn, were soon taken over by the larger and more powerful dynasties, kingdoms, and empires. Conquest, the accumulation and possession of land and people, dominating control, and the "planting" of colonies, the initial use of the term *plantations*, were the very signs, symbols, substance, and indications of being a "powerful" political entity.

Individual "human rights," if there were to be any, were granted by and at the whim of those at the top. Chiefs, pharaohs, kings, monarchs, dictators, patriarchs, popes, and emperors ruled, and the people, if they knew what was good for them, acquiesced, obeyed, and followed. Life could become toxic for anyone within those political entities who did not conform to the "acid-reign" of power coming down from above.

For those whose city or nation was conquered by a more powerful entity, life was even worse: they were either killed or forced into slavery, a subject we will deal with in a moment. Conquest and acquisition were the name of the political ego expansion game, while humanity lived through the epoch in which its adolescent Soul was in control and defining the rules.

Consequently, the Ottoman Empire developed and grew, and then the Holy Roman Empire had its day, eventually controlling most of mainland Europe and North Africa. That was followed by the Byzantine Empire. And then there was the Han Empire in China, the Mogul Empire in India, and imperial Japan.

The first to engage in overseas empire-building was the Portuguese and the Spanish who agreed among themselves, in 1494, to divide the world with each having the right to half, thus not getting in each other's way. That accommodation might have been a convenient arrangement for the Portuguese and the Spanish, but it was not, needless to say, a plan endorsed by the other nations who had ego-enhancing conquest in mind and were determined to build their own empires.

The nineteenth century was perhaps the most aggressively imperialistic century of all, overwhelmingly driven by the Europeans, with Japan being the only Asian nation to take part in empire building. By early in the twentieth century, the British and the Russians controlled fully one-third of this planet's land surface, with Europeans controlling most non-Europeans and whites colonizing the lands of most nonwhites. The British Empire, for instance, controlled about one-fifth of the human population at the turn of the twentieth century, some four-hundred-million people. The French controlled over fifty-million people outside their own borders. "The only places outside the Americas still not under direct white rule," writes Oxford University historian J. M. Roberts, "were China, the (much-shrunken) Ottoman and the Persian empires, Japan, and a handful of smaller countries."[2]

Once again, it is important to note that the acquisition of land and people by conquest was not seen as evil by those in power. In other words, far from feeling guilty about colonizing land and people and building vast empires, the nations and the leaders wielding such power were proud of their successful acquisitions and hostile takeovers. That was what was valued by the Epoch II Soul, the way a "great and powerful nation" was built. Great Britain, for instance, accumulated under its rule enough people and enough land around the world, so that it could say, *with considerable pride*, "the sun never sets on the British Empire."

Although "realists" would have said that such use of power was simply "the way the world works," change was on its way. The human journey was going to take the next step in its maturational process. At a very deep fundamental and causal level, the DNA of humanity's Soul was about to be transformed regarding the ideas and manifestations of power. The projection of power externally would lose its appeal, and the institutions based upon hierarchal wielding of power from on high and the acquiescence to such power from below would lose their legitimacy. Dictatorships, totalitarian regimes, colonialism, and imperialism were in their last days.

It was, in fact, rather dramatic how quickly the change began taking place. In the middle of the twentieth century, after several thousand years of "having its way with the world," Epoch II authoritarianism lost its political legitimacy virtually overnight. Most of the colonial empires that had ruled and bullied so much of the world until then vanished, and the Epoch III Soul began its ascendancy into prominence.

The word for the Epoch III maturation of power, the kind of power that will define the future, is *democracy*—the idea that power lies in and with the common people, that people have the right to collective self-determination, and that governments are "of the people, by the people, and for the people."

The Rise of Democracy

Robert A. Dahl, Sterling Professor of Political Science Emeritus at Yale University, considered to be one of the leading scholars on the history of democracy, writes:

> During the last half of the twentieth century the world witnessed an extraordinary and unprecedented political change. All of the main alternatives to democracy either disappeared, turned into eccentric survivals, or retreated from the field to hunker down in their last strongholds. Earlier in the century the premodern enemies of democracy—centralized monarchy, hereditary aristocracy, oligarchy based on narrow and exclusive suffrage—had lost their

legitimacy in the eyes of much of humankind. The main antide-
mocratic regimes of the twentieth century—communist, fascist,
Nazi—disappeared in the ruins of calamitous war or, as in the
Soviet Union, collapsed from within. Military dictatorships had
been pretty thoroughly discredited by their failures, particularly
in Latin America; where they managed to survive they often
adopted a pseudo-democratic facade.[3]

Because we are living within a chrysalis time in history, the
entire world is not yet democratic, but the trend is clear. Dahl may
be as authoritative a scholar as we can consult on this issue, and he
emphasizes how democracy has so replaced hierarchal and centralized notions of power and control that it now defines the essential
agenda for nearly all the two hundred countries in the world.
Democracy *is* now the operant value regarding political power,
Dahl suggests, even for those who have not as yet manifested it.

> For the nondemocratic countries, the challenge is whether and how
> they can make the *transition* to democracy. For the newly democra-
> tized countries, the challenge is whether and how the new demo-
> cratic practices and institutions can be strengthened or, as some
> political scientists would say, *consolidated*, so that they will withstand
> the tests of time, political conflict, and crisis. For the older democ-
> racies, the challenge is to perfect and *deepen* their democracy.[4]

For most of us, when we think of democracy, we think of ancient
Greece; after all, the idea did originate in Athens, probably the most
famous city-state of classical times. The Athenians invented the
word for the then-far-off Epoch III ideal of democracy (*demos*, the
people, and *kratos*, to rule). Nevertheless, because ancient Greece
was still so deeply embedded in Epoch II, its "democracy" was
extremely limited, both in its scope and in its history.

Greek democracy was only for those defined as "citizens,"
which did not include women, slaves, or legal aliens. Historically,
the human Soul was not yet providing the context within which the
democratic ideal could mature (we'll examine the United States of
America as a contrasting example shortly). The democratic idea and
ideal, initially "born" in Athens, simply could not survive the
"might-makes-right" propensity of the time. Democracy was an
idea whose time had not yet come.

In 321 BC, the Athenians were subjugated by a bigger and more powerful nation-state to the north, Macedonia. In like fashion, the Macedonians and the Athenians were subjugated by the more powerful Roman Empire. On and on it went: it was simply assumed that the bigger and more powerful had the right to gobble up the smaller and less powerful. True democracy had to wait until the Epoch III notion of political power began to emerge from the human Soul in the mid-twentieth century.

The Epoch II political caterpillar actually began its metamorphosis in the eighteenth century when the united British colonies in North America were the first to rebel successfully against its colonizers, to declare its independence from foreign power, and to establish a national democracy. Democracy was now an idea whose time had come, and the future of political power was to grow from the bottom up, rather than being "reigned" down from on high.

For our primary reference regarding the historical transformation of political power, we can turn to what may be the best and most exhaustive ongoing survey of democracy around the world, that conducted annually by Freedom House in Washington, D.C. Freedom House defines a country as a democracy when "there are reasonably free and fair elections characterized by significant choices for voters in a context of free political organization, reasonable access to the media and secret ballot elections."[5]

Using that definition of democracy, consider the history, the temporary retreats, and inexorable maturation of humanity's Soul in terms of political power:

> In 1776, there was one democracy in the world: the United States of America.
>
> By 1790, there were three democracies: France and Switzerland joined the United States of America.
>
> By 1900, there were thirteen democracies: Canada, Great Britain, Belgium, Netherlands, Denmark, Piedmont/Italy, Sweden, Greece, Chile, and Argentina joined the movement.
>
> By 1919, there were twenty-five democracies.
>
> By 1940, there were thirteen democracies. Whoops! During this twenty-one-year interval the maturation of power experienced a relapse, as France, Belgium, Austria, East and West Germany, Poland, Chile, Argentina, and others were not well enough

established in their democratic experiments in order to stay the course. However, focusing on this twenty-one-year trend, would give the false impression that democracy was simply a temporary aberration on the international political stage.

By 1960, there were thirty-six democracies. The number almost tripled in twenty years.

By 1975, there were thirty democracies: another "whoops," but not a trend.

By 1990, there were sixty-one democracies. The number more than doubled in fifteen years.

In the year 2000, there are 119 democracies.

The trend is unmistakable. As of this writing, more than sixty percent of the world's countries are now democratic. The world community may slip and slide or stumble and bumble along the way, but democracy is the spirit that will define the future.

Consider the way the democratization of power has changed a couple of the most horrendously brutal manifestations of humanity's adolescent soul—war and slavery.

War

War has been a thoroughly Epoch II phenomenon. As far as we can tell, there were no wars throughout the entire twenty-five-thousand years of Epoch I. Although we find that cities such as Jericho and Hacilar were walled-in enclaves during the ninth and eighth millennia BC, which might suggest purposes of protection and fortification, they were apparently exceptions to the rule. Most settlements and early city-states selected sites and built their communities with no apparent need for protection, and we find no evidence of actual battles or warfare prior to the sixth millennium BC. Egypt, for instance, apparently flourished for fifteen-hundred years before needing a standing army.

War, however, could be seen as a natural, understandable, exemplary, and inevitable manifestation of humanity's notions of power and control during its adolescent epoch. Consequently, as the DNA of the Epoch II Soul began shaping and conditioning human cultures around the world, a gradual reliance on warfare and violence became the method of choice for political entities to achieve their goals and to expand their egos. The accumulation of power and control over more and more people and more and more land were the applicable strategies.

The Epoch II deep-value system justified, indeed, encouraged territorial and population conquest, and war was simply the acceptable and appropriate means of accomplishing that goal. Consequently, wars of conquest virtually defined the history of political entities—city-states, nation-states, dynasties, empires, etc.—from the third millennium BC until the middle of the twentieth century AD. A nation became a great nation, an empire became a great empire precisely by conquering less powerful entities and taking power and control over greater numbers of people and larger quantities of land.

One popular interpretation regarding the cause of violent warfare, albeit apparently wrong, was that it was a necessary fight over land and resources in an increasingly crowded world. John Keegan, considered by many as the most distinguished military historian of the twentieth century, wrote that,

> Though the number of people in the world rose from about 5–10 million in 10,000 BC to perhaps 100 million in 3000 BC, they were almost nowhere densely concentrated. . . . Between 6000 and 3000 BC the scattered agriculture settlements in eastern Europe did not exceed a size of fifty or sixty households each. . . . Land was effectively free. . . . Yields, on the other hand, must have been so low as to produce little worth robbing.[6]

War was inevitable, not because of external needs for land or resources, but because of the nature and content of the human Soul throughout Epoch II. Interestingly enough, however, as the adolescent epoch began to lose its influence *the kind of war* that was considered legitimate began to change. In other words, even before war could be totally eliminated from the world, we began changing our minds and hearts about the type of war that was appropriate and for which there was general approval.

By the middle of the twentieth century, wars of conquest had lost legitimacy, whereas wars for the purpose of gaining independence, liberation, freedom, and self-determination were considered legitimate. Reflective of this shift of consciousness was the fact that the United States of America, in 1947, changed the name of its "War Department" to "The Department of Defense." As researcher

Bernard Nietschmann points out, during the last half of the twentieth century, three out of every four wars were wars of liberation.[7]

An interesting observation about the changing nature of warfare comes from Francis Fukuyama, a former deputy director of the U.S. State Department's Policy Planning Staff. In his widely heralded book *The End of History and the Last Man*, Fukuyama points out that a great deal of evidence now suggests that, since democracies began taking over the political stage, not one single democracy has waged war on another democracy.[8]

Pause for a moment to consider that carefully: *democracies do not wage war on other democracies!* Could it be that the incidence of war will be diminished or even eliminated precisely because the democratizing spirit is becoming ubiquitous throughout the world?

There is also evidence that totalitarian entities can mature into a democracy without a major war of liberation. Consider, for instance, the experience of the former Soviet Union.

The massive totalitarian state of the Soviet Union crumbled from the inside out, or from the Soul up, as it were. In a remarkably few short years at the end of the 1980s, a totalitarian philosophy was replaced by a democratic spirit and without an internal insurrection or war of liberation. As Fukuyama writes,

> Democratization in the USSR led directly to a belittling of earlier staples of Soviet foreign policy, such as fear of "capitalist encirclement" or NATO as an "aggressive, revanchist" organization. To the contrary, the Soviet Communist party's theoretical journal *Kommunist* explained in early 1988 that "there are no politically influential forces in either Western Europe or the US" that contemplate "military aggression against socialism," and that "bourgeois democracy serves as a definite barrier in the path of unleashing such a war."[9]

Advancement in technology provides an interesting subtext to this discussion. One might argue that the incredible progress in the technology of war made war no longer an appropriate or effective means of fighting; after all, we arrived at the point in the middle of the twentieth century where, if we used all the weapons we had developed, we would all be dead. The historic definitions of "winner" and "loser" lost their distinction when we arrived at the state of Mutually Assured Destruction. We had, after all, developed such a quality and quantity of weapons that we simply could not use them, unless we had some pathological compulsion for a species-wide suicide.

That is a tempting and seemingly logical argument. The suggestion here, however, is that it was a deeper matter that was the real causal factor—namely, the transformation of humanity's Soul and, in this particular case, the maturation of our notions of power. That Soul-change, and the process towards democratization, had started well before we had developed today's arsenals of weapons. If Fukuyama is right—and on this matter, I believe he is—then that process alone would sound the death-knell of warfare as we have known it, separate from the technology of violence.

It also would be a good guess to suggest that, as the democratic spirit becomes more pervasive throughout the world, we will find more women in positions of political leadership. And the more women involved in political decisions, the more likely it is that war will be considered an intolerable and undesirable method for handling international, ethnic, or religious conflict.

Slavery

War and slavery are inextricably connected, historically as well as causally at the level of deep values regarding power and control. Warfare, from its very inception, was not only about the accumulation of land. It was also about obtaining slave labor, slave sex—and, as a result, slaves *in* labor, which provided more slaves for labor, profits, and sex.

Historian Gerda Lerner suggests—rightly, I believe—that "slavery is the first institutionalized form of hierarchical dominance in human history":

> The "invention of slavery" consisted in the idea that one group of persons can be marked off as an out-group, branded enslaveable, forced into labor and subordination—and that this stigma of enslaveability combined with the reality of their status would make them accept it as a fact.[10]

Those of us in the United States associate slavery with the African slave trade and America's plantations but, in fact, it is a much bigger and more horrific legacy of humanity's adolescent deep values than just the African and American story, as bad as that story was and is.

Slavery began in the same prehistoric period as did the wars of conquest, midway through Epoch II. Although racism became a major factor in slavery in certain places at certain times, slavery itself was not a racial matter per se. Slavery was virtually universal, existing in almost every society, and condoned and supported by religions all across the human landscape and of every ilk. Every race and color engaged in slaving and were, in turn, enslaved.

It is important to reiterate that, during most of Epoch II, the arrangement of master and slave, dominator and dominated was not considered a social injustice to rectify. It was an arrangement believed to be ordained by the gods, and was accepted as simply the way the world was supposed to work. Milton Meltzer, one of the most prestigious and respected scholars on the history of slavery, comments on this:

> The institution of slavery was universal throughout much of history. It was a tradition everyone grew up with. It seemed essential to the social and economic life of the community, and man's conscience was seldom troubled by it. Both master and slave looked upon it as inevitable.[11]

The matter of ownership, involving absolute power and control, defined the nature of slaving and, once again, was closely tied to warfare. Captives were seen as the spoils of war with which the captors could do as they pleased, apparently without the interference of conscience. In the beginning, following wars of conquest, most of the men who were conquered were summarily killed—death was considered virtually inevitable if you lost the war, a seemingly necessary strategy so as to eliminate any threat of counterattack or insurrection from those just conquered. Thus, since most of the men were put to death for understandable reasons, most of the first slaves were women and children. If their life were spared, it was usually to provide cheap labor and available sex on demand.

Eventually, what was to become the driving force of slavery for millennia took over, namely, the *business* of slavery. Conquerors finally awakened to the fact that men were of more value to them alive than dead. Captive men could be put to work on tasks of hard labor, thereby accomplishing things that the captors certainly did not want to do themselves. In addition, the armies of the empires were primarily made up of slaves, fighting and dying on behalf of their masters.

If the men were not to be killed, however, the slave masters had the inevitable problem of security. How could male slaves be prevented from waging a counter-attack or simply running away? How could this valuable economic asset not be lost? How could one hold on to one's "property" (and property was definitely the applicable term)? Retention of one's property and the protection of one's assets were the primary security issues.

This is where an already ugly and almost unbelievably horrendous chapter in the human story becomes even more ugly and even more unbelievably horrendous. In order to keep one's human property from being able to fight back or to run away, the human imagination went to sadistic extremes.

One strategy for controlling male captives was that of blinding. Lerner reports that one Assyrian text, from about 1200 BC, tells of putting out of the eyes of 14,400 captives.[12] Others had tendons cut, either in their feet or in their ankles, so that they could not run away. Branding slaves, similar to cattle branding, and cutting off noses and ears were done, so that they could be easily recognizable, were they to run away. Public torturing of runaway slaves was also used to discourage others from trying to escape. Women were controlled primarily by threats about what would be done to their children if they ever tried to escape.

As the business of slavery grew, new means of obtaining slaves were created. Kidnaping was widely used, and courts would sentence people into slavery. Some people actually sold themselves into slavery in order to pay off a debt. And, of course, people were born into slavery, the "breeding" of slaves often being an intentional process by slave holders for the purpose of continually resupplying slave populations.

One incredibly ironic way of trying to reduce runaways was to charge them with thievery—after all, they had stolen their master's property, themselves. And, of course, there were severe penalties for such thievery.

As one reads extensively into the history of slavery throughout the world's past six-thousand years, one cannot help but be amazed at how widespread and thoroughly pervasive the institution of slavery was. Even though we now condemn such horrific practices and the institution of slavery is in its final days, nevertheless, few cultures can escape our judgment about the past. Virtually every major culture around the world shared the Epoch II deep values that created and sustained slavery, and virtually every major religion either participated in or condoned the practice of slavery.

There may be no greater monuments to the Epoch II need for ego-building, as well as the use of slave labor to serve that ego, than the Egyptian pyramids. The pyramids, of course, were built to house the pharaohs' tombs, and the Greek historian Herodotus, in the fifth century, claimed that it took one-hundred-thousand slaves twenty years to build the famous pyramid of Gizeh. No longer can we admire the task and the accomplishment of the pyramids without agonizing over what the ego-needs of those in power did to the lives of the slaves who were forced to build those monuments in their "honor."

The Egyptians, of course, were not alone. Greece, from very early in its history, relied extensively on slave labor. In the fifth century BC, Attica had a total of about 315,500 people, of which 115,000 were slaves. Athens had a population of about 155,000, 70,000 of whom were slaves. There was virtually no activity in ancient Greece, public or private, that was not performed by slaves. As Meltzer observes, appropriately, "[W]hat is surprising is that so few of the great thinkers and poets of Greece considered the abolition of slavery.[13]

And then there were the Romans. The Punic Wars, beginning in the third century BC, launched the Roman Republic, resulting in the rule of almost all the lands surrounding the Mediterranean. From these wars of conquest, as well as through piracy, slavery became a major force in making Rome rich and powerful. Although civil wars changed the Roman Republic into the Roman Empire, it did little to change the reliance upon slaves.

The Romans gave a unique twist to the institution of slavery: a special class of slaves trained to provide entertainment—the entertainment of human sacrifice. These specially trained slaves were the gladiators, trained to kill other slaves within the atmosphere of great public fanfare and ritual. Their own death, of course, was virtually assured, even though they might delay it for awhile if they

possessed extraordinary skill in the art of killing. Romans wou gather by the tens of thousands to watch men fight to their dead the slaughter would often run from dawn to dusk and sometime well into the night. Winners were often rewarded with costly gift and raucous glory, but they lived only to fight another day.[14]

Since slavery was the primary institution on which virtually all ancient civilizations were built, obtaining slaves dominated the business world—wars of conquest, piracy, purchase, breeding, kidnapping, and the punishment for debt or crimes. Slavery was central to the economies in Sumer, Babylonia, Assyria, Egypt, Israel, Greece, Africa, and Rome.

Slavery also persisted—in fact, flourished—throughout the world until modern times. The American and European slave trade of Africans to the New World may have resulted in the largest deportation of slaves over the greatest distance, but Africans were not unlike people from the rest of the world, practicing slavery themselves ever since prehistoric times. Slavery was fed and maintained by the wars between African empires.

Slavery was also practiced in America by the aboriginal populations long before the Europeans got involved. Similar to the Romans, the Aztecs in MesoAmerica engaged in widespread human sacrifice, although for religious purposes rather than for entertainment. The Aztecs had a large number of religious observances that required a continual supply of slaves for the purpose of human sacrifice.

In the Americas, as with much of slavery elsewhere, male captives were either killed, condemned to hard labor, frequently tortured, or permanently maimed. The women were used and abused for domestic labor and/or sexual service, including being made available for sex by visitors, sold into prostitution, or to breed future slaves.

The Pima and Papago Native Americans hunted down, captured, and sold Yuma, Apache, and Navaho slaves to the Mexicans. At the same time, the Navaho raided and captured the Pueblos. The Comanches, Kiowas, Cheyennes, and the Arapahoes also engaged in buying and selling slave captives, as did the Cherokees. Slavery was also prevalent among the Native Americans in the southeast, up the eastern coast, as well as in the Pacific northwest.

We could go on and on, documenting the widespread use of slavery throughout the world and discussing the slight differences in how the institution worked with various peoples. The primary

point, however, is that slavery was ubiquitous throughout the world as long as the Epoch II Soul was in control. Perhaps even more important to our discussion regarding the impending transformation of Soul, is the recognition of how pervasively slavery was accepted and condoned in the hearts and minds of people the world over, for more than six-thousand years.

Few people who were considered the wise and most religious of the times felt any compulsion to condemn the practice or to devote themselves to its abolition. For instance, we can find no aggressive or general condemnation of slavery from Buddha, Moses, Jesus, or Mohammed. In the great moral texts and scriptures of the great world religions, we find no moralizing about slavery or call for its abolition. Saint Thomas Aquinas, for instance, apparently believed that slavery was one consequence of Adam's sin, and that it was, therefore, both morally justifiable as well as economically necessary. As Meltzer sums it up,

> For many centuries, popes and bishops, churches and monasteries owned slaves. Pope Gregory I (590–604) used hundreds of slaves on the papal estates. He approved a law preventing slaves from becoming clerics or marrying free Christians. Early in the eighth century, the Abbey of St. Germain des Pres near Paris had 8,000 slaves and Martin of Tours had 20,000. . . .
>
> Slave trading was no vulgar or wicked occupation that shut a man out from office or honors. Engaged in the British trade were dukes, earls, lords, countesses, knights—and kings. . . . Many mayors of Liverpool were slavers, and so were the city's aldermen. Slave traders sat in both houses of Parliament.[15]

Nevertheless, after millennia of the human Soul's entrenchment in a deep-value system that saw slavery as a God-ordained, natural, and inevitable way of constructing human cultures, and justifiable as a way of using and abusing other human beings, a new Soul began to grow deep within; and humanity's next evolutionary purpose—spiritual maturation—began its ascendancy.

Spain abolished the enslavement of Indians in Cuba in the 1550s, and Britain, in 1662, made a treaty with Tripoli that banned the enslavement of British subjects in any of its territories. Nevertheless, the middle of the eighteenth century should be identified as

the true beginning of the end for slavery. Specifically, it could be argued that the Anti-Slavery Society, organized in England in 1765, started the inexorable demise of Epoch II power and control vis-a-vis slavery. The Society prepared the way for the 1772 history-making decision by Lord Chief Justice Mansfield regarding a West Indian slave named Somerset. Mansfield ruled that under English common law all people were guaranteed freedom:

> The Lord Chief Justice's decision did not affect slavery in the colonies, but it freed about 15,000 African slaves then living in England and gave hope to humanitarians that slavery could be abolished everywhere. Many societies sprang up in the colonies to carry on the fight. In 1807 Parliament declared the slave trade illegal for British subjects; four years later it passed another law to punish severely anyone who continued in the trade.[16]

Danish action in 1804 contributed to the international movement against the slave trade, the United States declared it illegal in 1808, the Dutch in 1814, and the French in 1815. As other nations joined in, the Atlantic slave trade was legally dead by 1842. Brazil abolished slavery in 1888, China in 1909, and West Nepal in 1948, just to cite a few examples. Today, every country that is a member of the United Nations officially deplores and has outlawed slavery.

Make no mistake about it, slavery is still with us. We should not be so naive as to think that it would be a quick or simple matter to eradicate slavery, given the powerful economic and sexual incentives to continue using and abusing the poor, the weak, the young, the vulnerable, and women, as long as the patriarchal deep value has any life remaining. Slavery has very deep deep-value roots, and more than six-thousand years of history, custom, and tradition. It will not disappear overnight or without a great deal of resistance. But it will disappear.

We should not underestimate the substantial shift that has already taken place and the momentum that is underway. We are not totally cleansed of the horrible institution of slavery as yet, but there is a powerful difference between the past when virtually everybody around the world considered slavery to be normal and God-ordained, and the present, when virtually everybody at least affirms the value of freedom and liberty and officially condemns slavery.

It is significant that, even where slavery is still occurring, the nations within which it is taking place want to hide that fact from the rest of the world. Every country now knows that the world's value system is against the very notion of slavery. Consequently, they abhor any publicity that leaks out suggesting that slavery is still taking place within their borders.

With slavery, as with other Epoch II staples of hierarchal power and control, we're still in the chrysalis period. The Epoch II caterpillar is not dead as yet, and the Epoch III butterfly has not completely spread its wings and experienced the joy of flight up and away from the chrysalis. But the organic propensity for maturation is clear, the Soul's transformation is evident, and the direction of our movement as a species is unmistakable.

A Microcosm of the "Chrysalis Phenomenon"

We hold these truths to be self-evident, that all men are created equal, that they are endowed by their Creator with certain unalienable rights, that among these are life, liberty and the pursuit of happiness. That to secure these rights, governments are instituted among men, deriving their just powers from the consent of the governed. That whenever any form of government becomes destructive of these ends, it is the right of the people to alter or to abolish it, and to institute new government, laying its foundation on such principles and organizing its power in such form.

The Declaration of Independence

The inevitability and direction of change, the time it takes for a transformation of Soul to be completed, and the simultaneous presence within the chrysalis of both the dying and the birthing—all these dynamics are illustrated in the history of the United States of America, a microcosm of the chrysalis phenomenon.

The Epoch II way of thinking was that everything should fit into neat categories, either/or, all or nothing, black or white. Real life, however, is usually a process, sometimes gradual, sometimes in fits and starts, but always a process. Consider the maturational process of the individual. We do not move from childhood to adolescence or from adolescence to adulthood overnight. We do not progress to the next stage of growth instantaneously. We usually grow gradually, step by step, one little punctuation by one little punctuation. Individually, we mature by a slow, sometimes agonizingly slow, process. So it is with collective humanity.

The United States of America was the first national democracy to open Epoch III, and the founders had a marvelous grasp of the democratic ideal—in theory. In practice, however, they, and we, have stumbled our way throughout the years, gradually moving towards a more mature understanding and integration of the democratic value.

Those who initially declared America's independence and instituted the spirit of democracy, liberty, and justice started out, in their own lives, with a severely restricted grasp of the notion that "all men are created equal." Democratic participation and freedom were not given to all persons; rather, at the beginning, it was given only to white, male landowners. If you did not own land, you did not have the vote. Thus, women, African Americans, or Native Americans did not share in the democratic ideal. Amazingly, the United States even continued the process of taking control of other lands and other people, in spite of the hypocrisy that entailed.

A study of our nation's beginnings leaves one with both an awe regarding the founders' vision of the ideal and an awful heartache regarding the actuality. It is amazing how people can be both ahead of their times, mature beyond their years, while simultaneously be thoroughly conditioned by the immaturity of their times. The awareness of this fact should, at the least, temper our arrogance and judgmentalism of other nations that fail to manifest ideal human rights on our time schedule. For a little humility and patience, we need only consider our own history.

Consider, for instance, the history of this country's relationship with the native and indigenous peoples of this continent. The version of history that most of us learned in school was that our European relatives discovered a new land that was free for the taking, a pristine unexplored territory ripe for the picking. How do you imagine we would have felt had we been the inhabitants of this land before the self-righteous and self-justifying invaders came in and took over with their might-makes-right value system?

How would we have felt if we had been betrayed by virtually every treaty we signed with the invaders? How would we have felt if there were fifteen million of us in 1492 when Columbus arrived, and through slaughter, slavery, relocation, disease, and the elimination of the buffalo, the occupying forces diminished our numbers to 237,000 by 1900? Would we not think that we were the victims of a well-orchestrated strategy of genocide? How would we feel about celebrating a national "Columbus Day" holiday? What would have gone through our minds if the European Americans referred to such expansionist behavior with such noble terms as "Manifest Destiny" and "the American Pioneering Spirit?"

The doctrine of Manifest Destiny, held widely throughout the United States in the nineteenth century, proposed that it was the European-American *destiny* to own and control all the land across North America. Where were the principles of democracy, self-determination, liberty, and justice when it came to the Native American population, the people who were here first?

Then there was also the matter of America's overseas imperialism. It was not without some internal debate; after all, some Americans argued, we had come into existence in a revolt against such colonialism. Yet, in spite of some disagreement, "the final annexation of Hawaii in July 1898 came in a burst of aggressiveness and expansion."[17]

Consider America's involvement in slavery and how that bred the racism that has plagued this country for its entire history. It is well documented that this nation's beginning, and particularly the economy of the southern states, depended heavily upon slavery. The United States was a major participant in the African slave trade to the Americas, the best estimates of which conclude that, between 1451 and 1870, about ten-million live slaves arrived into the Americas, with untold others dying during the trip across the Atlantic. By 1860, the United States alone had a slave population of about four million.[18]

As mentioned earlier, one of the critical and foundational beliefs in the slave trade was that a slave was a piece of property, not a person. With such a belief, it was easy to rationalize that the democratic ideal did not apply to slaves. Virtually all the Founding Fathers were slaveowners, including the "Father of our country" and first president George Washington, who was a fourth-generation slave holder. Washington never publicly condemned slavery and, at the time of his death, owned or had on lease more than one-hundred-sixty slaves. Recent DNA evidence suggests that our "founding fathers" were doing some other fathering as well.

The Constitution of the United States of America, article 1, section 2, paragraph 3, declared that, for purposes of representation and taxation, the Native American did not count at all, and the African-American was considered to be a mere sixty percent of a person. Those exercises in mathematics, believe it or not, were countenanced by the same men who declared, "We hold these truths to be self-evident, that all men are created equal."

The Reverend Dr. Martin Luther King Jr. pointed out how the writings of Thomas Jefferson revealed what King called the "haunting ambivalence" in the soul of early America:

> In his *Notes on Virginia*, Jefferson portrayed the African-American as inferior to the white man, yet, in the same document, commenting on the injustice of the institution of slavery, wrote: "Indeed I tremble for my country when I reflect that God is just, that his justice cannot sleep forever. . . . The Almighty has no attribute which can take sides with us in such a contest."[19]

It is remarkable, and quite hopeful for the future of humanity, that people like Thomas Jefferson who may in their actions fall far short of the ideal, still carry in their soul the knowledge that God "has no attribute which can take sides with us" in the dehumanization and disempowerment of others. We may be agonizingly slow at growing up, but the faith here is that the Soul has a built-in organic propensity for doing so. There is an evolutionary "within-ness" to the human Soul.

Nevertheless, America's "haunting ambivalence" lingered on for awhile. In 1857, the Supreme Court of the United States, in the Dred Scott case, concluded that African Americans had no rights that the white man had to respect. It was 1865 before slavery was abolished with the thirteenth amendment, to eventually be followed by the fourteenth amendment guaranteeing equal protection under the laws, and by the fifteenth protecting the right to vote. Nevertheless, unless one has been sleep-walking through the twentieth century, one cannot help but be aware of how long it has taken America to begin even to approach those constitutional ideals or to cleanse itself of the pathology of racism.

If anything is more ludicrous than the way the world's first Epoch III democracy dealt with Native Americans and African-

Americans, it has to be the way men, who were and are in the minority, dealt with the majority of the population, women. The very men who articulated the ideals of democracy, liberty, freedom, and justice for all at the same time considered it legal and appropriate to beat their wives, as long as the whip they used was no thicker than their thumb. Their wives' as well as their children's clothes belonged to the husbands and the fathers. Women could not buy property, rarely went to college, and were expected to stay at home, raise the children, and take care of the house. They had no say about the general role of women in the country, nor about the conditions of their own lives in particular. Men had the only opinions that counted—literally. The rationalization that men used was that, if women voted, they would lose their femininity. (In a true democracy, of course, women would have the right to "lose their femininity," if they wanted to do so. But, with patriarchal values, men think it is they who do the defining and grant the permissions.)

Nevertheless, some "uppity" women who, at least by the male definition, must have also been unrefined, undisciplined, and unfeminine, did not subscribe nor passively submit to those particular "family values." Nor did they remain in "their place." Instead, they boldly attended a gathering in Seneca Falls, New York, to hold the first Women's Rights Convention, on July 19 and 20, 1848.

It was not until thirty years later, however, that the first constitutional amendment intended to assure the vote to women was introduced into Congress, and victory was not achieved until 1920 when, at the last moment, a young Tennessee legislator, recalling his mother's request to vote in favor or the amendment, voted for ratification. Thus, the fourteenth amendment passed—by one vote.

All of this history notwithstanding, America has been progressing towards the ideals of democracy, freedom, and justice. Although one can argue that we still fall short—and we most certainly do—we have, nevertheless, been in the process of growing up. We can and should be impatient with the pace of our maturation, and activism on behalf of social justice is always necessary. Nevertheless, the big picture shows that the Epoch II caterpillar in America is definitely transforming into the Epoch III butterfly.

Examples of this maturation are far too numerous to delineate here: the simple observation of America as a microcosm of the chrysalis phenomenon is our only point. It is interesting to note, however, as just one brief example of this progress, the way in which European-Americans have changed their views regarding Native Americans' spirituality. In the history of this country, the problem for Native Americans has changed from the demonization and attempted eradication of their spirituality, coupled with demands that they convert to Christianity, to a growing appreciation of their nature-based spirituality and a frequently inappropriate appropriation of their sacred rites and customs. In our wisest moments, we know there is a great deal we can learn from the traditional spirituality of this "Turtle Island."

The current fear-based discrimination against anyone who does not neatly fit into the simplistic category of our sexual comfort zone—clearly, completely, and absolutely heterosexual—is but the most recent evidence that we still fall short of the Epoch III spiritual maturity. Nevertheless, we have grown beyond the fear of category pollution before—for example, John F. Kennedy's Catholicism in his 1960 run for the presidency, pluralistic spiritualities, interracial marriage, etc.—and I have no doubt we will on this matter as well. Frankly, however, I find it incredibly agonizing to know of the suffering, the discrimination, the injustice, and the lack of love and compassion that takes place "in the meantime." When it comes to basic human injustice, the meantime is a time that is just way too mean!

Communication and Computer Technology

Empowering the powerless, in virtually every area of human endeavor worldwide, has been aided substantially by the democratization of knowledge through communication and computer technology. The invention of movable type and the printing press in the fifteenth century was certainly a watershed in the history of the accessibility of knowledge and communication. But the awesome development of satelite communications all over the world, at the speed of light, coupled with the amazing progress of computer technology, provides the most recent symbol and substance of the shift in power from a central privileged elite to the empowered masses.

In a few years, we went from the mainframe to the personal computer, from centralized controlled access run by a skilled elite to a democratization of both access and knowledge. The World Wide Web came into existence as recently as the early 1990s, but now, in less than ten years, some fifty-two million people worldwide are "surfing the Web." As of this writing, sixty-thousand individuals every single day are jumping on their "surf-boards" for the first time and learning to surf the internet "wave of the future." If these figures are out-of-date by the time you read this book, and they most certainly will be, the figures will just as certainly be elevated rather than reduced.

One of the most amazing and fascinating subtexts of the World Wide Web has to do with its inventor—British-born physicist Tim Berners-Lee. In a world that is becoming obsessed with making fortunes through web-based businesses—personified by Silicon Valley's Jim Clark who has created three, separate, billion-dollar companies but who doesn't want to stop because he is not yet as rich as Bill Gates—Berners-Lee provides a refreshing contrast. Berners-Lee never chose to profit from his invention. Hailed by *Time* magazine as one of the one-hundred greatest minds of the twentieth century, Berners-Lee followed his passionate vision of a World Wide Web that could be a powerful force for social change and individual creativity. His focus was on an Epoch III kind of empowerment, rather than on worshiping the Epoch II god of power through wealth.

Berners-Lee wrote that his priority, from the beginning, was that the World Wide Web had to be "completely decentralized":

> That would be the only way a new person somewhere could start to use it without asking for access from anyone else. . . .
>
> Control was the wrong perspective. . . . Technically, if there was any centralized point of control, it would rapidly become a bottleneck that restricted the Web's growth, and the Web would never scale up. Its being "out of control" was very important.[20]

The genie of the democratization of knowledge cannot be forced back into the Epoch II bottle of centralized power and elite control. A human Soul that is being transformed in its valuation of power, when empowered by this democratization of access, rings the death knell to the Epoch II notions of hierarchal power and control. The revolution in communication and computer technology is the final nail in the coffin of Epoch II's deep value of power and control.

The Epoch III maturation of power began emerging on the surface of the human landscape long before these recent technological innovations, however important they are. One very impressive and prestigious study conducted by Duane Elgin of the Millennium Project, and sponsored by The Fetzer Institute, The Institute of Noetic Sciences, The Brande Foundation, The California Institute of Integral

Studies, and The State of the World Forum, appears to confirm this. The study was entitled "Global Consciousness Change: Indicators of an Emerging Paradigm." In the official report, Elgin writes that

> From this inquiry, we have concluded that a new global culture and consciousness have taken root and are beginning to grow in the world. This represents a shift in consciousness as distinct and momentous as that which occurred in the transition from the agricultural era to the industrial era roughly three hundred years ago. Because communications technologies are a powerful force driving the emergence of this new epoch, it would be convenient to call it the "communications era." But that name would be ill-suited since the most distinctive feature of this emerging era is not technological change, but a change in human consciousness.[21]

Religious Power

In the fateful, epoch-announcing words of Nietzsche's Zarathustra: "Dead are all the gods." One knows the tale: it has been told a thousand ways. It is the ... wonder-story of [humanity's] coming to maturity. The spell of the past, the bondage of tradition, was shattered with sure and mighty strokes. The dream-web of myth fell away; the mind opened to full waking consciousness; and [humanity] emerged from ancient ignorance, like a butterfly from its cocoon....

[Today's] hero-deed must be that of questing to bring to light again the lost Atlantis of the coordinated soul ... rendering the modern world spiritually significant ... [and] making it possible for men and women to come to full human maturity.

Joseph Campbell[22]

Religious power took virtually the same route through Epoch II as did political power—projecting power externally and hierarchically, as well as assuming that people in "positions of power" had the right to exercise power and control over those in positions of subservience and submission. And, just as with the democratization of political power, the democratization of religious power is the current name of the game.

The Epoch II political strategy was called colonialism and imperialism, while Epoch II religious strategy was called evangelism, converting "heathens" to the one and only legitimate faith.

The Epoch II political world was ruled by chiefs, kings, monarchs, patriarchs, pharaohs, and emperors, the religious world by popes, bishops, and a wide variety of gurus who claim power, control, and authority. We also participated by projecting power, control, and authority onto these figures.

The language and the metaphors we have traditionally used in the religions of Epoch II reveal how influenced this entire field has been by the Epoch II deep values. Max Black states the following:

> The monarchical model of God as King was developed systematically, both in Jewish thought (God as Lord and King of the Universe), in medieval Christian thought (with its emphasis on divine omnipotence), and in the Reformation (especially in Calvin's insistence on God's sovereignty). In the portrayal of God's relation to the world, the dominant western historical model has been that of the absolute monarch ruling over his kingdom.[23]

Vanderbilt University theologian Sallie McFague is among the best and most insightful in exploring our use of metaphors and models when thinking about God. She points out that such images of Lord, King, and a sovereign God have become so familiar that we fail to recognize them as metaphors. Familiarity, it would seem, breeds literalism. We become so accustomed to the metaphor we confuse it with fact, like thinking a map is the actual territory. McFague also reminds us that familiarity often blinds us to the fact that such metaphors are fundamentally oppressive.

We are familiar with, accustomed to, and sometimes defensive about our traditional metaphors. Heaven is up there; earth is down here. Hell is even further down. Matter and spirit, divine and human are separated and arranged hierarchically. God is a masculine Father figure, and we are "children of God." We have become accustomed to speaking of the divine/human relationship as between a king and his subjects or a shepherd and his flock, imagery that justifies our passive obedience and childlike dependence. It is imagery that fails to challenge us to accept adult responsibility for our own spiritual growth and development. But, whether we think of ourselves as theologians or not, we are doing theology with the images by which we understand our relationship with the divine. "In order to do theology," McFague writes, "one must in each epoch do it differently. To refuse this task is to settle for a theology appropriate to some time other than one's own. Are [the metaphors we use] . . . right *for our time?*"[24]

In Epoch II, we envisioned the Divine in a way consistent with the Epoch II Soul. But in Epoch III, we must theologize differently because we are in different spiritual territory. The old Soul is dying, and we are in the process of growing a new Soul. Patriarchal and hierarchal models are not compatible with the Epoch III Soul.

Once again, however, we can see hints of Epoch III spoken of and personified by the visionaries of Epoch III spiritual maturity, long before most of us were ready to grow beyond Epoch II. Such visionaries looked to the empowering images and metaphors that reflected a democratization of spiritual power, and they can be found in all religious traditions.

Stephen Mitchell, the eminent scholar and translator, has followed an unusual spiritual path, a combination of Judaism and Zen Buddhism. He writes:

> A couple of months after I began studying with my old Zen Master, he said to me, "You have three jobs here. Your first job is to kill the Buddha." I had read that phrase in the old Zen teachings, and I knew what it meant—to let go of any concepts of a separate, superior, enlightened being outside myself. Then he said, "Your second job is to kill your parents." (And), "your third job is to kill me."[25]

The use of the word *kill* may strike us as severe and unspiritual. Although we might be more comfortable with kinder and gentler words, consider the possibility that severe words are used for a good and precise reason: so that we will grasp the severity of the challenge. If we have, in good Epoch II fashion, worshipped the Buddha for a very long time, it is not an easy job to let go of that projection of power. If we have, at deep unconscious levels, allowed our parents to shape and determine who we are and what we do, it is not an easy task to become "our own person." If we have been dutiful students of great teachers, if we are humbled by their knowledge, it is not easy to realize that our task is not to know *their* truth, but to internalize and determine our *own* truth. Let's face it: spiritual empowerment is no small challenge, as we discussed in the previous chapter.

A student of Ramana Maharshi once said to him, "I want to give up my job and family and stay with you, sir, so that I can be with God." Maharshi said, "God is always with you, in you. That is what you should realize."[26]

It is not our purpose here to survey all the visionaries of Epoch III spiritual maturity, in all the various religions of the world. But, as an example, listen to what Jesus is reported to have said in the Gnostic Gospel of Thomas 70:1–2, and consider how it reflects an Epoch III democratization of spiritual power rather than the imperialistic Epoch II notions of salvation or a concept of an external God:

> If you bring forth what is within you, what you bring forth will save you. If you do not bring forth what is within you, what you do not bring forth will destroy you.[27]

Jesus scholar John Dominic Crossan of DePaul University writes that Jesus' strategy,

> implicitly for himself and explicitly for his followers, was . . . a religious . . . egalitarianism that negated alike and at once the hierarchical and patronal normalities of Jewish religion and Roman power. . . . He was neither broker nor mediator but, somewhat paradoxically, the announcer that neither should exist between humanity and divinity. . . . He announced, in other words, the unmediated or brokerless Kingdom of God.[28]

The difficulty, of course, was that, since the people running Christian institutions were still operating out of the Epoch II Soul, they thought that their reason for being was to be "God's representatives" in the hierarchal arrangement of heaven and earth, the one and only conduit between the divine and the human realms. They thought that the "Kingdom of God" was to be brokered by them—apparently, different notions than those held by Jesus himself.

Another Jesus scholar, Marcus Borg, suggests that Jesus' primary message "was not about himself or the importance of believing in him . . . [and] did not consist of seeking to convert people to believe certain things about him." Borg, along with many other biblical scholars, does not think that Jesus made special claims for himself, and that the oft-quoted phrase from the Gospel of John—"I am the way, the truth, and the life; no one comes to the Father but by me"—was a statement by and for his followers, and not something that Jesus would have said.[29]

Walter Wink, professor of Biblical Interpretation at Auburn Theological Seminary, has conducted a wide-ranging study of power and domination and has written widely on the subject. Related to our topic here, Wink documents extensively how Jesus' life and ministry were not only the opposite of hierarchical power and domination, but were a direct challenge to those prevalent values.[30]

Of course, Christianity is not the only religion to be influenced profoundly by Epoch II deep values which were, apparently, in stark contrast to the one around whom the religion was founded. It is simply the religion I know best.

It will take courage on our part to confront our deeply held spiritual and theological habits that have disempowered us in the past. It will take courage to stop denying our inner power. It will take courage to stop looking for someone else to save us. The time has come for us to grow up, to mature, and to accept the responsibility of adult spirituality. The time has come for us to engage in what Gandhi called "enlightened anarchism."

If we want to participate in the transformation of humanity's Soul, we will take back our power, withdraw legitimacy from any "religious authorities" who claim to dictate our spiritual meaning and purpose. It is time for us to start "author-izing" our own spiritual autobiographies. In Epoch III spiritual maturity, we have to write our own life story—it simply cannot and should not be plagiarized from some saint or savior out of the past. It can't be lived by proxy—we have to live it ourselves.

Once again, we can see evidence of this emerging all across the human landscape, flowering from the soil of souls in every nation, culture, ethnic group, and religion. This is confirmed by the massive "World Values Survey."

Conducted by the global coordinator of the survey Ronald Inglehart, as well as by more than eighty principal investigators, the survey covers forty-three societies that represent seventy percent of the world's population. The investigators found "deep rooted changes in mass world views [that] are reshaping economic, political, and social life."[31]

Relevant to our discussion is the fact that the survey detected a major shift throughout the world "away from *both* religious and bureaucratic authority, bringing declining emphasis on all kinds of authority"[32]:

> An empirically demonstrable cultural shift is taking place. The great religious and ideological metanarratives are losing their authority among the masses. The uniformity and hierarchy that shaped modernity are giving way to an increasing acceptance of diversity. [There is a] greater tolerance for ethnic, cultural, and sexual diversity and individual choice concerning the kind of life one wants to lead.[33]

There is, however, a special challenge for religious authorities in the midst of a Soul's transformation. If they see their role as conserving, preserving, and promoting answers from the past, the people who feel the democratic spirit emerging from their souls, those who are feeling more and more comfortable with quests and questions, as well as less and less tolerant with simply accepting the old answers—well, to put it bluntly, these people will walk their own meaning-filled spiritual path, while the "authorities" are left lonely, frustrated, and talking to themselves.

In contrast, those in religious leadership positions who affirm and facilitate the quest, who are not threatened by doubts and questions, and who will be "on the path" in communion with other seekers—those are the leaders of Epoch III religions.

Wade Clark Roof, a widely read and well-known observer of the American religious scene in particular, suggests that:

> To emphasize quest is to make the point that in an age when boundaries are especially permeable, when exchanges freely occur, spiritual searching should come as no surprise. . . .
>
> . . . [W]hat a person chooses, rather than what one is born into, becomes decisive. . . . [T]he notion that the individual is freed from the tutelage of religious institutions and therefore fully enfranchised for making religious decisions is widely accepted. . . .
>
> . . . [A]nother theme is introduced: self-authentication. For Americans, this means that one can—indeed, one ought to—choose how to engage the religious question, that is, how to think about believing and practicing, on the basis of one's own deepest spiritual sensibilities.[34]

Remember that the word *heretic* literally means "to choose." Sounds like what used to be cause for getting burned at the stake by the church—acting as if one were free to choose an unorthodox or a very personal spiritual path—has now become the Epoch III individual's burning desire for stoking the fires of enlightenment.

A Personal Quest for the Sacred

It seems as if I have always known that personal empowerment was an important ingredient in my spiritual journey. The powerful mystical experience that I described earlier, the experience that completely turned my life around at age twenty-two—my "call" to ministry, if you will—was *so* powerful and *so* personal that I felt I simply had to answer with as powerful and personal response as I was capable of. That meant that I needed to live as authentic a life as I could—authentic in discovering my power and authentic in offering my power in service to the world.

I felt certain that what I now call the Epoch II kinds of power—disempowering myself by projecting power externally or the ego-need to wield power over other people—had absolutely nothing to do with the authentic discovery and use of power to which I had been called.

Nevertheless, because we are still partly within Epoch II, there are two ways in which the value of this quest for one's power can be misunderstood. One is that to take this approach is to engage in some sort of self-centered, immature, or selfish endeavor. I completely reject that interpretation. After all, the experience that turned my life around was not an ordinary or generalized experience. It was not a group experience. It was not a cookie-cutter kind of experience. It was, rather, an extraordinary experience, specific, and powerfully personal. In that moment, *it was I* who was being called into a ministry of service—not a group, not a religion, not a community, not a gender, not a species, not any category at all: just I. The only appropriate response to that, it seemed to me, was to respond with all the capacity that God had created within me.

The other misunderstanding, or perhaps temptation, that sometimes flows out of having personal power-awakening experiences is the assumption that one's experience is, or should be, a model for others. It is not only arrogant for someone to think that his or her experience should be the experience of another, but it denies the principle of authenticity that I believe is at the heart of personal empowerment. Each of us must find our own power in the way that is authentic to our own sacred quest.

The following are some of the guideposts in my sacred quest for empowerment.

Establish Your Own Authenticity

Far too often, we deny authenticity by trying to emulate someone else's spiritual awakening. Instead of truly being oneself, one becomes a "wannabee" via imitation. Simply because the Buddha obtained his enlightenment while sitting under a bo tree, people should not assume that they will become enlightened if they can just find that particular tree and sit under it. Just because Jesus' life was turned around during and following his baptism in the River Jordan, we should not immerse ourselves in those waters with the assumption that we will have a similar experience. Just because Paul had a powerful mystical experience on the road to Damascus and Black Elk had his seminal vision on Harney Peak in South Dakota does not mean that we should return to those places and expect to duplicate their experience.

Each of us is unique, and our sacred quest must, at least to a great extent, be authentic to our uniqueness. We are each a special case of spiritualized matter, materialized spirit, and God incarnate. That special-case incarnation has a soul with unique power and responsibility, unique meaning and purpose. Our spiritual task, it seems to me, is to find out why, when, how, and where God is calling us personally to serve the world with the special power that is incarnate within us.

This is not to deny the value of community and shared worship and ritual. It is simply to say that, unless it involves empowered persons' coming together and respecting each other's authentic sacred quest, the relationships and communities will not be as empowered as they can be. The world needs the powerful synergy that results when individually empowered souls join together in shared celebration and in common tasks. Carbon copies of one authentic life, even if that were possible, and I believe it is not, do not enrich the world. What enriches the world and what contributes to the spiritual synergy between us are not duplication but addition and multiplication: one authentic life in relationship with another authentic life, and another and another, wherein the whole becomes more than the sum of the parts.

Clarence Page, the journalist and frequent television pundit, wrote a book entitled *Showing My Color: Impolite Essays on Race and Identity*. The title, he said, came from his parents' admonitions not to "show your color." Such advice is understandable given the discrimination, humiliation, abuse, injustice, and disempowerment that African Americans have had to endure in a racist culture. Page's "Impolite Essays," however, make the statement that his color is an important part of who he is and that he is not about to diminish his essential nature. Bravo, Mr. Page!

The spiritual empowerment of Epoch III challenges all of us to take pride in who we are and to contribute to the world that uniqueness. Our spiritual maturity is in need of, indeed matures because of, a world of human beings that live out a vibrant tapestry of texture and color.

Epoch II was filled with disempowering conventions, conformities, and discomforts thrust upon other people, constricting and restricting demands that you "don't show your colors," "stay in the closet," and "know your place." Or, as the British would say it, "keep your station." Charles Dickens wrote a mocking hymn regarding the latter in *The Chimes, Second Quarter*:

O let us love our occupations,
Bless the squire and his relations,
Live upon our daily rations,
And always know our proper stations.

Epoch III will be a time when we will show our colors, come out of the closet, intentionally leave our "place," and have no idea what it means to keep our proper station. It will be an epoch of profound and courageous spiritual liberation.

We have heard it said many times: we are made in the image of God. The way we honor that divinity within is not to blaspheme the God who looks like me, nor blaspheme the God who looks like you, or you, or you. This is what Patricia Reilly is getting at in a book directed at women: *A God Who Looks Like Me*. And it is what Native American Vine Deloria Jr. is getting at in his book: *God Is Red*. God is versatile and incognito in each of us. If you want to know what God looks like, look in the mirror—*and* look into the face and into the soul of all your brothers and sisters throughout the world. God has a plethora of personae, speaks many different languages, and worships in a wide range of rituals and songs.

Cultivate the Peregrine Spirit

One day I found myself flying next to the fastest animal on this planet—a peregrine falcon, whose very name means "beyond the borders." Well, okay, so I wasn't actually flying myself; I was aboard a Boeing 777 heading for Chicago and in the seat next to me was the falcon, tethered to, being cared for, and sitting majestically on the gloved hand of a young Air Force cadet.

The cadet was the falcon's trainer, and they were on their way to South Bend, Indiana, for a demonstration during half-time of the Air Force Academy and Notre Dame football game. In the demonstration, the cadet-trainer explained to me, the peregrine falcon would fly away from her hand, circle around and above the football stadium, soaring so high as to almost be out of sight, and then dive at speeds up to 220 miles per hour as it returned to her gloved hand, which held a morsel of food.

I was thrilled to spend a couple of rapturous hours within a few inches of this magnificent raptor. What a handsome profile! What a powerful countenance! And I communed with a sense of awe about the natural abilities that enabled this falcon to transcend borders and to fly at such incredible speeds.

I wondered what the world would look like through the peregrine's eyes. I wondered how my companion was different from her wild brothers and sisters, due to human controlling, blindfolding, tethering, and training. On the one hand, were it not for the latter, I would not have this close-up communion. On the other hand, I wonder if all that human intervention into the life of this bird transformed it into something other than true falcon-nature. There is something sad about that: for me to have a close-up appreciation of its magnificence, it might have to compromise its true nature.

I eventually found myself meditating on the wonderful symbol that the peregrine falcon spirit provided for spiritual empowerment in general and for my own quest in particular. We have all grown up, albeit to varying degrees, within an aura of "proper" boundaries and appropriate borders. Ideas about being civilized, appropriate, legitimate, reasonable, orthodox, safe, likable, agreeable—all to some extent are like fences keeping us within approved territory.

The wild uniqueness within us can be tamed by official religious dogma, institutional rules and regulations, family customs and traditions, or our own self-imposed shackles. The lives of "authorities" are made much easier and institutions tend to run much more efficiently if we are tame rather than wild. But a priority for tameness, comfort, efficiency, and ease may be dangerous to our soul-life, a hazardous ingredient that, when consumed, stunts the growth, development, maturation, and well-being of our sacred quest.

Ken Kesey's 1962 novel *One Flew Over the Cuckoo's Nest* is about the inmates of an insane asylum who live passive and obedient lives under the tyrannical and watchful eye of Big Nurse. McMurphy, one of the inmates, has the peregrine spirit, however, and is constantly breaking the rules and wants to lead the other inmates to freedom, to help them fly, if you will, beyond the borders of the asylum. In the process of trying to be a liberator, however, McMurphy discovers that none of the inmates is being kept there against his will. They *like* the security of Big Nurse's being in charge. They *like* the simplicity of having Big Nurse tell them what to do and when to do it. They fear freedom and choose childlike dependence over adult responsibility.

Voluntary incarceration can be just as disempowering as forced incarceration. But you and I live in one of the special transformational moments in history, when the case could be made that it is especially dangerous to our souls if we choose stasis and safety, comfort and conformity, order and orthodoxy. It is a time for the peregrine spirit to fly out over all the restricting and constricting borders that fence us in. The peregrine soul flips a wing at the borders and the boarder guards. The peregrine soul simply flies above and beyond them. The view is liberating and empowering.

I mentioned in the previous chapter my use of doubt early in my spiritual journey as a means of finding my authenticity spiritually and religiously. It has been a useful ongoing strategy, a process that keeps me aware of the necessity of humility in the face of the inevitable temptation to solidify and build rock walls around any religious answers that may make sense to me at a given time. It is a process that keeps me dancing with the Lord of the Dance, rather than idolizing monuments of my mind. And it is a process that keeps the peregrine spirit alive in me so that I do not voluntarily incarcerate myself within theological or philosophical prisons. The "Big Nurse" incarnation that most of us face is the "Big Authority" in a given religion, but our own legitimation of that authority imprisons us.

Someone a long time ago said that the trouble with editorial cartoons is that they cannot offer the "but, on the other hand." There is, of course, almost always a "but, on the other hand" for virtually any subject. The "other hand" in this subject is the value that comes from sitting still long enough so as to glean the depths of a tradition. The flighty life can sometimes forget the value of a nest. Spiritual dilettantes may be good at flying around, but they miss the value of a sustained encounter with a great tradition.

As much as I value doubting, searching, seeking, questing, and questioning, I also value my long and deep encounter with Christianity. I am all too aware of the historical warts on the face and the pathology in the soul of Christianity from time to time, but there is a spiritual depth and sacred power there for those who are willing to dive deeply into it. Certainly, the life and ministry of Jesus are models of spiritual maturity; he was at least one of God's major hints that Epoch III is both possible and probable. Today's noisy, antihistorical, fearful, and resistant Christian fundamentalists should not drown out the clear clarion call from within the Christian faith for an exodus and resurrection faith in the future.

My Christian faith never put shackles on my imagination, never tethered my spirit, and certainly never gave me a fear of exploring the unknown. Contrary to giving me a fear of the future and a desire to put my spiritual gears in reverse, Christianity as I have known it has provided a powerful hope in what God is creating before us. My faith has always drawn me to love the quest and the questions, the doubt and humility, as well as to love the discovery of the meaning and purpose in my soul's journey.

One of the most influential books in my spiritual journey was the wonderful 1972 book by John S. Dunne, a theologian at the University of Notre Dame, entitled *The Way of All the Earth*. I think part of why I liked it so much was that Dunne gave voice to that peregrine spirit within me, before I fully understood it myself. He affirmed the process of "passing over" to other cultures, viewpoints, religions, etc., learning from them, and then "coming back" to one's own roots. In the preface, Dunne summed up what would be the major thrust of his book, something that he saw emerging from the human Soul, and what he remarkably envisioned some three decades ago:

> The holy man of our time, it seems, is not a figure like Gotama or Jesus or Mohammed, a man who could found a world religion, but a figure like Gandhi, a man who passes over by sympathetic understanding from his own religion to other religions and comes back again with new insight to his own.[35]

I would add—and I suspect Dunne would also if he were writing that book today—that the phenomenon is, of course, just as applicable to women as to men.

Listen to Your Own Soul

There is an ancient fable in which God, angered that humanity had violated its divinity, decided to make it inaccessible and to conceal it in a place where the human being would least likely look. The council advising God first suggested that divinity be placed upon the highest mountain, higher than humanity could climb. "No," said God, "eventually they will learn to climb the highest mountain." "Then, let's hide divinity in the deepest sea, deeper than humanity can dive." Again God rejected the idea, saying that eventually humanity would learn how to dive into the deepest sea. Finally, the council hit upon the best idea: hide divinity down deep within the human soul, for that would be the last place people would think to look.

If one buys the basic assumption of the fable, which I don't— that God would *want* divinity to be inaccessible to humanity—then the story has great merit. However, even if we believe that God wants us to find, to awaken to, and to develop the divinity within, the story is right in that it seems to be the last place we tend to look.

Consider Epoch II Christianity, for instance, and the way most churches emphasized "attending" worship, "studying" the Bible, "participating" in the official rituals, "confessing" the ancient creeds, and "listening" to the preacher's sermons. But how many give equal emphasis to encouraging people to listen to their own souls through meditation, dreams, and intuition and to examine carefully the synchronicities and serendipities in their lives?

The latter disciplines have been central to my spiritual journey and my quest for the sacred. I believe that God has embedded in my soul a knowledge of its meaning and purpose, the reason for my particular special-case incarnation of divinity, the unique powers that God has given me. Nobody else can tell me what those are: I need to give priority to paying attention and to listening to my soul.

The left-brain intellectual capacity has obviously played an important role in my life's journey, which makes it all the more important that I give a balanced role to the skills and propensities of the right brain. A half-brained approach to discovering one's soul-power—either left or right brain alone—is simply not adequate. If I am not mistaken, Jesus, when asked what was the greatest commandment, did *not* say that we should "love the Lord our God with all our heart, all our strength, and just the left hemisphere of our minds."

Sometimes our soul speaks to us in harsh ways, perhaps because we have not heard the more gentle messages. Sometimes it is through failures, disasters, accidents, diseases, divorces, or even our dream nightmares that it communicates with us most effectively. The famous Swiss psychologist Carl Jung had it right when he said, "We do not become enlightened by imagining figures of light, but by making the darkness conscious."[36]

Most of our Epoch II left-brained approaches to religion have not encouraged such listening. Most of academia does not consider it legitimate, and certainly mainstream medical care would not put disease in the category of a soul's message. But Epoch III will bring us some surprises and blow out the walls of some of our orthodoxies.

If we will listen to all of its many voices, our soul will give us lessons of empowerment. I have written before of how one of my major lessons in empowerment came through a health crisis that resulted in years of severe pain, depression, and increased crippling, with medical authorities telling me that I would spend the rest of my life in pain, on strong drugs, and confined to a wheelchair. Eventually, however, I discovered the power that the experience was trying to communicate to me—the power within me to "author-ize" a new story of healing.[37]

And, speaking of a crisis . . .

A Case of Unexpected Empowerment

Before it happened, if you would have asked me if a sixty-four-year-old man could stop an enraged and charging momma bear in her tracks, I probably would have said, "No." I certainly would not have volunteered to give it a try.

In June of 1999, we became aware of a family of black bears being "in the neighborhood." Papa Bear was pretty much off doing his own thing, coming in from time to time to see if there was any food around and then leaving. Momma Bear and her three cubs, however, were my primary concern. Her obvious and total dedication to protect and safeguard her three cubs was fascinating and admirable, but also cause for me to make sure that our dog, Gypsy-Bear, was inside the house when they were around. (I was soon to discover the irony of our naming the dog Gypsy-Bear.) I knew that the most volatile situation, if not potentially a disastrous one, would be to have Gypsy-Bear chase or make any move that would appear to threaten those cubs.

The degree of sensitivity on the part of Momma Bear and the intensity of her commitment to the cubs' protection were evident when I would slip out onto the far side of our upper deck and quietly move to where I could get a picture of any or all of them. The moment she would hear the shutter click on my camera, even though I was sometimes forty or fifty yards from them, she would immediately chase the cubs back to the wooded ridge to the west of our home, periodically stopping to check if I, or anyone else, were following them. The slightest sound or smell would set this frantic retreat into motion, and although I did not intend for it to happen, I was impressed at Momma Bear's total dedication to her cubs' safety and amazed at how quickly her cubs knew when she wanted them to run to the ridge and down the side of the mountain.

Consequently, during this volatile time, I would let Gypsy-Bear outside only after I had carefully checked to make sure Momma and her cubs were not around, and then would go out with her. But then it happened—I made a terrible mistake and Gypsy-Bear and I were in a major crisis.

It was about 5:00 PM when Gypsy-Bear let me know that she needed to "go" outside. I had, a couple of hours earlier, seen Momma Bear and her cubs head off in their usual westward direction and down the side of the mountain. So I looked in that direction, did not see them, and thought it was safe to let Gypsy-Bear out to the front of our house, which is to the south. As usual, I followed her out.

I stood on the front porch watching Gypsy-Bear head to the south when, all of a sudden, I saw her head turn quickly to her right, and she was immediately off and running to the west, barking all the way. I instantly knew that we were in big, big trouble. I yelled at her to stop, but she was consumed with the chase. I ran after her, continuing to yell for her to stop, but she soon was out of my sight around the west side of our house. As I got to the southwest corner of the house, I was confronted with a scene that I did not want to see.

The three bear cubs were running to their usual exit spot on the western ridge. Gypsy-Bear was doing a very rapid 180-degree turn, with an enraged Momma Bear, foaming at the mouth, with eyes afire, totally enraged, and completely consumed with getting Gypsy-Bear. They were about twenty yards away from me, both coming right at me in a full sprint. Gypsy-Bear is a Belgian Sheepdog, and she can run very fast. However, I understand that black bears can almost instantly be running at about thirty to thirty-five miles an hour. Needless to say, I did not have a radar-gun in my hand, but I can tell you that they were both coming directly at me at a substantial rate of speed.

There was no time to think, and the following reactions and instincts seemingly took place instantaneously. But imagine, if you will, the following all happening at once, with Gypsy-Bear and Momma Bear bearing down on me at warp speed.

The first thought I had was that I was about to see Gypsy-Bear killed. Since they were running directly at me, I cannot be sure of the distance between them, but my guess is that there was no more than three or four feet between the tail end of my dog and the foaming mouth of Momma Bear. I was also amazed at how instantly Momma Bear could be foaming at the mouth and with such incredible volume. It was not a trickle. It was not a flow. It was like Niagara Falls pouring out of her mouth. She was really, and I mean *REALLY*, enraged.

My immediate instinct was that the only way I could save Gypsy-Bear's life was if I could get the Momma Bear's attention, and the only way I could do that was if I could match or exceed the intensity and the power of her rage.

I jumped up on the picnic table that was beside me and started waving my arms, yelling as loud as I possibly could, trying to project all the power and intensity of which I was capable.

When the two were seemingly a split-second from being on top of me, Momma Bear took her eyes off Gypsy-Bear, glanced at me with a surprised look in her eyes, put on the breaks, reared up on her hind legs, and came down on all fours, with her and me eyeball to eyeball. I later measured it, and we were about eight feet apart when she came to a stop.

Something quite phenomenal happened in that next moment. I have no idea as to how long we actually looked into each other's eyes—probably only a very few moments—but time seemed to stand still, and I spent what felt like an eternity in communion with the spirit in and behind those eyes. There was a profound sense of communication with her. I felt that she understood my respect for her desire to protect her cubs and my admiration for her intensity and power on behalf of their defense. At the same time, she seemed to understand that I, too, intensely wanted to protect my "child."

Gypsy-Bear had streaked past me when Momma Bear and I had this confrontation and, when I got to thinking about it, I presumed she had run to our front door.

Thinking that the confrontation was at least neutralized, I wanted to let Momma Bear know that I meant no aggression or harm to her, that my only concern was to end the encounter. Consequently, I slowly stepped down from the picnic table and gradually started backing up towards our front door, still watching Momma Bear very intently.

She stayed where she was as I slowly backed up, and I was beginning to relax, thinking that the crisis was about over. But then, Momma Bear's head turned suddenly to her right, and her attention was on something out in front of our house. I made a quick glance to see what had drawn her attention—it was Gypsy-Bear who, instead of waiting at the front door for me, had circled back around to the south. It almost looked like Gypsy-Bear was now trying to distract the Momma Bear and return the favor of saving me. But now I thought that the entire crisis would resume since it was Gypsy-Bear, who had been the initial cause of Momma Bear's anger.

I yelled at Gypsy-Bear to "get into the house," and out of the corner of my eye saw her start running towards the front door. My attention was still primarily on Momma Bear, and as I recall, I was still verbally and telepathically trying to assure her that I meant no harm and just wanted us all to go home safely. I was still only about fifteen feet from her, however, and she still looked very angry, with fire in her eyes and foam pouring profusely out of her mouth.

I continued to back up slowly towards our front door. I knew that I needed to get both Gypsy-Bear and myself inside the house before I could be sure the danger would be over. Trying to time my move with Gypsy-Bear's arrival at the front door, still watching Momma Bear very closely, I finally turned and ran the final fifteen feet or so to the door. Gypsy-Bear was, indeed, there waiting for me and we both got inside.

Finally inside, safe I thought, I turned only to see that Momma Bear was at the door looking in at us. Knowing that that flimsy front door would not stop that bear and knowing that it was Gypsy-Bear at whom she was raging, I looked to see if Gypsy-Bear was still in sight. Fortunately, she had done the smart thing: she had run upstairs and was hiding under the dining room table.

The next scene was Momma Bear's pacing back and forth out on the west side of the house and my pacing back and forth on our second-floor deck—both of us having an excessive amount of adrenalin pumping through our bodies and both of us having more to say. I can't describe the heaving sounds that came out of Momma Bear, but we had some more "conversation" before she eventually went to the western ridge where her cubs were waiting, disappeared down the mountainside, and I went into the house to reflect on what had just happened.

Diana was not at home during this entire event—thankfully. Interestingly enough, however, she called just a few moments after it was all over, to ask if everything was all right. She had intuited that something was going on. Indeed!

In the days following that confrontation, I thought about and meditated on the experience a lot. There were three particular ingredients that I wanted to understand more fully. One was why I would instinctively assume that I could muster the power and intensity with which to stop a raging black bear. Friends to whom I would tell this story would ask me, quite understandably, if I was frightened. Or they would simply assume that I was scared to death throughout the experience. All of that would seem logical. Or they would offer the advice that I should have run and simply sacrificed Gypsy-Bear, so as to make sure that I would get into the safety of my home.

All the logic and joking aside, however, that is not what happened. In fact, I never experienced a moment of fear throughout that entire crisis. Nor do I recall a single thought about saving myself and letting Gypsy-Bear fend for herself. But why? Why did I not have any fear? It's not as if I had previous experiences in stopping raging bears—at least, not in this lifetime. I eventually came to believe that the answer to that question was related to my second question.

Where did that power come from, to be able to generate enough intensity to match Momma Bear's? How and why did I trust it so much that I had no fear? I have had other experiences in my life, although this may have been the most extreme, in which I somehow felt that there was virtually an unlimited source of power on which I could draw. Following a number of meditations on this, I now believe that all of us have that source of power available to us: it just takes a crisis sometimes to remind us of that.

Think about it. If each of us is truly spiritualized matter and materialized spirit and if the theological idea of panentheism is right—that the power of God is incarnate within every cell of our being—then doesn't it follow that the power of God is somehow available for us? I am aware that in normal, ordinary, regular consciousness—the consciousness within which most of us spend most of our days—this sounds quite outrageous. Nevertheless, it just may be that you and I have access to much more power than we have traditionally thought. It may be that we have allowed some of the Epoch II habitual ways of thinking to convince us of our powerlessness and that part of the emerging spiritual maturity is to recognize and trust the enormous resource of power on which we can draw. While today it may take a crisis to awaken us to that power, in some tomorrow, some day in the future of Epoch III, neither you nor I will look upon this as skeptically as we do now. We will know God's power and trust the democratization of access to that power.

The third matter on which I have spent a good deal of time meditating was that moment when time seemed to stand still, and Momma Bear and I were eyeball to eyeball. Some extraordinary communication took place in that moment. Once again, there has been nothing in my current lifetime that would seem to make sense of it. But what I felt was a profound shamanic at-one-ment with the spirit and energy of that bear.

Remember our earlier discussion, in chapter one, about how some contemporary research suggests that some of the paleolithic cave wall paintings were done while in a shamanic trance? And remember that, while in that altered state of consciousness, the shaman can communicate with his or her power animal and, in the final stage, becomes one with the animal.

I don't presume to understand completely what happened in that moment of communication; I only know that it was extraordinary. What came through to me in meditation was that it was a shamanic experience. There was a deep and profound sense of mutual understanding and communication—my respect for and understanding of the bear's instinctual protection of her cubs and the reason for her rage against the dog, while at the same time, her understanding of and respect for my need to protect my "child."

In some mysterious way, all three of those questions are tied together. It was a profound experience, and I feel extremely fortunate to have had it. I still have a lot to learn from it; but, in some way, it exemplifies the power available to all of us, as well as the powerful communication possible between the human and the animal worlds. It was, all in all, an incredibly privileged experience.

It would seem that most of the empowerment that awaits us in the Epoch III evolutionary purpose of spiritual maturation will come simply by eliminating the barriers that humanity's adolescent epoch erected. We eliminate the barriers and we expand our sense of self—empowered, we will be uncommon as well as common, paranormal as well as normal, supernatural as well as natural, metaphysical as well as physical, esoteric as well as exoteric, and right-brained as well as left-brained. We will have a shamanic experience with our peregrine nature and fly high over restrictive borders and boundaries. But, most of all, we will have the courage to be our unique selves and serve the world with that gift.

I conclude this discussion on empowerment with a benediction I first heard when it was given by the Reverend Nancy Bauer-King of Racine, Wisconsin:

May you live until the word of your life is fully spoken.

Questions for Those on a Quest

To quest is to question,
and sometimes the quality of our spiritual quest
has more to do with the questions we ask today
than with answers entombed within past dogma.

1. What do you think are the primary threats to democracy in the twenty-first century?
2. What do you believe will be the future of warfare? Of slavery?
3. How do you feel about America's past failures regarding its democratic ideals, as well as its progress? What do you believe are the strongest forces resisting democracy in America today?
4. How do you see technology's role in the future of democracy?
5. What has been your experience of religious authoritarianism?
6. What traditional religious language do you find disempowering?
7. How will you think about God in Epoch III? What new theological language and metaphors do you think will be helpful and liberating?
8. In what ways, if any, have you remained voluntarily disempowered or been afraid of your own spiritual power?
9. How are you taking over the author-izing of your spiritual autobiography?
10. What means do you use to discover your soul's purpose?
11. What constitutes an authentic life for you?
12. How do you manifest the "peregrine spirit" in your life?
13. What role do dreams, meditation, intuition, and serendipities play in discovering and manifesting your spiritual power?

Chapter Seven

The Spirituality of Time

In any attempt to bridge the domains of experience belonging to the spiritual and physical sides of our nature, time occupies the key position.

Arthur Stanley Eddington, *The Nature of the Physical World*[1]

The human Soul is on the grow—and it's about time.

Time, in fact, is central to our entire discussion about the human journey. Both the maturational and journey metaphors assume the passage of time. The fundamental paradigm of science—evolution—is just another way of saying that time is central, that there is a process of development in the universe, on planet Earth, for life in general and for human life in particular.

This entire book is about spiritual evolution, my conviction that humanity's Soul is on a journey of maturation—that it is evolving, changing, periodically going through major punctuations or radical transformations; that we are currently living in the midst of just such a transformation; and that individuals on the sacred quest can grow an integrity between their lives and the larger evolutionary time of their lives. It is about change and maturation. It is about evolving and growing a humanity capable of greater love, justice, equality, and empowerment. In other words, it is about becoming more fully human by growing into greater maturity. It is all about time.

It is not surprising, therefore, that one of the primary emergent Epoch III deep values has to do with changing our relationship with time. The experience of time for an adolescent is not the same as the experience of time for a mature adult. As a species, humanity has gone through a ten- thousand-year adolescent epoch in which we feared time, denied that time existed, or trivialized time by claiming it was an illusion. (We'll look at the details of that fear, denial, and trivialization in just a moment.) Adult spiritual maturity is now our evolutionary challenge, and growing a more mature relationship with time—discovering the spirituality in and of time—is the fourth and final emergent deep value of Epoch III.

Because the spirituality of time is the most recent of all the Epoch III deep values to emerge from the human Soul, we are less familiar with it than we are with the other three, and it may very well turn out to be the most difficult for us to confront. It may, in fact, be the most controversial of all four. At an emotional level, time may be the most threatening of all the Epoch III deep values and may call for more religious and spiritual courage than we have had to muster on all the other emergent deep values put together.

At first blush, that warning may sound ridiculous. After all, we deal with time every day. The flow of time is certainly not unfamiliar to us. In fact, a case could be made that we like time so much we are totally preoccupied with it. We constantly ask, "What time is it?" We wear watches on our wrists and have clocks in virtually every room of our homes, in our cars, and in our computers. Calendars are big business. We love to spend time massaging memories about the past. We worry about or regret what we have said or done in the past. We invest time in planning, wishing, hoping, and dreaming about the future. We *must* absolutely love time because we talk about it constantly—we try to be on time, we don't like to waste time, and, once in a while, we just feel like killing time.

We certainly make a big deal about our creation stories—stories about when time began. We seem determined to describe different generations in time—the "me" generation, the baby boomer generation, generation X, etc. We recently spent a great deal of time considering the end of a decade, concentrating on the end of a century, and becoming downright manic about the turn of the millennium. And consider the money and energy expended on exterminating the Y2K computer bug. The evidence from our daily existence seems to suggest that we really love time. So how can it be said that we fear, ignore, or trivialize the role of time?

We need only look a little more deeply. When we consider the issue just a little more carefully, we can see that, in spite of all the superficial preoccupation with time, when it comes to the largest contexts within which we live or what we consider to be the really important levels of human existence, we don't want anything to do with time. We may have to deal with time in the here and now, in the daily, seasonal, and annual cycles; but in the fundamental structure of the universe or in our ideas about God, heaven, and "eternal life"—in other words, in the hereafter—we have not wanted time to play any role at all. At those levels, we have desperately wanted—indeed needed—stability, certainty, and dependability, all of which make time the enemy. If time is real, we can't have stability. If time is real, we can't have certainty. If time is real, we can't have dependability.

On the other hand, if we want creativity, novelty, change, a journey of discovery, maturation, evolution, revolution, or transformation, then we have to reconcile ourselves to the flow of time.

The extraordinary South American writer Jorge Luis Borges wrote about how modern science had apparently proven that time is an illusion:

> And yet, and yet . . . denying temporal succession, denying the self, denying the astronomical universe, are apparent desperations and secret consolations. . . . Time is the substance I am made of. Time is a river which sweeps me along, but I am the river; it is the tiger which destroys me, but I am the tiger; it is a fire which consumes me; but I am the fire. The world, unfortunately, is real; I, unfortunately, am Borges.[2]

Borges recognizes that time is real; he just thinks it is an unfortunate realization. What is unfortunate, however, is that Borges is not alone—the human species has a long-held and deeply entrenched discomfort with time. We have existentially feared time because it involves aging and dying, we have conceived of the ultimate religious reward as being an escape from time, and we have scientifically trivialized time because it got in the way of what Epoch II science considered to be the primary goal—obtaining the holy grail of scientific certainty, control, and repeatability.

"And yet, and yet. . . ." We have now arrived at the point in the human maturational journey when our primary evolutionary purpose is that of spiritual development, and one of the four major ingredients in becoming spiritually mature is discovering the positive role of time. We are on the threshold of discovering that time is in everything sacred, and the sacred is in everything having to do with the flow of time. The time has come for us to confront and deal with our fear, discomfort, and trivialization of time, so that we can begin to experience the spirituality in and of time.

In may be helpful to clarify what our Epoch II adolescent experience of time has been, before considering what a spiritually mature experience will look like—a look back at where we have been, before envisioning where we are going.

The Epoch II Experience of Time

The Cyclical Experience of Time

The ancient Greeks, astrologers, as well as native and indigenous peoples began with assuming that time ran around in circles. Time was "real" only in bringing us back to where we started. Who would have thought otherwise? After all, we had no science back then that contradicted our primary experience of daily, monthly, and annual cycles within cycles within cycles. The sun came up today just as it did yesterday, and then it disappeared just as it did yesterday, only to repeat the cycle again and again. The moon waxed and then waned in a regular monthly cycle, and then did it again, again, and again. Planting season came around, predictably, just as it did last year. The solstice and the equinox were regular and dependable. Time and change, it appeared, repeated in a timely fashion, so that the fundamental structure of the universe remained essentially timeless, stable, predictable, and dependable.

Although changes were seen and experienced, it was thought that those changes existed within a larger unchanging reality of predictable and recurring cycles. "There is necessarily some change in the whole world," wrote Aristotle, "but not in the way of coming into existence or perishing, for the universe is permanent."[3]

Consequently, when people thought about the really big picture, they simply enlarged the same cyclical pattern. The larger the context, the larger the cycle. Daily cycles were part of monthly cycles, which were part of annual cycles, which were part of universal and heavenly cycles. There was no real sense of history, no fundamental passage of time. Time was thought to be a renewable resource, running around in circles and eventually coming back to the same place. Reflecting on this ancient paradigm of non-time, Henri-Charles Puech writes:

> No event is unique, nothing is enacted but once . . .; every event has been enacted, is enacted, and will be enacted perpetually; the same individuals have appeared, appear, and will appear at every turn of the circle.[4]

Then, the ancient Israelites came along with a major innovation regarding time.

The Jewish Invention of the Concept of History

The Israelites, the people who were to become the Jews, were the first to break the cycle. They invented history and introduced the idea that there was a beginning of time, a flow of time and, presumably therefore, an end of time.

As important as the invention of history was—and make no mistake about it, this was an important and seminal invention—the critical part for our discussion here is that the Israelites only went half-way with the idea of time. In their invention of historical time, they envisioned it as applicable only to the human and earthly realms, whereas Yahweh and the heavenly realms were still assumed to be timeless and eternal. We will return to the implications of going only half-way in a few moments, but for now, let's stick to the remarkable and influential side of their invention.

The stories of Abraham and Moses, and by implication the entire Jewish people, were stories of Yahweh's acting in human history, calling them to a journey with a particular destiny. "Let my people go" was not only a call liberating the Israelites from slavery in Egypt, but it was also a call for escaping the endless cycles of time. This invention of history and the start of taking the flow of time seriously turned out to be one of the most significant innovations in human history—in fact, we would probably not even use that phrase "human history" were it not for this gift from the Jews. Christianity and Islam grew out of the same soil of Soul and also counted themselves as heirs of Abraham. And, although Eastern religions continued to think in cyclical terms, the idea of history and the flow of time in the human realm have had a wide influence throughout the world.

The implications of the invention of history are huge. Thomas Cahill writes:

> The Israelites, by becoming the first people to live—psychologically—in real time, also became the first people to value the New and to welcome Surprise. In doing this, they radically subverted all other ancient worldviews.[5]

Before the Israelites, the stories people told were for the purpose of keeping the archetypical and eternal wisdom alive, so that we would know it when and as it returned again and again. With the Israelites, however, genealogy became serious business. So, too, did the process of writing an accurate account of the past, not because it would be repeated, but precisely because the past is important in helping a people to know the journey they are on and to understand the trajectory of where they are going. Past, present, and future took on a whole new level of meaning as a result of the Jewish conception of time.

The Jews put the lie to the old phrase "history repeats itself." Myth repeats itself. Cycles repeat themselves. But history is precisely the realization that *nothing* repeats. Every moment is a new moment in history. Human experience is always new, alive, changing, and different with every moment. Another lie is "there is nothing new under the sun." *Everything* under the sun is becoming new and changing again every moment. Again, Thomas Cahill comments:

> The future will not be what has happened before; indeed, the only reality that the future has is that it has not happened yet. . . . For this reason the concept of the future—for the first time—holds out promise, rather than the same old thing. We are not doomed, not bound to some predetermined fate; we are free.[6]

This was a bold step in the growth and maturation of the human Soul. For the first time, there was a context for hope: hope in an open future pregnant with possibilities of new life, hope in the promise that something new is not only possible but inevitable, and hope rooted in the fact that not only individuals but entire peoples are called to live out unique spiritual journeys. We will be exploring these and other Epoch III implications of taking time seriously later in this chapter.

An interesting side note to our discussion of "human history" is the fact that the Sumerians, the very people who invented one of the most important tools for recording history—namely, writing—did not themselves believe in history. The culture of Sumer was like the rest of the ancients, a timeless culture assuming endless cycles within cycles.

It is not terribly surprising that, when the Jews invented history, their first steps into that bold understanding of time were, certainly by today's standards, very small steps. The Jews assumed that God created the world in 3760 BC, thus starting the flow of all history at that time. Christians, following in the footsteps of the Jews, took the scriptural record of genealogy to be an accurate and literal account of history. Consequently, counting back the biblical "begats," Christians came up with some interesting conclusions regarding the beginning of time. And, interestingly enough, they were not all the same. Eusebius, chairman of the Council of Nicea, in the fourth century AD decided that there were 3,184 years between the births of Adam and Abraham. Saint Augustine decided that the moment of creation occurred in 5500 BC; Isaac Newton chose 3988 BC, whereas Johannes Kepler picked 3993 BC.

The most fastidious and fascinating estimate, however, came from the seventeenth century. Bishop James Ussher of Armagh, Ireland, decided, with great care and in ludicrous detail, that "the beginning of time . . . fell on the beginning of the night which preceded the 23rd day of October, in the year . . . 4004 BC."[7] We modern and postmodern Americans know, of course, that Bishop Ussher was terribly wrong—the world could not possibly have been created in October, since football season begins in September!

As we mentioned earlier, the invention of history was conceptually applicable only to human history—the human realm may be within the flow of time, but God and heaven still existed beyond and outside of time. While that represents a fundamental trivialization of time, it signifies an understandable emotional need, during humanity's adolescent epoch, to want the ultimate context to be dependable, reliable, stable, unchanging, and safely eternal. In other words, we might have to put up with the vicissitudes of time while in this earthly life, we may have to deal with unpredictability and change in the here and now, but if we are good and religious little boys and girls, we will be rewarded with an escape from time in the eternal hereafter.

That trivialization and reduction of time, limiting history to the human realm while maintaining eternal timelessness in the heavenly and Godly realms, is not the fault of the Jews per se. The adolescent emotional need to split human-time and God-time preceded the Jewish people. The Jews, in their bold invention of history, simply did not take it all the way.

Virtually all of Epoch II humanity assumed the human and divine differentiation regarding time. Western religions accepted the Jewish notion of human history but kept the notion of God's eternal timelessness. Eastern religions kept the cyclical notion of time in the human realm, but they, too, considered the ultimate spiritual reality to be timeless. Jews, Christians, and Muslims call the timeless hereafter eternity, the Hindus call it *moksha* (which means total release), and the Buddhists call it *nirvana* (which means to extinguish). Huston Smith, whom many consider to be the greatest living authority on world religions, defines nirvana in Buddhism as "permanent, stable, imperishable, immovable, ageless, deathless, unborn, and unbecome . . . the shelter, the place of unassailable safety."[8]

Few of us in Epoch II, even great spiritual gurus, saints, saviors, seers, and prophets, had the courage to take time seriously enough to take it all the way. Adolescent humanity had the immature emotional need for a security blanket, needed the ultimate spiritual realm to provide us with comforting stability, the sense of certainty, theological absolutes, and emotional dependability. Even when the flow of history and the seriousness of time were introduced into Western religions, we could only take it half-way.

It may shock some religious sensibilities to see us using terms like "adolescence," "security blankets," and "immature emotional needs" when referring to the world's great religions and the most esteemed of religious figures of the past. Those words are used, however, not simply to be harsh or to shock. Our purpose here is to try to be as accurate as possible regarding the nature and content of the history of the human Soul in general and the new emerging Soul in particular. As we have already suggested, this deep value may be the most controversial of all four, precisely because it may be the toughest for us to handle emotionally. One of the most interesting historical phenomena is how fundamentalism flairs up when changes threaten traditional religious principals or when chaos rips emotional security blankets out of our hands. Fundamentalists are easy targets for those of us who do not share their fear of change. But can we, or should we, learn something from them?

It may be that fundamentalism, of whatever ilk, provides a mirror that reflects some of the deepest fears and insecurities that we all share. It is a mirror, and we should not be thrown off by the fact that it is a *magnifying* mirror. Fundamentalists accurately perceive some of the toughest emotional challenges brought about by change. They just react to change in an exaggerated, magnified manner.

Fundamentalism is blatantly antihistorical, believing, as one pundit quipped, that God wrote the Bible and then died. Thus, instead of being open to the fact that spiritual reality might be evolutionary, that God might be creating the world via the process of evolution, they must hold tightly to the idea of creationism, the notion that God created humanity, as Genesis suggests, just six-thousand years ago looking precisely as we do now. The idea that God could be creating life over time is rejected because time itself is a scary prospect to the Epoch II Soul. But we have all been antihistorical in some regards.

The effects of needing to preserve timelessness are pernicious. Consider violence as just one example. One does not have to read very far in the Bible to find a God who is extraordinarily vindictive and violent, commanding the Israelites to kill all the Canaanites, even their children. If we do not believe that God changes over time or if we do not believe that, with the passage of time, our understanding of God can progress, grow, change, or evolve beyond what it was in biblical times, then how will we ever move beyond our violent behavior? Violence, in the antihistorical mind, was—therefore, is—ordained by God. If God dealt with enemies violently, why shouldn't we adopt the same divine strategy?

Throughout Epoch II, the past was worshiped. Religious scriptures, ancient wisdom, past revelations of "truth," the lives and experiences of founding religious icons, traditional doctrine and dogma—all held central and important positions. Epoch II religions excommunicated members, defrocked clergy, and fought to the death to defend the past and to insist upon conformity to past beliefs and ideals. Creativity and individualism were, therefore, enemies of and threats to the well-defined boundaries of faith. Fundamentalism simply takes this attitude to the extreme.

There is a particularly dangerous pitfall, always lurking in the unconscious underbrush of religions—the conviction that religion or spirituality possesses divinely revealed truth, unfiltered and unblemished by human interpretation. "God says" is the preface to our moral and theological pronouncements, rather than any humble admission that such pronouncements are our *interpretations* of divine will and purpose. "The Bible says" frequently baptizes our own biases and our own wishes with supposedly sacred and infallible holy water. We use, abuse, and misinterpret scripture because we need the security blanket of an absolute and unchanging, unaltered and unadulterated past.

When we fear the flow of time and when we idolize the past, we fall all too easily into such pits. Ken Wilber says it is time to climb to the surface:

> It is time, then, to have done with our sickly yearning for yesteryear, our morbid fixation to Mother Past, our preposterous groveling at any doctrine whose only authority comes from the fact that it was uttered by a really really ancient sage, centuries or preferably millennia ago. For, ironically enough, our fixation to the past comes only from our fear of death in the present: unable to die to our egos, we latch onto the permanence and fixity of the past as a substitute immortality project. The corpse of yesteryear becomes our morbid refuge, our rancid immortality.[9]

Wilber's words may strike us as rather harsh, somewhat like our earlier consideration of the admonition to "Kill the Buddha." But, as we suggested in the previous chapter, harsh language may indicate that we face a tough challenge. In that regard, Wilber is not overstating the issue.

The challenge of changing our notions about time, however, is not limited only to the religious and spiritual realms. Epoch II science played the same game, participated in the same ambivalence, and demonstrated some of the same fear in taking time seriously.

The Epoch II Scientific Fear of Time

As we discussed in chapter two, the historical period that we identified as the Prodigal Son era saw the emergence of modern or classical science. The Bubonic Plague of the fourteenth century and the resultant enormous sense of helplessness, of hopelessness, and of being out-of-control gave birth to the Prodigal Son. Worship of God did not give us the security and safety we needed nor the control and predictability over our lives that we wanted.

It is not surprising, therefore, that certainty and predictability became the central premise, the strongest promise, and the most powerful expectation of classical science. One of the most influential architects of classical science was René Descartes, who thought that the purpose of science was to obtain certainty. Even more than that, he thought that such certainty was possible and achievable.

Science became our late Epoch II defacto religion, our truth-giver and our salvation. Clearly, if the holy grail of classical science was certainty and predictability, time would be feared, discounted, and necessarily trivialized.

We also considered how Isaac Newton, another of the prime architects of Epoch II classical science, conceived of the universe as strictly deterministic, a theory and an emphasis that makes it impossible to take time's unpredictability seriously.

The consequence was that, in the classical Cartesian–Newtonian scientific paradigm, time was neither a factor nor a threat. With the basic premise, promise, and expectation of certainty, control, and repeatability, time had to be irrelevant to the basic "laws" of science. And so it was.

Ironically, in the use of mechanistic metaphors that were, and are, so prevalent in scientific and popular thinking, the clock was a favorite mechanistic device. We live in a clockwork universe, our scientific fathers told us, created by the Master Clockmaker who then retreated into the background so that the universe could run on its own. A healthy human being, as Descartes put it, is like "a well-made clock." Nevertheless, since time on the clock just goes around in circles—this was before digital clocks—there was nothing to fear. Clock time never really took classical scientists to any uncertain or unpredictable place.

Science, therefore, although coming onto the human scene with such promise to save us from the premodern religious ignorance and superstition, actually ended up with the same fear, denial, and trivialization of time. Epoch II modern science had the same emotional need for stability, dependability, predictability, and control, as did Epoch II religion before it.

Science eventually did awaken to the reality of time—but it, too, could only take it half-way.

Just as the Israelites brought history into the religious sphere, but only took the flow of time half-way, classical science, in the nineteen century, also invented a half-way flow of time. In the nineteenth century, science discovered evidence for the flow of time in certain areas, but still maintained that the universe at large was in a "steady state"—in other words, the largest context that science could consider, it believed, was timeless, unchanging, and eternal.

Science discovered that "down here" there was "an arrow of time," suggesting that time was actually going somewhere. The problem was that two different sciences—physics and biology—discovered the arrow as pointing in two very different directions.

Physics, in its second law of thermodynamics, said that the arrow of time pointed downward, what is popularly known as entropy. Everything is running downhill toward "heat death." It was a very pessimistic notion of time, with time "going to hell in a handbasket" and taking all of us with it.

Biology, on the other hand, discovered that life over time progressed from the simple to the complex. Life was evolutionary, and the evolutionary "arrow of time" pointed upwards. It was an optimistic notion of life and time: we are, indeed, going somewhere, biology asserted, and that somewhere is not down but up. Instead of going to hell in a handbasket, we are going to heaven on the wings of evolving life.

We do not need to get into a thorough discussion here of entropy or of biological evolution; our purpose is simply to point out how the two concepts came along late in our adolescent epoch and began transforming the scientific notions of time. Still, both physics and biology began taking time seriously, but with the same attitude that characterized the Jewish notion of time.

Two "E" words—entropy and evolution—applied to some of the universe, but the really big "E" word—eternity—applied to only the largest and most important context. Time and change may take place in the down here, but in the up there, time is irrelevant and nonexistent. The universe, Epoch II science maintained, is in a state of timelessness and eternal stability. It was, to use the scientific term for it, in a "steady-state."

Cosmology and theology are two ways of trying to describe the biggest context we can consider. Cosmology is the way science tries to talk about the largest and ultimate context, whereas theology (God talk) is the way most religions try to describe the largest and ultimate context. In Eastern religions, human time goes around in cycles, but the ultimate spiritual sphere is timeless and eternal. In Western religions, after the gift of the Jews, humanity is thought to be on a historical journey, but God and heaven are timeless and eternal.

Regarding scientific cosmological thinking, another "E" word—Einstein—provides a fascinating illustration of the transition from Epoch II science to Epoch III science, particularly in regard to time. Albert Einstein, the very name we use to symbolize intellectual genius, dramatically illustrated how strong the emotional need may be for dependability, stability, and changelessness. In fact, Einstein showed us how emotional need can overwhelm even the greatest of minds.

In a cosmological frame of reference, an expanding universe would be the opposite of a "steady-state" universe. In the former, time would be real; in the latter, time would be irrelevant.

Einstein was deeply attached to the emotional need for a steady-state universe, certain that the universe *must* be stable, static, and dependable. "God," he said in a famous and oft-quoted statement, "does not play dice with the universe." Consequently, Einstein concluded and proclaimed over and over again that "time is an illusion." So much did Einstein need a steady-state universe that he actually fudged his mathematics in order to conceive of a universe that would behave as he wanted.

Cambridge University professor Stephen Hawking, the man who is widely regarded as the most brilliant theoretical physicist since Einstein, explains: "[W]hen he formulated the general theory of relativity in 1915 [Einstein] was so sure that the universe had to be static that he modified his theory to make this possible, introducing a so-called cosmological constant into his equations."[10]

In 1924, Einstein wrote a letter to fellow physicist Max Born, in which he said that, if he had to abandon strict causality—another way of saying that time was a nonfactor—he "would rather be a cobbler, or even an employee in a gaming house, than a physicist."[11] Einstein desperately needed the universe to be stable, static, steady-state, dependable, and predictable. But Einstein's scientific conviction and emotional need were the same as the Epoch II religious conviction and emotional need. Einstein used a mathematical "cosmological constant," Epoch II religion used various forms of a theological constant: in all cases, it was rationalizing adolescent emotional need.

To Einstein's credit, and what reveals his true greatness, he was willing to have his mind changed. He was open to being convinced by the evidence, and he later humbly admitted that his emotional need for a "cosmological constant" led him into distorting his own theory of relativity—what Einstein called "the biggest blunder" of his entire career.

Like us duffers watching a professional golfer miss a two-foot putt, knowing that Einstein let his emotional needs override his brilliant intellect—well, it sort of lets us common folk feel like our blinders and our blunders are not that bad after all.

Epoch III: Taking Time All the Way

By the early twentieth century a galaxy of minds . . . sought new meaning in the very processes of change. Abandoning the breathless quest for absolutes, exhilarated by the flux of the unexpected, they learned to enjoy the mystery in the flow of experience. . . . In place of eternal ideas, they would adore the vitality of an ever-changing world.

Daniel J. Boorstin[12]

Twentieth-century sciences—particularly relativity and quantum physics, chaos and complexity theory, nonequilibrium physics, and the dynamics of unstable systems—revolutionized Epoch II science, introduced Epoch III science, and provided us with a dramatically new and different understanding of time. The entire universe, it seems, is thoroughly evolutionary—it had a beginning in the so-called "Big Bang" and it has been evolving, expanding, and changing ever since. The universe and everything in it are on the move, and we cannot be sure where it is taking us. We know simply that *nothing* is static, *nothing* is absolutely predictable, and *nothing* is certain. Even our understanding of evolution is, well, evolving.

Once again, without getting extensively into the details of the various new sciences or engaging in indepth analysis of even the time-related insights, let's take a brief overview of how Epoch III science takes time all the way.

As stated earlier, even Einstein's own general theory of relativity implied that the universe as a whole could not be static, in spite of the fact that Einstein could not, at first, handle that implication. Nevertheless, Einstein should be given credit for initially intuiting a theory that implied an expanding universe—what was, in Timothy Ferris's words, "a completely novel idea, and one for which there was, at the time, no observational evidence whatever."[13]

Russian physicist and mathematician Alexander Friedmann first discovered Einstein's algebraic error—the cosmological constant. When correcting the error, Friedmann said that "general relativity broke free of its fetters and the relativistic universe, to Einstein's frustration, once again took on wings."[14]

> Connoisseurs of irony's serrated edge will appreciate that it was in 1917, the very year that Einstein besmirched his general theory of relativity by introducing the cosmological term, that the American astronomer Vesto Slipher published a paper containing the first observational evidence that the universe is in fact expanding.[15]

The discovery that the universe is expanding—which means, as we have noted, that time is real in its ultimate context—was dependent upon several earlier discoveries.

First we had to discover that our Milky Way galaxy was not the only galaxy in the universe. What appeared in some cases to be fuzzy distant stars in our own galaxy were actually other "island" galaxies that, in and of themselves, contained billions and billions of stars. Then came the realization that galaxies were speeding away from each other. Edwin Hubble, the astronomer after whom our telescope in the sky is named, is credited with clarifying the expansion issue in the 1920s. Hubble was able to measure only nine galaxies, all of which were speeding away from each other, whereas today's telescopes have shown us some hundred-thousand-million galaxies—and still counting—with each galaxy containing some hundred-thousand-million stars.

The more our knowledge of the universe has expanded, the more we have realized that the entire universe itself is expanding. The flow of time, it seems, is real all the way.

Time, of course, is involved in another way as we look out into the universe. Because it takes time for light to travel, the farther out we look, the farther back in time we are going. Consequently, we do not see things as they are, but as they were. The light from the sun, for instance, takes eight minutes to get to the earth. Consequently, if the sun exploded, we would not know it for eight minutes. In what astronomy calls "lookback time," we see the nearest star beyond our sun, Alpha Centauri, as it was some four-and-a-half years ago. Our nearest galaxy, Andromeda, can actually be seen with the unaided eye but is some two-million light years away. How wondrous it is to stand outside on a clear dark night, looking at the Andromeda Galaxy and thinking about how the light entering our eyes left Andromeda before our ancestors began making stone tools and a very long time before they discovered fire or started painting on cave walls.

With the aid of powerful telescopes, the galaxies in the Como cluster are seen as they were seven-hundred-million years ago. Quasars are seen out, and back, about one-billion lightyears. In other words, what we know about quasars is only about a billion years out of date! Mind-and-spirit boggling stuff!

It was inevitable, once astronomers discovered that the universe is expanding, that they would wonder not only where it is going but where it has been. If the galaxies are speeding away from each other, where did they start? In other words, if the "movie" taken of the expanding universe were to be run backwards, what would have preceded this current frame?

This is basically the same questioning in which Deep-value Research has been involved. I began Deep-value Research by wondering why our current world is so chaotic and whether there are meaning and purpose in the chaos. I discovered that the chaos is the result of the human Soul going through a major transformation—the dying of one deep-value system while, at the same time, the emergence of an entirely new deep-value system.

The questions that then emerged were two: (1) when did the currently dying deep-value system emerge from humanity's Soul to shape and influence human societies, and (2) what preceded that? If we ran the "movie" of spiritual evolution and the history of the human Soul backwards, how far back could we go, and what would we learn? It has been the process of discovering what we have called the Soul's DNA, that which determines why humans create culture in the way they do.

The same "movie-in-reverse" concept is what led to the current scientific creation story. A Belgian priest and mathematician, Georges Lamaitre, was the first to propose that, if we ran the history of an expanding universe in reverse, we would discover how it all began. The logical assumption was that galaxies rushing away from each other must have all started out at the same point. The universe must have begun with all space, matter, and energy concentrated into one single pinpoint. It was time zero. Lamaitre called it, in the title to his book on the subject, "The Primeval Atom." The assumption was that this starting point, this primal atom, erupted in the mother of all explosions—an explosion that gave birth to the universe and that had an expansive energy that even some fifteen-billion years later is still pushing entire galaxies away from each other. Now, *that* was a powerful explosion!

Lamaitre, presuming that such an explosion would have accompanying sound, dubbed it the "big noise." Later, astrophysicist Fred Hoyle, who did not like the idea of a scientific creation story at all and despised Lamaitre's theory, called it by the most insulting and derisive name he could think of, the "Big Bang."

Since a catchy title is everything, the "big noise" got lost in the shuffle, and the public picked up on "The Big Bang," no doubt to the consternation of Fred Hoyle. It remained, however, only a theory. It may have been a logical theory based upon the reasonable reversal of the imaginary "movie" of an expanding universe, but no actual evidence supported it. Not, that is, until two American physicists at the Bell Telephone Laboratories in New Jersey, in 1965, akin to the legendary three princes of Serendip, stumbled onto an unexpected and wonderful discovery.

You may recall that the three princes of Serendip kept stumbling across unexpected good fortune during their travels. What has since become known as a "serendipity," therefore, may be the most common uncommon occurrence in all branches of science. Serendipity led Arno Penzias and Robert Wilson stumbling along until they bumped into the Nobel Prize.

Penzias and Wilson were testing a very sensitive microwave detector and became worried when they picked up too much of some kind of background noise. It was a bothersome noise, and they wanted to get rid of it. They explored every possible reason for the noise that they could think of, including cleaning bird droppings off their equipment. They checked and double-checked the calibration of their equipment but still could find no way to eliminate the background noise. After a great deal of frustration, exasperation, and experimentation to get rid of the bothersome noise, Penzias and Wilson eventually discovered that the background noise was actually radiation left over from the original big noise—er, excuse me, the Big Bang. The radiation noise was coming from the universe itself, an equal amount coming from every direction: it turned out to be radiation noise left over from that original explosion some fifteen-billion years earlier, still permeating the universe. Eureka! Serendipity!

The most recent scientific theoretical work regarding time, however, and what may turn out to be the most impressive, important, and influential, is currently being done by Nobel laureate Ilya Prigogine and his team of research scientists at the University of Texas and at the Solvay Institute in Brussels. They have been working for several years on a synthesis of entropy and evolution, on what Prigogine calls a "science of becoming."

Prigogine calls time "the forgotten dimension" in classical science. He says that, far from being an illusion as Einstein suggested, time is very real, indeed, and that control, certainty, and predictability are the illusions.

> I believe that we are at an important turning point in the history of science. We have come to the end of the . . . deterministic universe. We now see the erosion of determinism and the emergence of a new formulation of the laws of physics.[16]

> [W]e are actually at the beginning of a new scientific era. We are observing the birth of a science that is no longer limited to idealized and simplified situations but reflects the complexity of

the real world, a science that views us and our creativity as part of a fundamental trend present at all levels of nature.[17]

"Time is our basic existential dimension," writes Prigogine, and "the idea of certainty is . . . a denial of time and novelty." But, "in accepting that the future is not determined, we come to the end of certainty."[18]

Prigogine and his colleagues are contributing to a new science of time. They are helping us awaken to the fact that we live in a world that is profoundly and thoroughly evolving—always becoming, always in process, and always presenting us with newness and surprise. Creativity and novelty are, therefore, fundamental to our understanding of the universe.

Prigogine credits the philosophers who thought these thoughts before him—among them Henri Bergson who said that human existence consists of "the continual creation of unpredictable novelty" and Alfred North Whitehead who conceived of existence as a process and who saw that creativity was the basic property of nature. Just as we have seen throughout our examination of the Soul's evolution, voices of vision have articulated an Epoch III truth before humanity in general was ready to hear or understand it—like a Buddha or a Jesus living and teaching Epoch III spiritual maturity before most of us were ready to hear it or live it. Eyes to see and ears to hear are historically determined for most of us, with only the rare person being ahead of her or his time.

Why is it, for instance, that process theologians like John Cobb Jr., professor emeritus at Claremont School of Theology, can have a long and productive career, making brilliant Epoch III intellectual and theological contributions, teaching decades of students who go out into ministry, and yet the spirit of process theology has made such little impact at the local church or general public level?

We have always, it seems, had prophets who saw ahead of their time, who caught a glimpse of the dawn before the rest of us, and whose wisdom and words no doubt helped prepare us for our time of awakening. But regarding the flow of time, creativity, novelty, and the possibilities within process, the time for all of us is now. It is time for the people, not just the prophets, to awaken to the spirituality in and of time. It is the time in humanity's evolutionary journey for our collective Soul to awaken to a celebration of time. It is time to leave behind the fear and the trivialization of time.

Our contemporary prophet, Ilya Prigogine, dreamed, ever since his youth, that he might "contribute to the unification of science and philosophy by resolving the enigma of time. Nonequilibrium physics," the field in which he won the Nobel Prize, "shows that this is entirely possible."[19] We have come, he says, "to a new formulation of the laws of nature, one that is no longer built on certitudes . . . but rather on possibilities."[20]

That, as we have seen, may be a difficult awakening. But leading theologians and scientists, as well as the common you and me who are trying to live spiritually conscientious lives, would be well served to repeat the following line by Prigogine several times, over and over, until it is emblazoned upon our souls:

> To deny time may be a consolation . . . [but] it is always a denial of reality.[21]

Epoch III Spirituality Takes Time All the Way

Why would we ever choose rigidity or predictability when we have been invited to be part of the generative processes of the cosmos?

Margaret J. Wheatley[22]

To deny time, whether in science, religion, or spirituality, is to deny the real world. Science has now awakened to the real world; but, by and large, religion and spirituality still exist in a world of adolescent need for stability, dependability, and control. It is now time for us to get real. It is now time for religion and spirituality to grow up, to leave behind adolescent fears and to develop a mature sense of the sacred that takes time all the way.

We can no longer think that time is a bad thing, that time applies only to the human and earthly realms, whereas timelessness rules all the good stuff—God, heaven, eternal truths, and life everlasting. It is time now to grow into a mature faith, a faith courageous enough to celebrate the processes of life, a faith that delights in rather than fears creativity, and a faith that brings God, heaven, and eternity into the creative realm of new possibilities, novelty, change, growth, development, evolution, and yes, even radical transformation.

This is not to suggest that this growing up will be easy—particularly for religion and spirituality regarding the issues of time. In one sense, science has a leg up on religion in dealing with change and, therefore, time. Science, after all, has a method and a habit for questioning past answers, developing new evidence, and allowing new findings to challenge and change old answers. Religions and spiritualities, in contrast, have often relied on defending the past at all costs, resisting any change or challenge, and demonizing anyone who had the audacity to think independently or creatively. The experiences as well as the pronouncements of past saviors, sages, and seers have been sacrosanct—rigidified into sacred ritual, dogma, and "traditional wisdom."

But nobody of any maturity and intelligence ever said growing up spiritually would be easy. An epoch-sized transformation of Soul—in this case, a ten-thousand-year wait for a growth spurt—is no trivial matter. We would be well advised, therefore, to relax a bit, take a deep breath, and swallow a large dose of humility, patience, and forgiveness—for ourselves, as well as for our companions on the journey. It will, no doubt, take some time for us to grow up and accept time.

Most of us allow scientific discoveries about the universe to shape our theologies and our spiritualities—at least to some extent. And most of us realize that materialistic science cannot provide a complete spiritual understanding of reality. Nevertheless, we accept the need to have a religion or spirituality that takes into consideration what science has discovered about the material universe.

But religious and spiritual people have also been notoriously slow in accepting the "real world" into their minds and hearts. We were slow, agonizingly slow, in accepting the Copernican revolution in astronomy, because our theologies were rooted in a rock-solid, stable, and unmoving Earth. If the Earth moved, we thought, God could not be stable and dependable—and we needed "him" to be so. If the Earth was not the center of the universe, we thought, our lives and God's activity in our lives could not be as important as we needed them to be. To displace the Earth, and us, from the center felt like trivializing God's activity on the planet and in our lives.

"And yet, and yet . . . ," we eventually let scientific discovery reshape our theologies.

In similar fashion, religious and spiritual people were slow, agonizingly slow, in accepting the Darwinian revolution in biology. The theory of evolution directly conflicted with a literal understanding of the Bible's creation stories and with an adolescent emotional need for "absolute truth." "Bible-believing" folks could not tolerate the relativizing of the Bible or conceive of a God who might be creating humanity and the world over time, via an evolutionary process. Even to this day, local school boards are intimidated by fundamentalists who want to make "creationism" on a scientific par with evolution. The former is "biblical fact," they say, the latter "only a theory." "And yet, and yet . . . ," most of us have grown into a spirituality that includes evolution, change, and the passage of time—at least part of the way.

The question now before religious and spiritual people is this: how much time will it take for us to reconcile with time, spiritually and totally? Science has been awakening now for about eighty years to the profound reality of time all the way to the largest possible context. Recent discoveries of science regarding time emerge from a human Soul that is calling us to grow up out of our adolescent emotional need for a static universe. When will religion and spirituality hear that same Soul-calling?

It may be ironic, but not terribly surprising, that nonreligious people often hear the calling of Soul before religious people. The same, of course, could be said of many other fields, where official dogma yells so loud into the ears of professionals and "true believers" that they cannot hear a new word—as when medical professionals stick to a reductionistic Epoch II dogma regarding disease and healing, while common ordinary people simply intuit Epoch III and *know* that they are whole persons—mind, body, and spirit—whether in health or in illness.

Since nothing in the observable universe is static, the burden of proof shifts to any religious or spiritual claims of eternal stability. Certainly, we have been accustomed, for a very long time, to thinking that God, heaven, and the hereafter exist beyond time; but what evidence is there for that belief? That a belief has been held long and hard does not correlate with its veracity. How does a belief in eternal timelessness, for instance, differ from earlier beliefs that the Earth was flat or that the Earth was at the center of the universe, or that humanity was placed upon this Earth some six-thousand years ago looking just as we do today?

It is time to accept the fact courageously—and it will take courage—that everything is in a state of flux, a state of becoming.

Sacred Chaos—Far from Equilibrium

We mentioned earlier that chaos theory and nonequilibrium physics are two of the new sciences changing our understanding of time. They are also metaphors for understanding the role of time in spiritual maturity.

The science of chaos refers to the fact that, underlying what looks like random and unrelated events, there is a fundamental interconnectedness. A theology of chaos would say that we need not fear the free and unrestrained questioning of questers, maverick meanderings of mind, heretical hunches, or speculations of spirit, because underneath it all is our faith in a God who holds it all together.

The science of chaos affirms that there is both death and birth, destruction and creation, within a fundamental universe of order. A theology of chaos does not fear the death or destruction of ideas, dogma, rituals, or institutions, because it has faith in the larger context that is the divine order.

Science writers John Briggs and F. David Peat also serve us as theologians when in their recent book on the science of chaos they write:

> Chaos is evolving from a scientific theory into a new cultural metaphor. As a metaphor, chaos allows us to query some of our most cherished assumptions and encourages us to ask fresh questions about reality. . . .
>
> The idea of chaos opens up radical new ways of thinking and experiencing reality. At the same time, chaos as a metaphor has a built-in humility that previous scientific metaphors did not. Chaos, it turns out, is as much about what we *can't* know as it is about certainty and fact. It's about letting go, accepting limits, and celebrating magic and mystery. . . .

> Chaotic systems lie beyond all our attempts to predict, manipulate, and control them. Chaos suggests that instead of resisting life's uncertainties, we should embrace them.[23]

The mature religions and spiritualities of Epoch III will ditto that! In Epoch III, within the realms of religion and spirituality, we will have far more humility, a quality in short supply during humanity's adolescent epoch. The need for certainty virtually assures arrogance. The openness to mystery, the willingness to let go of the need for control, and the acceptance of limits to what we can know allows a profound humility to enter the sacred quest.

Prigogine won the Nobel Prize in chemistry for demonstrating that, when chaotic systems reach a state far from equilibrium, non-equilibrium itself becomes the source of new order. Perturbations far from equilibrium can create the new and the novel. In other words, nonequilibrium can bring, to use the title of one of Prigogine's earlier books, "order out of chaos."

Consider how much the religions of Epoch II have felt threatened by chaotic change. Consider how often their reaction has been to hunker down, to circle the wagons, to "dampen" the threatening fluctuations, and to eliminate all perturbations. There has an desperate desire for safety and stability, for the dependability of the "good old values," and for the clarity of former certainties. Religions do not like people to disturb or perturb the equilibrium, to "rock the boat," to threaten the "tried and true," or to challenge the traditional established practices. "Jesus Christ," say some Christians, quoting the Bible, "was the same yesterday, today, and forever."

But what if the very nature of Christ is dynamic change? Would it not be, then, that change itself would be the quality of yesterday, today, and forever? What if the Divine Spirit of the universe is not only the ground of Being, but also the ground of Becoming? What if God is a "becoming" God, currently transforming humanity's Soul? If so, then to resist change would be to deny Christ, and to preserve and conserve the status quo would to undermine God's current work in the world. The mature spiritual response to our chaotic time in history may be—in fact, may be precisely the reason for the chaos—to learn a new spiritual skill, to resonate with fluctuations far from equilibrium, and to flow into the new order emerging out of chaos.

The spiritual maturity of Epoch III will be a daring spirituality, following in the spirit of Helen Keller who said, "Life is a daring adventure, or it is nothing." The spiritual maturity of Epoch III will be oriented more to living faithfully into an unknown future than in believing in the known past.

It will not be a safe spirituality: it will be daring and dangerous. As Alfred North Whitehead put it, "It is the business of the future to be dangerous." And it is the business of religion and spirituality to be courageous, faithfully futuristic, and daringly dangerous. Religion and spirituality will be so, or they will be nothing at all. Religion and spirituality will be so, or they will be relegated to the pathetic and apathetic archives of a musty museum.

Belief: An Excuse for Not Having Faith

In the past, we have been confused about two words, *belief* and *faith*. We have often said that a person's religious faith consisted of, indeed was synonymous with, a certain set of beliefs. To belong to a particular "faith," one presumably held certain "beliefs."

For our discussion here, however, beliefs are the intellectual and verbal formulations of what we think we know for certain about religion or spirituality, while faith, on the other hand, is trust in the ultimacy of divine reality when we don't know things for certain, when mystery is the most convincing reality, and when doubt seems most credible.

Epoch II religions and spiritualities often based their security, indeed their identities, on beliefs. They would establish the proper and defining orthodox set of beliefs and then insist that "followers" give ascent to those beliefs. A rigid belief system became the central priority. The identity of the religion or spirituality, as well as its safety, security, stability, and control, were threatened by nonconformists. Many a heretic—the very name means "to choose"—has been demonized, ostracized, excommunicated, and/or burned at the stake for that threat.

Epoch III religions and spiritualities will have a faith that emphasizes that divinity is the essential energy of the universe, that divine order underlies all the seeming chaos and, therefore, that has no fear of experimentation, fluctuations, perturbations, non-conformity, creativity, novelty, or people who stray from the equilibrium of the group. Faith is knowing that we are all one, that the universe at its core is spiritual, and that God's love embraces even the most maverick, the most unconventional, the most unorthodox, and the most nonconforming. A mature sacred quest, therefore, is not threatened by all the various forms of religious and spiritual seeking, for it knows that all our lives are richer precisely because of that diversity. God is incognito and speaks many different languages.

Belief, on the other hand, needs certainty and is threatened by a faith that thrives on doubt and uncertainty. Belief needs answers and is threatened by the faith that lives and loves the questions. Belief needs a security blanket, whereas faith is comfortable even when our blanket is in the dryer. Belief needs the bar the trapeze artist holds on to, whereas faith is found soaring in the air when there is nothing solid to grasp. Needing belief for security and certainty is the epitome of cowardice, whereas faith is the expression of courage. Belief is the excuse for not having faith; and if our fear is increased because of belief's being threatened, we will never know the glorious liberation of faith. Emphasizing belief in the individual pieces prevents us from knowing the peace that passes all understanding.

The Death of Dogma

From what we just stated it goes without saying that dogma is unnecessary when one has faith. There are two particular dangers when religion or spirituality gets preoccupied with dogma. One is idolatry, worshiping something that is less than God. The other is that dogma, like fundamentalism, is antihistorical, presuming that the spiritual reality of the past is better and more important than the spiritual reality of the present, that the past must be protected against any and all assaults, changes, or trivializations.

All too often, when we think that dogma, doctrine, orthodoxy, or "confessional norms" are crucial, we slip and slide into thinking that religious gatekeepers are needed to defend and protect the purity, stability, certainty, and perpetuity of that "truth." Dogma becomes authoritative, which generally means that authorities are needed to protect and preserve it, to be, in other words, guardians of the truth, gatekeepers of "The Pearly Gates," and possessors of the "keys to the Kingdom."

Matthew Fox tells of a local school district in New Hampshire where the Christian Coalition had gained control of the school board. One of the first acts of business, once they were in control, was to ban the word *imagination*, prohibiting any teacher to use that word in the classroom.[24] It is soul-boggling to see such instances where dogmatic minds express such incredible fear of creativity. It seems that the very people who talk of being "born again" want that new birth, or anything else that is new, to be predictable, controllable, and unimaginative.

In Epoch III, when the deep values of empowerment and the creativity of time are taken seriously, people will be constantly "born again"—each time more imaginatively than before. Creativity will be celebrated in individual as well as communal questing and questioning. People will be encouraged and supported in authorizing their own version of the sacred quest. We will also share with and learn from one another, without having to judge or change another person's quest and without demanding conformity of others to our own style of questing.

Traditions out of the past and former formulations of spiritual quests can certainly play helpful roles in our personal authorizing— but, as we emphasized in the previous chapter, the final authorizing comes from within each unique individual, for everyone is a unique materialization of spirit and a special spiritualization of matter. We embody spirit in important and special ways, and we must have our sacred quest manifested and authorized in special ways. Spiritual authorization cannot be conferred from on high or from the outside. It is a soul-level, inside job. Epoch III spirituality will certainly not fear the past but will see the past as catalytic rather than capturing, a springboard rather than a stumbling block, and a launching pad rather than a padded cell.

Dogma was understandable in Epoch II, for it was a logical manifestation of Epoch II deep values. Dogma was to Epoch II religion what Descartes was to Epoch II science—the preoccupation with certainty and the discomfort with mystery and wonder. As Karen Armstrong writes, "Descartes . . . had no time at all for wonder. A sense of mystery was to be avoided at all costs because it represented a primitive state of mind that civilized man had out-grown."[25]

As Epoch III dawns within religion and spirituality, however, there will no longer be the need to explain everything with clarity and with certainty. There will no longer be the need for dogma—encapsulated "truth," cemented into rigid and unchanging form and hoisted onto an altar to be worshiped like an idol.

A rigid past and dogmatic truth simply have no effective place in Epoch III, an epoch that will resonate with the spiritual maturity that the prophet Micah spoke of when he said, "What does the Lord require of you? To do justice, to love kindness, and to walk humbly with your Lord" (6:8). The humility of Epoch III realizes that God is on the move, so what we saw and thought at one point in time will be changing and flowing and moving on to another timely perception of the journey. Like Einstein's emotional need for a "cosmological constant," Epoch II religion and spirituality had the emotional need for a "theological constant"; its name was dogma. Epoch III will see the death of dogma.

A Personal Quest for the Sacred

To be consistent with everything said previously in this book, I can-not avoid the personal challenge to apply this emergent deep value to my own life, nor do I presume that my attempts define anyone else's path into spiritual integrity. Consequently, as with the three previous deep values, the following expressions of my quest for spir-itual integrity are shared simply with the hope that, in some small way, they might contribute to your own quest for a sacred integrity between your life and the time of your life.

For me, the discovery of the sacred in and of time involves a quest in and through three words. One is the Greek word *chronos*, the root of our concept of chronological time, our typical and most familiar experience with time, such as clock time, calendar time, and our per-sonal lifetimes. The second is also a Greek word, *kairos*, which refers to a very special moment in time, the right moment, a moment that is atypical, unusual, and powerful. The third word that I explore is a word often used in religious language, *eternity*, a word I have derided in this chapter so far, but a word that I want to reinterpret so that it can continue to be used in Epoch III. In that order, then, ...

A Sacred Quest in Chronological Time

In ancient Greek mythology, Homer's Odysseus was given a choice: he could choose immortality and remain the lover of Calypso or he could choose to return to the human condition, which involved aging and death. He chose mortality over immortality and time over timelessness.

Throughout Epoch II, we wanted desperately to choose immortality and timelessness—at least for the important stuff—but in Epoch III, we will discover what we have been missing because of that adolescent need for certainty and stability. We will redeem our relationship with chronological time as we discover the sacred inherent within *chronos*. Because of that redemption, we will transform our experience with aging and death, two of the greatest fears that have plagued us.

When it comes to my personal attempt to resonate with the Epoch III evolution of Soul, I try to live my days in a coordinated effort between the theoretical and the visceral and between the theological and the existential, and never to let the thinking about the former keep me from feeling the latter. On the one hand, I want to spend some of the time "in my head" trying to understand and conceptualize an integrity between thought and action. On the other hand, I want to spend some of my time "out of my head" where I can check in with how I actually feel. In other words, can I actually live in this Epoch III deep value and not just think and write about it? Regarding the processes of aging and the inevitability of death, like every other emergent deep value, I have both thoughts and feelings. Let's first address the matter of aging.

I live in and am consequently influenced by, at least to some extent, a culture that is afraid of aging. Ponce de Leon, the Spanish explorer who looked for the fountain of youth, should be proclaimed the patron saint of the United States. Our culture has an extraordinary fear of aging, tries to avoid it or reverse it at all costs, and carries a plethora of ageist attitudes. For many in our country, it is somehow bad to be old, and to be "old hat" is to be out of date.

I will, therefore, intentionally refer to myself sometimes as an "old man"—not particularly inaccurate, given that I turned sixty-five shortly before this book was published—but I do it just to see what kind of reaction I will get. Some let it pass, whereas some others scold me for thinking badly about myself or "putting myself down."

The fact is that I don't consider old as either "bad" or a "put-down." It is, after all, a fact of life and quite a bit better, as the "old saw" has it, than the alternative. And just as there are some "young codgers," there are also some of us "old whippersnappers."

Aging has been thought to be a disease by many in the medical culture, and dying represents a failure of the professionals. Enormous amounts of money have been, and are being, spent to "cure the ravages of time"—to have a surgeon suck out any amount of fat, tuck this or that, or cut away any amount of skin, implant or dye one's hair in order to hide the evidence that we are getting older. We give guru status to people who define aging as a failure to eat or think right and who promise to help us get over such mistaken notions or improper nutrition. If we buy their advice or their product, we can correct such errors, "reverse the aging process" and "recover our youth."

When it comes to such products, procedures, books, or workshop gurus, I'd like to see a little truth in advertising—but then, I don't buy anything from those who think that aging is something to be avoided, cured, or reversed. A culture obsessed with recovery from real ills such as various forms of abuse and addiction wants to talk us into a recovery from the natural process of aging. What we need recovery from, however, is the abuse of ageism and the addiction to remaining "forever young."

Of course, I want the highest quality of aging possible for me, so I take physical exercise as seriously as my body will allow, I take mental exercise as a given—in both the mind and the body, the old adage is true: "If you don't use it, you lose it." Plenty of research, as well as personal experience, verifies the fact that much of what we have taken for granted as the inevitable infirmities of aging has simply been the result of disuse. And nutrition is also important to put the most life in our years, as well as years in our lives, even though this one is the hardest area of wisdom for me to translate from my head to my stomach. My mind, you see, is in health-conscious Boulder, but my stomach never did leave the good old meat, potatoes, and gravy of Iowa. Basically, however, it comes down to this: I want to make my aging more holistic and more empowering and my dying more faithful.

What do I mean by making my aging more holistic? Well, our culture's bias, as well as our own physical pain and infirmities, tends to make aging simply a matter of the physical body. As a materialistic culture, we have become totally preoccupied with *physical* aging. My existential attempt is to balance it all out, to be more holistic and consider the mental, emotional, and spiritual aspects of aging as well as the physical and material.

At sixty-five, I cannot play handball as I did when I was twenty-five or forty-five, but I know a lot more about life now than I did then. Which is more important? At sixty-five, I am not as capable at throwing a football or a baseball as I was forty or fifty years ago, but I am a lot better at loving than I was then. Which is more important? At sixty-five, I'm not as strong physically as I once was—after all, some of the macho muscle has turned to mucho mush—but I am psychologically stronger in a lot of other ways. Which is more important? As an Epoch II male, I thought that virtually everything about my life was to be hard work, but now, trying to discover what it would be like to be an Epoch III male, I live much more softly and faithfully. Which is more important? At sixty-five, my eyesight is weaker than it used to be, but my insight is stronger. Which is more important?

This is not to ignore or trivialize the adjustments, the disappointments, the loss, or the pain and discomfort that accompany physical deterioration. I have had, and continue to have, a fair sampling of all that. It is simply to say that, if I consider the whole picture, there are gains as well as losses, and a little more emphasis upon the former puts the latter into proper perspective.

All the above obviously deals with empowerment as well.The more holistic my approach to aging is, the more empowering I find it to be. But there is another empowering approach that I take into my aging process. It has to do with anticipating the coming year. I use two symbolic occasions—my birthday and New Year's Eve—to meditate upon what I might learn and experience in the coming year that I never knew or experienced before. I have never lived next year before, so the questions of my quest involve the future.

What can I learn or experience this coming year that transcends anything in previous years? When I am thinking or doing something that I have done before, can I think or do it more deeply, more meaningfully, more purposefully than before? And the most important question of all: can I learn to give, live, and receive love with a greater infusion of the sacred than I ever did before?

My friend Bob Raines has written a wonderful book about aging entitled *A Time To Live*. I have always known Bob to bring a great deal of intelligence, wisdom, and skill to any writing or speaking project he undertakes, and this book is no exception. In fact, if I were writing a more lengthy discussion of aging, I would probably be quoting most of his book. Among the many things I liked was Bob's reference to Meister Eckhart's sermon, "Sinking Eternally into God," in which Eckhart said, "Let your 'being you' sink and flow into God's 'being God.'"[26]

The other aspect of empowering the aging process for me has to do with what I call "historical integrity." Because I dealt with this subject at such length in my earlier book *Sacred Eyes*, I will only touch briefly on it here. What I mean by that phrase is that I do not believe that the historical time in which we are living is an accidental or unimportant relationship. Is there meaning and purpose in:

1. My embodiment. What is the meaning and purpose of this particular version of spiritualized matter known as Bob Keck?
2. My historicity. Why is my life occurring at this particular time in history? Can I discover an integrity between my life and the time of my life?
3. My place. Why was I born in Minnesota, raised in Iowa, find the most meaningful living in Colorado, and the most refreshing renewal of my soul in Door County, Wisconsin? Am I hopelessly a "Middle American," or is there some spiritual meaning and purpose in those questions and those realizations?

There is something else about historical integrity, something that Schopenhauer observed in the middle of the nineteenth century and something that Carl Jung and Joseph Campbell agreed with:

[I]n the later years of a lifetime, looking back over the course of one's days and noticing how encounters and events that appeared at the time to be accidental became the crucial structuring features of an unintended lifestory through which the potentialities of one's character were fostered to fulfillment, one may find it difficult to resist the notion of the course of one's biography as comparable to that of a cleverly constructed novel, wondering who the author of the surprising plot can have been.[27]

Indeed, the older I get and the more experiences I have to reflect back on, the more my life seems to be a story that has a meaningful flow to it. As a typical "Type A," I usually had my life all planned out—the only problem was that my life never followed the script I had written. I think someone had my life in mind when they crafted the old joke, "Want to know how to make God laugh? Tell God your plans." If God is ever reported to have died laughing, I'm afraid that I will have to confess to being the cause.

Speaking of dying, I mentioned earlier that I want to be more faithful in the way that I face the inevitability of dying.

Frankly, I've been too busy living to give much thought to dying. But when I do think about it, I am sure about at least two things. One is that I just flat out do not agree with the biblical notion that death is God's punishment for human sin. Death was obviously around long before human beings conceived of the idea of sin, and death has always participated in the ongoing flow of life as we know it: birth, life, death, and rebirth. The blunt fact is that death is a natural part of an evolutionary world.

The other thing that I am sure of is that I do not want to participate in the "American way of death"—namely, to do everything possible to hide the actuality of death, to attempt to preserve a corpse "for eternity," and to take up a section of good earth with a casket that tries to interrupt the natural processes of participation. Participation is a very important aspect of life—one might even say, it is *the* process of life—and most of what our culture does about death is an attempt to stop participation. Preservation of a dead body, trying to maintain a static physical state, is antitime, antichange, and antiparticipatory.

When I die, I want to be allowed to participate in the grand recycling program of the universe. I want to participate in the air and in other lives. I want to participate in the salt of the earth, to be a solid rock, and to sail on the inspirited winds. I want to participate in the soil of our Soul that is the ground of all Being, as well as the ground of all our Becoming. I love what Hildegarde of Bingen was feeling when she wrote:

I am that supreme and fiery force that sends forth all the sparks of life. . . . I am that living and fiery essence of the divine substance that flows in the beauty of the fields. I shine in the water, I burn in the sun and the moon and the stars. Mine is the mysterious force of the invisible wind. . . . I am life.[28]

No species on this planet lives in isolation from all the rest; only Epoch II humanity with its agenda of ego development even thought it possible. I want to live out, and to die into, the Epoch III realization of profound participation. When the time comes to die, I want to dance death's dance in the rhythm of exchange.

I love the obituary for Carr Kaoru Suzuki, about whom it was said:

[He] died peacefully on May 8th. He was eighty-five. His ashes will be spread on the winds of Quadra Island. He found great strength in the Japanese tradition of nature-worship. Shortly before he died, he said: "I will return to nature where I came from. I will be part of the fish, the trees, the birds—that's my reincarnation. I have had a rich and full life and have no regrets. I will live on in your memories of me and through my grandchildren."[29]

That's the kind of hereafter I would want. If I have been loved by those who live beyond my time, and if I have lived a life worth remembering, I would want it to be remembered in their living minds and warm hearts, not on a cold tombstone and a buried casket that tries to interrupt my participation. Well, okay, to be perfectly honest, I would love it if my books hang around for just a little while before they are recycled.

A Sacred Quest in Kairotic Time

The word *kairotic* is probably not an actual word, so, I am going to make it up. It does, however, come from an actual word, the Greek *kairos*. "It was a fine feeling," wrote Paul Tillich, "that made the spirit of the Greek language signify *chronos*, 'formal time,' with a different word from *kairos*, 'the right time,' the moment rich in content and significance."[30]

In our overview of spiritual evolution and the history of the human Soul, we earlier suggested a parallel with a theory in physical evolution, namely, punctuated equilibria. We have seen how, after a period of relatively stable Soul-level activity, stable in terms of evolutionary purpose and deep values, a rather sudden transformation takes place that includes a radical change in evolutionary purpose and deep values. It was kairotic time for humanity, "the right time" for a growth spurt, a "moment rich in content and significance" regarding our evolutionary and maturational journey. A transformation of Soul—either the first that took place ten-thousand years ago or the second taking place right now—is a sacred kairotic moment in the big picture of human evolution.

The same thing happens in our individual lives. We have the usual and regular flow of time, moment after moment, hour after hour, day after day. Then, a special kairotic moment breaks through, and we know for certain that something extraordinary just happened. It was a moment unlike those that preceded it, and it needs a different name.

We experience kairotic moments in a wide variety of ways. Sometimes it may be a creative "Ah-ha," a eureka or serendipitous kind of *kairos*. Sometimes it may be an orgasmic moment, erotic and kairotic at the same time. And sometimes it can be a mystical moment, that extraordinary experience when you feel divinity break through the ordinary with a sudden and new level of meaning and purpose in life, a moment of perception regarding the interconnectedness of all life, or a soul-level kairotic "call" to a particular mission.

We all change over time. Chronological time changes us slowly, but kairotic time can change us suddenly. For me, it may very well be the fact that, because of a extraordinarily thick skull and an extraordinarily wide streak of stubbornness, God decided that the shock of kairotic moments might be the only way to get my attention, let alone actually to change me.

I have had some wonderful, powerful, and life-changing kairotic moments, when I felt that I wasn't writing my own life story, as mentioned earlier, but was being forced to live a life planned by God who was fooling around in my soul—and not always with my permission or at my request. They were occasions when my life took radical and unexpected turns. They were moments when I suddenly found myself on "a road less traveled," feeling as if the road had picked me rather than my choosing the road.

The only way I can make sense out of my kairotic experiences—and the very nature of a kairotic experience is that it defies explanation and description—is to say that I felt eternity had just erupted up into my *chronos*. Which brings us to what I mean by *eternity*.

A Sacred Quest for Eternity

For me, eternity takes on an entirely different meaning from the one we have used in the past. Instead of timelessness, eternity for me refers to the spiritual depth within time. Instead of an escape from time into the hereafter, eternity is the divine availability in the here and now. Eternity, I believe, is undergoing an epochal time change. We thought and talked about eternity in one particular way in Epoch II, and we will think and talk and experience eternity in a very different way in Epoch III.

The experience of eternity does not involve going somewhere, like "going to heaven." The experience of eternity is simply waking up—waking up to the divine presence that always has been, is now, and always will be available in the depths of life and, therefore, in our own depths. The Ground of our Being and the Ground of our Becoming is always down there in our souls; we just need to wake up to that fact and to do everything we can to open the channels of communication.

Jesus, as it turns out, demonstrated once again that he was an Epoch III man ahead of his time when it came to the subject of eternity. When asked *where* heaven was, Jesus scoffed at those who looked to the skies, saying, "then the birds of the sky will precede you" (Gospel of Thomas 3). He said that heaven was inside every one of us, as well as outside every one of us. When his disciples asked him *when* they would get to eternity, he responded with some rather blunt words: "What you look forward to has already come, but you don't know it" (Gospel of Thomas 51). In similar fashion, and on another occasion, he said that eternity is "spread out upon the earth, and people don't see it" (Gospel of Thomas 113).

Jesus, almost two-thousand years ago, was saying something that we are only now ready to understand—time and eternity are not mutually exclusive. Time is not the enemy of divinity. Heaven and earth are one. Human and divine are one. Eternity is available for us right now, right here, spread throughout the earth, inside us, and all around us. We need simply to awaken to the Epoch III democratization of access to the ever-present heaven, the eternal now.

Many other prophets, also ahead of their time, caught a vision of Epoch III's realization that eternity is hidden in every moment of time. Among the more famous and familiar observations are those of the eighteenth-century poet and artist William Blake:

> If the doors of perception were cleansed everything would appear to man as it is: infinite.
>
> *The Marriage of Heaven and Hell,* Plate 14

> To see a World in a Grain of Sand,
> And heaven in a Wild Flower,
> Hold infinity in the palm of your hand
> And Eternity in an hour
>
> *Songs and Ballads, "Auguries of Innocence"*

The sacred quest involves cleansing our perceptions—seeing anew with sacred eyes, hearing anew with sacred ears, and feeling anew with sacred palms as we hold infinity in our hands. It means that, if we wake up and pay attention, we can experience the depth of eternity within the flow of chronological time.

For me, that means not only searching through the living of my own life in chronological time, but searching for the eternal depths within humanity's chronological time. That is what led me to look as deeply as I can into what is causing the chaos at this particular time in history. That is what led me into developing Deep-value Research. And that is what led me into tracing the eternal in the human Soul as far back in history as I can find evidence, what turned out to be some thirty-five-thousand years.

As we have already stated, the two major kairotic eruptions of the eternal in humanity's chronological time are the two historic transformations of Soul. There are, of course, lesser kairotic moments in history as well, moments when something spiritually unusual or significant happened. Many people would feel, and legitimately so, that the lives and contributions of certain people fall into that category: Buddha, Moses, Jesus, Muhammad, as well as a host of other saints, sages, and prophets past as well as present. Any life of exemplary spiritual maturity could be said to be a kairotic event for humanity-at-large.

My experiences of kairotic eternity, as I have already stated, did not feel as if I were in charge, in control, or at the planning helm. No effort of mine in any way made them happen. They seem to just happen, totally out of my control, usually at a time that I would not have chosen.

Nevertheless, I suspect that we can live lives that cultivate the soil of soul, that give the eternal a better chance of breaking through, like the sprouts of spring emerging from the winter of our souls. Perhaps that is at least part of the value in having specific religious and spiritual disciplines—cultivating the soil of soul for the transition from winter to springtime, preparing our lives to be receptive to eternal "happenings."

Meister Eckhart spoke to such cultivation:

> The seed of God is in us. If you are an intelligent and hard-working farmer, it will thrive and grow up into God, whose seed it is, and its fruits will be God-fruits. Pear seeds grow into pear trees, nut seeds grow into nut trees, and God seeds grow into God.[31]

Eckhart's image also suggests the balance between God's activity and ours. Because of God's grace, we have the seed in the first place, as well as the soil, the sun, and the rain that enable it to grow. "And yet, and yet . . . ," there is a role for the farmer in cultivating the soil of soul. We certainly do not control eternity, but we can choose to live deeply and perhaps make it just a little more likely that we will recognize the eternal when it breaks through.

To conclude this brief reflection on my personal quest for living into the new deep value of time, I want to return to the image and metaphor of the chrysalis. As we explored in chapter three, the chrysalis may be the best metaphor for understanding the chaos in our time in history, a chaos created when the caterpillar of Epoch II is in the process of dying and, simultaneously, the butterfly of Epoch III is in its birth pangs. But this metaphor is also rich in relevancy for our consideration of spirituality in all times.

If the emerging butterfly represents Epoch III spirituality, it is important to note that it is an organic form of life that lives by the flight. If we try to rigidify our religious and spiritual meaning, we stop the movement. If we think that what has been meaningful to us, perhaps even something that has been particularly joyful in our spiritual experience, should be killed and put on display, we not only lose the life of that experience, we miss the daily sunrise of enlightenment as eternity takes flight in every new day of our lives.

William Blake's words, from the poem "Eternity," sum it all up:

He who binds to himself a joy
Doth the winged life destroy
But he who kisses the joy as it flies
Lives in eternity's sunrise.

Questions for Those on a Quest

To quest is to question,
and sometimes the quality of our spiritual quest
has more to do with the questions we ask today
than with answers entombed within past dogma.

1. When you deeply consider your own feelings, where do you find the Epoch II fear of time? Would you be able to take time all the way to the eternal?

2. If you were seriously to ask how God is active in our time, how do you deal with religious and spiritual expressions of the past? What do you think about dogma? How do you relate to the experiences of ancient sages, seers, prophets, and saviors, around which religions are founded? How do you deal with the scriptures of your religion?

3. Can your religious and spiritual meaning shift from the certainty of past answers to the uncertainty of "living and loving the questions" involved in a dynamic quest? Can you resonate with a spirituality of chaos, far from equilibrium? If so, how will that change you? Can you "kiss the joy as it flies?" If not, what are the implications of your trying to maintain stasis in a time of chaos?

4. As you look back over your life, is there a sacred story with a sacred plot being written? Think about it. Talk about it. Perhaps even write about it.

5. Have you had experiences of the kairotic sacred? What were they like? What do you do to cultivate a soil of soul that might increase your experiences of those eternal breakthroughs?

6. What do you do to witness and praise the eternal within and about you?

A Future in Question

It would seem appropriate to conclude a book about questing and questioning with a few additional questions. Allow me to presume to guess what some of the most urgent questions are that occur to you as you finish reading this book.

How Do We Know That Epoch III Will Arrive?

We don't. We cannot be certain that humanity will grow up, leaving adolescent immaturity behind and living abundantly within a spiritual maturity. After all, humanity has now developed into a substantial player on the world's stage, and we have it within our capacity to commit a "teenage suicide" and take a number of other species down with us. That would be one hell of a legacy, wouldn't it? And, no doubt about it, we are capable of doing just that. We are very experienced in self-destructive behavior.

But we are capable of heaven as well as of hell. We have demonstrated the capacity for self-transcendence, self-reorganization, and self-transformation. It certainly is possible that we can grow out of an adolescent self and into a mature adult self. More than just possible, it is probable—not absolutely certain, but probable. The passionate search and research that I have been engaged in for over forty years—the desire to find meaning and purpose in my life within the context of the time of my life—all that led to the writing of this book has convinced me that the evidence is pointing in a very hopeful direction.

How Long Will It Take?

I don't know. I'm afraid that if I make any specific guess, I'll just give God another side-splitting, down-on-the-floor, hilarious, jaw-breaking, laughing fit. But I do feel there are at least four relevant thoughts about that question.

First of all, we live in a world of rapid change, in fact, a world in which the very rate of change is escalating. Consequently, it only makes sense that the transformation from adolescence to adulthood for humanity will not take several millennia as it did when we moved from our childhood into adolescence. I don't believe it will take even centuries. I suspect we are looking at decades as the time-frame within which this "punctuation" of Soul will be completed.

Second, as we just discussed in the previous chapter, things may be speeding up precisely because we *need* to have a radical confrontation with the spirituality in and of time. As long as time moved slowly, we tended to ignore it. Now, we can't.

Third, to presume to know exactly when Epoch III will be fully present, to think that we can predict the future in any specific way, is to deny the role of creativity, novelty, change, and innovation. It is the cosmic "uncertainty principle"—God's way of keeping us humble.

And, fourth, it depends—on a lot of things. But most of all, it depends on what, if any, God's role is in this transformation of Soul, and it depends on how responsibly humanity handles its role. That forms the next two questions.

What Is God's Role in the Current Transformation of Soul?

We have to be really careful with this one. There is a very long and arrogant history of people's thinking they knew, with certainty, what God's will is and with no hesitancy to inform us, in capital letters, of their certainty.

With the necessary humility noted, however, this entire book is based upon the belief that God has given us at least some hints regarding the divine within-ness to the human evolutionary journey. Deep-value Research has been my best attempt to discern and articulate those hints. There is an obvious faith in these pages, therefore, that God is in and with us as we journey, individually and

271

collectively, into our dawning future. But even more than that, the faith expressed here is that the love of God creates a particular direction to and intention for that journey—a bias, if you will, for our health and wholeness.

The reason for the maturational metaphor in this book is that I believe that, just as in our individual lives, humanity collectively has a built-in propensity for growth and maturation, a normal process— if we don't screw it up—to move from childhood, through adolescence, and into adulthood.

What Is Our Role?

Our role, it seems to me, is to show up, pay attention to what God is doing in our souls, participate in both the personal and the collective journey, and mature into a greater capacity for love and justice. We are significant players in co-creating the future: it is a tremendous responsibility but one that spiritually mature adults will accept. It is a very serious matter. It is also one in which we can have a little fun along the way, as well as a lot of meaningful communion with each other and with the world at large.

What an incredible privilege!

Notes

Introduction

1. The relatively new science of memetics is not a materialistic science, and it also makes the claim to be a science discovering the DNA of culture; but memetics, as it has been described by its primary proponents, lacks the spiritual paradigm that is basic to Deep-value Research. Nevertheless, it is probably the closest thing to Deep-value Research, and scholars may be interested in exploring the similarities and differences. The term *meme* was introduced first by Richard Dawkins in his 1976 book *The Selfish Gene* (Cambridge: Oxford University Press, 1990) and was picked up by the distinguished philosopher Daniel Dennett to be the cornerstone of his theory of mind, articulated in both *Consciousness Explained* (Boston: Little, Brown and Company, 1992) and *Darwin's Dangerous Idea: Evolution and the Meanings of Life* (rpt. New York: Touchstone Books, 1996). Other books devoted to the subject of memes are Susan Blackmore's *The Meme Machine* (New York: Oxford University Press, 1999), Richard Brodie's *Virus of the Mind: The New Science of the Meme* (Seattle: Integral Press, 1995), and Aaron Lynch's *Thought Contagion: How Belief Spreads through Society* (New York: Basic Books, 1999).

Because the science of memetics is virtually unknown outside the academy, I have chosen not to include a discussion of it in this book, which is intended primarily for the wider public.

2. N. Eldredge and S. J. Gould in *Models in Paleobiology*, edited by T. J. M. Schopf (San Francisco: Freeman, Coper and Co., 1972), 82–115.

3. *The Portable Jung*, edited, with an introduction, by Joseph Campbell, trans. R. F. C. Hull (New York: The Viking Press, 1971), 17–18.

Chapter 1

1. Riane Eisler, *The Chalice and the Blade: Our History, Our Future* (San Francisco: Harper & Row, 1987), xv.

2. Richard Leakey and Roger Lewin, *Origins Reconsidered* (New York: Doubleday, 1992), 316.

3. Ian Tattersall, *Becoming Human* (New York: Harcourt Brace & Company, 1998), 188.

4. Those who would like to explore the details of this controversy should consult the following books, especially their references, endnotes, and bibliographies: Robert Wenke, *Patterns in Prehistory* (New York: Oxford University Press, 1980); Donald Johanson and James Shreeve, *Lucy's Child* (New York: William Morrow & Co., 1989); Richard Leakey and Roger Lewin, *Origins Reconsidered*; Ian Tattersall, *The Human Odyssey* (New York: Prentice Hall, 1993); Ian Tattersall, *Becoming Human*; Christopher Stringer and Robin McKie, *African Exodus* (New York: Henry Holt & Co., 1996); and Brian Fagan, *The Journey from Eden* (London, Thames & Hudson, 1990).

The single best summary of the debate may be in *Origins Reconsidered* by Leakey and Lewin. The argument, and their references to other material, however, must be accepted strictly on the basis of their reputations, which is considerable, for the book offers no documentation. Fortunately, the other books cited above do provide that assistance.

5. Leakey and Lewin, 219.

6. Stringer and McKie, 11.

7. What I am identifying as the awakening of the human Soul corresponds closely, in terms of both timing and content, to what Jared Diamond, professor of physiology at the UCLA School of Medicine, calls "The Great Leap Forward." Diamond does not, however, share my particular interest in spiritual evolution, and we tend to interpret the evidence in slightly different ways. Diamond does makes a convincing case, although he is not the first or only one to do so, for the notion that it was a slight change in throat anatomy and the appearance of speech that launched "The Great Leap Forward." Speech and the appearance of Soul activity may be closely related, but whether the former caused the latter is something we simply don't know. Archaeologist Richard Leakey also suggests that speech was a key distinction between humans and pre-humans. For those interested in Diamond's theories and the evidence supporting them, see his *The Third Chimpanzee* (New York: HarperCollins, 1992) and *Guns, Germs, and Steel* (New York: W. W. Norton & Company, 1997).

8. Diamond, *Third Chimpanzee*, 44.

9. Stringer and McKie, 215.

10. Colin Renfrew, "People of the Stone Age," in *The Illustrated History of Humankind* (HarperSan Francisco, 1993), 9.

11. Leakey and Lewin, 322.

12. Tattersall, *Human Odyssey*, 159.

13. Goran Burenhult, ed. *The First Humans: Human Origins and History to 10,000 B.C.* (HarperSan Francisco, 1993), 118–121.

14. Leakey and Lewin, 314.

15. Ibid., 312 .

16. Ibid., 325–326.

17. Ibid., 325, 327, and 335.

18. Henry de Lumley, quoted in "Behold The Stone Age," *Time*, February 13, 1995, 54–62.

19. Burenhult, 97.

20. Ibid., 115.

21. Stringer and McKie, 214.

22. Tattersall, *Becoming Human*, 18.

23. Mircea Eliade, *Shamanism: Archaic Techniques of Ecstasy* (London: Routledge and Kegan Paul, 1972).

24. Joan Halifax, *Shamanism: The Wounded Healer* (New York: Crossroad, 1982).

25. Jean Clottes and David Lewis-Williams, *The Shamans of Prehistory: Trance and Magic in the Painted Caves* (New York: Harry N. Abrams, Inc., 1996).

26. Ibid., 329.

27. Ibid., 13.

28. Ibid., 112.

29. Ibid., 41.

30. Leakey and Lewin, 318.

31. Ann Baring and Jules Cashford, *The Myth of the Goddess* (New York: Penguin Books, 1991), 25.

32. Tattersall, *Human Odyssey*,168

33. Clottes and Lewis-Williams, 92.

34. Ibid., 110.

35. Ibid.

36. Raymond Dart, "The Predatory Transition from Ape to Man," *International Anthropological and Linguistic Review* 1, no 4 (1953): 204–207.

37. Stringer and McKie, 30.

38. Ibid.

39. Leakey and Lewin, xvii.

40. Robert Ardrey, *African Genesis* (New York: Atheneum, 1961), 9.

41. Diamond, *Third Chimpanzee* (New York: Harper Perennial, 1992), 52.

42. Leakey and Lewin, 233.

43. Eisler, 20.

44. Melvin Konner, *The Tangled Wing* (New York: Holt, Rinehart, and Winston,1982), 5–6.

45. Ibid., 7.

46. Ibid., 8.

47. Joseph Campbell, *Primitive Mythology* (New York: Penguin Books, 1959), 315; 139; and 6.

48. Marija Gimbutas, *The Language of the Goddess* (New York: Harper & Row, 1989), xix and 141.

49. Merlin Stone, *When God Was a Woman* (New York: Harcourt Brace Jovanovich), 11–12.

50. Gimbutas, xxii.

51. Eisler, 2.

52. Campbell, 313.

53. Baring and Cashford, 11–12.

54. There are a few exceptions, such as the twenty-five-thousand-year-old female head carved delicately in mammoth ivory—known as the "Lady of Brassempouy"—but such exceptions are rare.

55. Baring and Cashford, 25.

56. Ibid., 8.

Chapter 2

1. Brian Swimme and Thomas Berry, *The Universe Story* (San Francisco: Harper San Francisco, 1992), 199

2. Marija Gimbutas, *The Language of the Goddess* , op. cit., 271–273.

3. Ann Baring and Jules Cashford, *The Myth of the Goddess*, op. cit., 50.

4. Merlin Stone, *When God Was a Woman*, op. cit., 3.

5. Gimbutas, 321.

6. Baring and Cashford, 79.

7. Richard Heinberg, *Memories and Visions of Paradise* (Los Angeles: Jeremy P. Tarcher, Inc., 1989), xxvi.

8. "Foreword," Ibid., xxii.

9. John C. Neihardt, *Black Elk Speaks* (Lincoln, Neb.: University of Nebraska Press, 1968), 3–4.

10. In academic circles, we would be talking about dualism at this point, with the word *reductionism* usually reserved

for the later emphasis upon division, separation, specialization, etc., that emerged as part of the scientific revolution in the seventeenth century. Nevertheless, we will continue to use *reductionism* in this discussion for the entire Epoch II deep value, because this book is directed primarily to the general public and because the dictionary definition of reduction is "the act of reducing or the state of being reduced." That dictionary definition, and not the academic more specialized use, is what is applicable for our discussion. This book suggests that reducing wholes to parts was initiated ten-thousand years ago when humanity split the human/nature unity, and that it has been one of the most influential deep values for the entire Epoch II, not only for the past four-hundred years or so.

11. Goran Burenhult, "People of the Stone Age" in *The Illustrated History of Humankind* (San Francisco: HarperSan Francisco, 1993), 13.

12. Jared Diamond, *The Third Chimpanzee*, op. cit., 186–187.

13. Max Charlesworth, *Religion in Aboriginal Australia* (Queensland, Australia: University of Queensland Press, 1984), 5.

14. Anthony Harding, "People of the Stone Age" in *The Illustrated History of Humankind*, op. cit., 105.

15. Mats Malmer, ibid., 106–107.

16. Chellis Glendinning, *My Name is Chellis and I'm in Recovery from Western Civilization* (Boston: Shambhala, 1994), 64.

17. Rosemary Radford Ruether, *Gaia and God* (San Francisco: Harper San Francisco, 1992), 174.

18. Gimbutas, xx.

19. Boyo G. Ockinga, "Old World Civilizations" in *The Illustrated History of Humankind*, 43.

20. Gerda Lerner, *The Creation of Patriarchy* (New York: Oxford University Press, 1986), 8.
21. Ibid. 183.
22. Elizabeth Johnson, *She Who Is* (New York: Crossroad, 1994), 26–27.
23. Sherry Ruth Anderson and Patricia Hopkins, *The Feminine Face of God* (New York: Bantam Books, 1991), 127. Dr. Bolen is quoted in this book from a personal conversation.
24. Christiane Northrup, *Women's Bodies, Women's Wisdom* (New York: Bantam Books, 1994), 4.
25. Jared Diamond, *Guns, Germs, and Steel*, op. cit., 273.
26. Charles Redman, "Old World Civilizations" in *The Illustrated History of Humankind,*. 31.
27. Ian Glover and Himashu Ray, "Old World Civilizations" in *The Illustrated History of Humankind*, 69.
28. Shashi Tharoor, *India: From Midnight to the Millennium* (New York: Harper-Perennial, 1997), 104.
29. Ockinga, op. cit., 41; 54.
30. News story in the *Daily Camera* (Boulder, Colorado), August 20, 1997.
31. *The Christian Century*, March 22–29, 1995: 324.
32. Alice Walker, *Anything We Love Can Be Saved* (New York: Random House, 1997), 191.
33. Ibid., 41–42.
34. Ibid., 34.
35. Barbara Tuchman, *A Distant Mirror: The Calamitous 14th Century* (New York: Ballantine Books, 1978), 99.
36. Ibid., 95.
37. Richard Tarnas, *The Passion of the Western Mind* (New York: Harmony Books, 1991), 319–320.
38. Peter Berger, "Towards a Sociological Understanding of Psychoanalysis," *Social Research* 32 (Spring 1965): 32.
39. Karen Armstrong, *A History of God* (New York: Alfred A. Knopf, 1993), 296.
40. George Marsden, *The Soul of The American University: From Protestant Establishment to Established Non-belief* (New York: Oxford University Press, 1994).
41. James Wall, *The Christian Century*, April 24, 1996: 443.
42. Ibid.
43. David R. Boldt, "Why is there such fear of religion in the U.S.," *Sunday Camera* (Boulder, Colorado), March 31, 1996.
44. Owen C. Paepke, *The Evolution of Progress* (New York: Random House, 1993), vii; xviii.
45. Charlene Spretnak, *The Resurgence of the Real* (New York: Addison-Wesley Publishing Company, 1997), 40 .
46. Neil Postman, *Technopoly* (New York: Alfred A. Knopf, 1992), 179.
47. Alan Durning, *How Much is Enough?* (New York: Norton, 1992), 119.
48. Sam Keen, *Hymns to an Unknown God* (New York: Bantam Books,1994), 13.

Chapter Three

1. Sam Keen, *Hymns To An Unknown God,* op. cit., 3.
2. Joanna Macy, "The Great Turning" in *The Fabric of the Future: Women Visionaries of Today Illuminate the Path to Tomorrow*, edited by M. J. Ryan (Berkeley, Calif.: Conari Press, 1998), 77.
3. L. S. Stavrianos, *The Promise of the Coming Dark Age* (San Francisco: W. H. Freeman and Company, 1976), vii.
4. Vaclav Havel, president of the Czech Republic, received the Philadelphia Liberty Medal at Independence Hall on July 4, 1994. His acceptance speech was printed in *The New York Times*, OP-ED, July 8, 1994, from which this quote was taken.
5. Charlene Spretnak, *The Resurgence of the Real*, op. cit., 1.

6. Newt Gingrich, *To Renew America* (New York: Harper Collins, 1995), 3–7.
7. Roger Rosenblatt, essay on "The Triumph of Liberalism" reprinted in the *Daily Camera* (Boulder), January 21, 1996.
8. Huston Smith's chapter, "Jesus and the World's Religions," in *Jesus at 2000*, edited by Marcus Borg (Boulder, Colo.: Westview Press, 1997), 111. Reprinted by permission of Huston Smith.
9. Emily Nussbaum, "A Question of Gender," in *Discover Magazine*, January 2000: 93.
10. Garry Wills, *A Necessary Evil* (New York: Simon & Schuster, 1999), 252.
11. Bernard Schwartz, *The Bill of Rights: A Documentary History*, vol 2 (New York: McGraw-Hill, 1971), 1026.
12. Wills, 121.
13. Michael Gartner, "I have a right not to be shot," *USA Today*, July 19, 1994.
14. Wills, 252.
15. Richard Bach, *Illusions* (New York: Delacorte Press, 1977), 134.
16. Havel, op. cit.
17. Albert Einstein, "Strange is Our Situation Here on Earth," in *Modern Religious Thought*, edited by Jaroslav Pelikan (New Haven, Conn.: Yale University Press, 1990) 204.
18. Loren Eiseley, *The Firmament of Time* (New York: Atheneum, 1985), 5.
19. Duane Elgin, *Global Consciousness Change: Indicators of an Emerging Paradigm* (San Anselmo, Calif: The Millennium Project, 1997), 17.
20. Ibid.
21. Trina Paulus, *Hope for the Flowers* (Mahway, N.J.: Paulist Press, 1972), 75.

Chapter Four
1. Albert Einstein, quoted in *Peace: A Dream Unfolding*, edited by Penney Kome and Patrick Crean (New York: Somerville House Books, 1986), 143.

2. Union of Concerned Scientists, "World Scientists' Warning to Humanity," November 18, 1992.
3. Thomas Berry, *The Dream of the Earth* (San Francisco: Sierra Club Books, 1988). This is a quotation from Berry that appears on the back jacket cover.
4. See Morris Berman, *Coming To Our Senses* (New York: Simon & Schuster, 1989); Chellis Glendinning, *My Name is Chellis and I'm in Recovery from Western Civilization* (Boston: Shambhala, 1994); Robert Jay Lifton, *Survivors of Hiroshima: Death in Life* (New York: Random House, 1967); Paul Shepard, *Nature and Madness* (San Francisco: Sierra Club, 1982); and David Suzuki, *The Sacred Balance* (Amherst, N.Y.: Prometheus Books, 1998).
5. David Abram, *The Spell of the Sensuous* (New York: Pantheon Books, 1996), ix.
6. Charlene Spretnak, *Resurgence of the Real*, op. cit., 129. The italics are Spretnak's.
7. Alice Walker, interviewed in the *Utne Reader* (January-February, 1996), 53.
8. Robert Greenway, "The Wilderness Effect and Ecopsychology," in *Ecopsychology*, edited by Theodore Roszak, Mary Gomes, and Allen Kanner (San Francisco: Sierra Club Books, 1995), 122.
9. Marcus J. Borg, *Jesus: A New Vision* (San Francisco: Harper San Francisco, 1987), 36.
10. David Abram, 260.
11. R. Costanza, R. dArge, R. deGroot, et al, "The Value of the World's Ecosystem Services and Natural Capital," *Nature* 387 (May 15, 1997): 253–260.
12. Donella Meadows, *Timeline* (Palo Alto, CA, A bimonthly publication of the Foundation for Global Community, September/October 1998),12.
13. Glendinning, 19.
14. Spretnak, 72.

15. Bernard Campbell, *Human Ecology* (Westport, Conn.: Heinemann Educational, 1983), 72.

16. As of this writing, there is still a great deal of uncertainty as to precisely when the Americas were populated by human beings. Some evidence suggests that it could be as "recent" as about fifteen-thousand or twenty-thousand years ago, whereas there are some scholars who believe that it could have been as long ago as thirty-thousand years.

17. Michael W. Fox, *The Boundless Circle* (Wheaton, Ill.: Quest Books, 1996), 134–135.

18. John G. Neihardt, op. cit., x. In my earlier book, *Sacred Eyes*, I commented on that vision as told by Black Elk to Neihardt. It was, therefore, a very special, delightful, and surprising moment when a letter arrived one morning from Hilda Neihardt, John's daughter. She told me how she accompanied her father during those visits with Black Elk and had sat with the two men as they talked. Her father prepared her for those meetings by a reading and study program so that she might better understand the wisdom she was to hear from Black Elk. Apparently, Black Elk was impressed by the fourteen-year-old young woman: he gave her a special name, Day-break Star Woman.

19. Joseph Epes Brown, *The Spiritual Legacy of the American Indian* (New York: Crossroad, 1982), 39.

20. Glendinning, 211–212.

21. Berry, 8.

22. Charlene Spretnak, *States of Grace* (San Francisco: Harper San Francisco, 1991), 90.

23. Brian Swimme, *The Hidden Heart of the Cosmos* (Maryknoll, N.Y.: Orbis Books, 1996), 108.

24. Diane Ackerman, *The Moon by Whale Light* (New York: Random House, 1991), xiv.

25. Mike Davis, *Ecology of Fear* (New York: Henry Holt & Co., 1998), 201.

26. Ted Andrews, *Animal-Speak* (St. Paul, Minn.: Llewellyn Publications, 1993), 259.

27. Wallace Stegner, in his foreword to Karen McCall and Jim Dutcher, *Cougar: Ghost of the Rockies* (San Francisco: Sierra Club Books, 1992), iv.

28. Quoted in David Suzuki, op. cit., 38.

29. Ibid.

30. David Abram, 229.

Chapter Five

1. David Bohm, *Wholeness and the Implicate Order* (London: Routledge & Kegan Paul, 1980), 124–125, and 1.

2. Paul Davies, *The Cosmic Blueprint* (New York: Simon & Schuster, 1988), 2.

3. Bohm, 134. The italic are Bohm's.

4. John Briggs and David Peat, *Looking Glass Universe* (New York: Simon & Schuster, 1984), 94.

5. Paul Davies, *The Mind of God* (New York: Simon & Schuster, 1992), 21.

6. Fritjof Capra, *The Web of Life* (New York: Doubleday, An Anchor Book, 1996), 37.

7. Kevin W. Kelley, ed. *The Home Planet* (New York: Addison-Wesley Publishing Company, 1988), Mitchell, 52 and 137; Kovalyonok, 76; Faris, 76; Bartoe, 85; and Sharma, 80.

8. Bohm, 144–145.

9. Marcus Borg, *The God We Never Knew* (San Francisco: Harper San Francisco, 1997), 35.

10. James F. Lawrence, "The Swedenborgian Church," in *Gnosis Magazine* (Summer, 1989): 56.

11. George Dole, *A Thoughtful Soul* (West Chester, Penna.: Chrysalis Books, 1995), xxi.

12. For information on the entire range of Swedenborg's life and thought, I suggest one book: Robin Larsen, ed., *Emanuel Swedenborg: A Continuing Vision* (New York: Swedenborg Foundation, 1988).

13. Lawrence, 56.

14. James F. Lawrence, ed., *Testimony to the Invisible* (West Chester, Penna.: Chrysalis Books, 1995), 3.

15. Ibid., 22.

16. D. T. Suzuki, *Swedenborg: Buddha of the North*, translated by Andrew Bernstein (West Chester, Penna.: Swedenborg Foundation, 1996), 3.

17. Lawrence, "The Swedenborgian Church," 57.

18. Ibid., 57–58.

19. As mentioned earlier, K.F.C. Krause, in the nineteenth century, coined the word *panentheism*. In a conversation with Swedenborgian scholar Robert Kirven, I learned that Krause came up with the word because he was trying to find a way of explaining Swedenborg's holistic theology.

20. Gordon Kaufman, *God, Mystery, Diversity* (Minneapolis, Minn.: Fortress Press, 1996), 56.

21. Ken Wilber, *A Brief History of Everything* (Boston: Shambhala, 1996), 21.

22. Matthew Fox, *The Coming of the Cosmic Christ* (San Francisco: Harper-San Francisco, 1988), 228.

23. Interview of Bishop Tutu by Zia Jaffrey, *Daily Camera* (Boulder), March 1, 1998.

24. Ken Dychtwald, *Age Wave* (Los Angeles: Jeremy P. Tarcher, 1989), 13.

25. Ibid., 13, 19–20.

26. Ibid., 15.

27. Ibid., 17.

28. Wade Clark Roof, *A Generation of Seekers* (San Francisco: Harper San Francisco, 1993).

29. Ibid., 244.

30. Ibid., 245; 8.

31. Ursula King, *The Spirit of One Earth* (New York: Paragon House, 1989), 176.

32. Brian Swimme, *The Universe Is a Green Dragon* (Santa Fe, N.M.: Bear & Co., 1984), 44–45.

33. George Leonard, *The Silent Pulse* (New York: E.P. Dutton, 1978), 15.

34. Ibid., 17.

35. Mitchell M. Waldrop, *Complexity* (New York: Touchstone, 1992), 11. The italics are Waldrop's.

36. Mike Davis, *Ecology of Fear* (New York: Holt & Company, 1998), 329.

37. Rita Nakashima Brock, *Journeys by Heart* (New York: Crossroad, 1988), xiv.

Chapter Six

1. Marilyn French, *Beyond Power* (New York: Summit Books, 1985), 545.

2. J. M. Roberts, *A Short History of the World* (New York: Oxford University Press, 1993), 371.

3. Robert A. Dahl, *On Democracy* (New Haven, Conn.: Yale University Press, 1998), 1.

4. Ibid., 2

5. *Freedom in the World—1997–1998.* Annual reports are published by Freedom House, 1319 Eighteenth Street N.W., Washington, D.C., 20036. The statistics here are gleaned from pages 7 and 8 of this report, as well as from a news release of the 1999 report, published in the *Daily Camera* (Boulder), December 22, 1999.

6. John Keegan, *A History of Warfare* (New York: Random House, 1993), 125–126. This may be the best single source for a more thorough and nuanced examination of warfare than is possible in my generalizing, holistic, and synthetic summary.

7. Bernard Nietschmann, "Third World War," *Cultural Survival Quarterly* 11, no. 3 (1987): 1–15. See also Cultural Survival Center Staff, *State of the Peoples: A Global Human Rights Report on Societies in Danger* (Boston: Beacon Press, 1993).

8. Francis Fukuyama, *The End of History and the Last Man* (New York: The Free Press, 1992), 263.

9. Ibid., Page 262–263.

10. Gerda Lerner, *Creation of Patriarchy*, op. cit., 76–77. Incidentally, the derivation of the word *slave* comes from the time when Germans enslaved the Slavs—thus, perverting a national name that meant "glory" into a word that meant servitude and a complete loss of freedom.

11. Milton Meltzer, *Slavery: A World History* (New York: Da Capo Press, 1993), 6. Most of the information, and particularly the statistics, used in this chapter is drawn from this comprehensive and prestigious work.

12. Lerner, op. cit., 82.

13. Meltzer, 91.

14. One interesting subtext in Roman history, however, is how they unexpectedly created a problem for themselves by training skilled professional killers. A gladiator in Capua in 73 BC by the name of Spartacus recruited some seventy other gladiators in plotting and carrying out the greatest slave revolt in history, what became known as the "War of the Gladiators." Other slaves ran away from their masters and joined Spartacus' liberation army, which eventually grew to a total of 120,000 men. They conquered many Roman legions and enjoyed making many of their captives perform the same rituals of human sacrifice to which they had earlier been subjected.

Eventually, however, after two years of humiliating defeats, the Romans pulled out all the stops and massed enough troops by which they could finally defeat Spartacus and his fellow rebels. In order to teach all potentially rebellious slaves a lesson, the Romans lined the Appian Way, from Rome to Capua, with 6,000 of the rebels nailed to crosses.

15. Meltzer, 211; 44.

16. Ibid., 245.

17. Roberts, op. cit, 380.

18. Meltzer, 51, 161.

19. Martin Luther King Jr., *Where Do We Go from Here: Chaos or Community?* (New York: Harper & Roe, 1967), 77.

20. Tim Berners-Lee, *Weaving the Web* (San Francisco: HarperSan Francisco, 1999), 16, 99. For the story about Jim Clark, to which I referred as a contrast to Berners-Lee, see Michael Lewis, *The New New Thing* (New York: W. W. Norton, 2000).

21. Duane Elgin's report may be obtained from the Millennium Project, P. O. Box 2449, San Anselmo, CA 94960 (e-mail: report@awakening earth.org).

22. Joseph Campbell, *The Hero with a Thousand Faces* (Princeton, N.J.: Princeton University Press, 1949), 287–288.

23. Max Black, *Metaphors and Model* (Ithaca, N.Y.: Cornell University Press, 1962), 41–42.

24. Sallie McFague, *Models of God* (Philadelphia: Fortress Press, 1987), 30. Italics are McFague's.

25. Stephen Mitchell, *The Gospel According to Jesus* (New York: Harper Collins, 1991), 46–47.

26. Ibid., 47.

27. The Gospel of Thomas can be found in several translations. The text I use throughout when quoting Thomas comes from *The Five Gospels: The*

Search for the Authentic Words of Jesus,
translation and commentary by Robert
W. Funk, Roy W. Hoover, and The
Jesus Seminar (New York: Macmillian
Publishing Co., 1993).

28. John Dominic Crossan, *Jesus: A
Revolutionary Biography* (San Francisco:
Harper San Francisco, 1994), 198.

29. Marcus Borg, *Jesus in Contemporary
Scholarship* (Valley Forge, Penna.:
Trinity Press International, 1994), 145.

30. See particularly, Walter Wink's *Engaging
the Powers* (Minneapolis, Minn.: Fortress
Press, 1992), or the brief synthesis of his
three books on "the powers," intended
more for the general public, *The Powers
That Be: Theology for a New Millennium*
(New York: Doubleday, 1998).

31. Ronald Inglehart, *Modernization and
Postmodernization: Cultural, Economic,
and Political Change in 43 Societies*
(Princeton, N.J.: Princeton University
Press, 1997), 3.

32. Ibid., 39.

33. Ibid., 22–23.

34. Wade Clark Roof, *Spiritual Marketplace*
(Princeton, N.J.: Princeton University
Press, 1999), 44–45, 157.

35. John S. Dunne, *The Way of All the
Earth* (Notre Dame, Ind.: University
of Notre Dame Press, 1972), ix.

36. C. G. Jung, *Psychological Reflections*
(Princeton, N.J.: Princeton University
Press, 1970), 220.

37. I told some of this story in my first
book, *The Spirit of Synergy* (Abingdon
Press, 1978), which is now is out-of-
print. I then told some of the story in
my next book, *Sacred Eyes* (Knowledge
Systems, Inc., 1992). The book I am
currently working on, tentatively entitled *The New Sacred Quest for Healing,*
will summarize what I have learned in
thirty-five years of trying to understand
the role of spirituality in health, illness,
and in the processes of healing.

Chapter 7

1. A.S. Eddington, *The Nature of the
Physical World* (Ann Arbor, Mich.:
University of Michigan Press, 1958), 38

2. J. L. Borges, "A New Refutation of
Time," *Labyrinths* (New York: Penguin
Books, 1970), 269.

3. Aristotle, "Meterology," 352b, quoted
in Timothy Ferris, *Coming of Age in the
Milky Way* (New York: William
Morrow & Co., 1988), 220.

4. Quoted in Thomas Cahill, *The Gifts of
the Jews* (New York: Doubleday, 1998),
5.

5. Ibid., 128.

6. Ibid., 131. Cahill may be overstating
his case a bit, although he is not
entirely wrong either, when he suggests
that, among the gifts of the Jews are
some of our best words and concepts—
"new, adventure, surprise; unique,
individual, person, vocation; time,
history, future; freedom, progress,
spirit; faith, hope, justice" (p. 241).

7. Wolfgang Yourgrau and Allen D. Breck,
eds. *Cosmology, History, and Theology*
(New York: Plenum Press, 1977), 307.

8. Huston Smith, *The Illustrated World's
Religions* (San Francisco: HarperSan
Francisco, 1986), 77.

9. Ken Wilber, *The Eye of Spirit* (Boston:
Shambhala, 1997), 66.

10. Stephen Hawking, *A Brief History of Time*
(New York: Bantam Books, 1988), 40.

11. Albert Einstein and Max Born, *The
Born–Einstein Letters* (New York:
Walker, 1971), 82.

12. Daniel J. Boorstin, *The Seekers* (New
York: Random House, 1998), 245.

13. Timothy Ferris, 205.

14. Ibid., 206.

15. Ibid.

16. Ilya Prigogine, *The End of Certainty*
(New York: The Free Press, 1996), viii.

17. Ibid., 7.

18. Ibid., 13, 183.

19. Ibid., 72.

20. Ibid., 29.

21. Ibid., 187.

22. Margaret J. Wheatley, *Leadership and the New Science* (San Francisco: Berrett-Koehler Publishers, 1992), 73.

23. John Briggs and David F. Peat, *Seven Life Lessons of Chaos* (New York: Harper Collins, 1999), 6, 7, and 8.

24. Matthew Fox, *Creation Spirituality* (Autumn 1995): 4.

25. Karen Armstrong, *A History of God* (New York: Alfred A. Knopf, 1993), 301.

26. Robert Raines, *A Time To Live* (New York: Dutton, 1997), 170.

27. Quoted in Joseph Campbell, *The Inner Reaches of Outer Space* (Toronto: St. James Press, 1986), 110.

28. Quoted in David Suzuki, *The Sacred Balance*, op. cit., 105.

29. Ibid., 198.

30. Paul Tillich, *The Protestant Era* (Chicago: University of Chicago Press, 1948), 33.

31. Quoted in Stephen Mitchell, *Gospel*, op. cit., 141.

Index

About the Author

L. Robert Keck has a master's degree in theology from Vanderbilt University and a doctorate in the philosophy of health from Union Graduate School. Professionally, he has been a United Methodist minister in Iowa and Ohio, served on the medical school faculty at The Ohio State University, founded and managed a corporate wellness consulting firm, and was president of Boulder Graduate School. Today, he is an independent scholar, a philosopher of health, and an evolutionary theologian. For more information, contact his website: www.robertkeck.com.

About the Cover

This is not a book about the labyrinth, per se. But after considering many other possibilities, I came to feel that it is the one symbol that comes closest to expressing the spirit of this book—a quest for the sacred.

We have ranged far and wide throughout this discussion—35,000 years of history and a worldwide sensitivity to the evolutionary human journey. No image that is restricted to one time in history or is too parochial, whether religiously, culturally, or ethnically, would be appropriate.

The circle, however, is both an ancient and contemporary symbol of wholeness. The mandala, which is also suggested in the image of the labyrinth, has long been associated with the human unconscious. And the labyrinth itself is both a symbol and a practice that crosses many boundaries and unites a wide range of humanity in "walking a sacred path," the title of the book by Lauren Artress which is at the center of a remarkable resurgence of interest in walking the labyrinth.

It is significant, I believe, that the labyrinth has become prevalent in the sacred quest of so many people in just the past decade, after essentially laying fallow in the human unconscious for centuries. It is reflective of the increasing interest in spirituality in general and in the intuition that a holistic quest is what is appropriate in particular. The labyrinth engages the body, mind, and soul, the right as well as the left brain, in questing for spiritual meaning and purpose. It seeks insight by going into the center and affirms service by coming back out into the world.

I am indebted to the visual and graphic skills of Caroline Kulp Kline for the artistic rendition of the jacket cover. It is now for you to use that symbol to go within the pages of this book, gain the insights that are appropriate for your own spiritual journey, and then bring a more empowered you back out to contribute love and justice to a world in need.

For information on Bob's earlier book, *Sacred Eyes,* check his website:

www.robertkeck.com

or write to

Synergy Associates, Inc.
P. O. Box 4589
Boulder, CO 80306